Praise for Krishna

"An IT professional has caught this master of mysteries in the net of this enchanting volume by pursuing him relentlessly on earth. Immensely readable and ofcourse enjoyable."
— Amazon, USA

"An excellent biography of sorts of the most loved face of Hindu religion and culture revered not only in India, but all the world over."
— *Afternoon Despatch & Courier*

"Dev Prasad has tracked Krishna in the maze of myths, legends, holy places and popular conceptions with a single-minded zeal."
— *Deccan Herald*

"Everyone wants to write for *Lonely Planet*, and if that's not possible, heck, write your own travel book."
— *The Hindu*, Bangalore Edition

"Prasad explores the lesser known but significant places that Lord Krishna visited."
— *The New Indian Express*, Hyderabad

"There is a story that is waiting to be discovered and narrated in every nook and corner of this country, whether in the form of mythology, folk tales and literature."
— *The Hindu*, Chennai Edition

"To those who believe in Him and want to worship Him, the book is a treasure house. There has never been a book like this."
— Late Mr. M.V. Kamath, in *Organiser* Magazine

"Helps a traveller to plan his journey."
— *Tourism India*

"The book is a travelogue, giving information about these places of religious importance, juxtaposed with their associated legends."

— Techgoss Magazine

"This innovative book blends the Legends of Krishna with the places where the pastimes occurred."

— Asian Traveller

"A very positive blend of the historical and mythological in Lord Krishna."

— Vijaya Karnataka, The Times of India Group

"This publication is an example of the systematic study by the author."

— Praja Vani, Deccan Herald Group

"A perfect balance of past and present — goes beyond the religious aspects of historically renowned places, making it an interesting travelogue with practical information."

— Maharashtra Times

"The valuable results of a 5 year journey of a Computer Professional."

— Eenadu Newspaper

"Most essential for every tourist. The Author presents the book in his own unique style, which makes the book very interesting to read."

— Vaartha Newspaper

"The author in simple but beautiful English has presented the core of Krishna Leela's in this book."

— Dina Malar

"Dev Prasad takes us on a travel on the footsteps of Sri Krishna through his words."

— *Sandesh Newspaper*

"Sri Krishna's lifestyle has been revealed in an excellent and manner."

— *Vijaya Karnataka, The Times of India*
Group on Book Release Function, Bangalore

"Dev Prasad's Book *KRISHNA: A Journey through the lands & legends of Krishna*, was released by retired Chief Justice of Supreme Court, M.N. Venkatachaliah.

— *Kannada Prabha, Indian Express*
Group on Book Release Function, Bangalore

"The writer has been excellent in explaining various locations and events related to Krishna's life."

— Mr. J.A. Chowdary,
former STPI Director, during the Book Reading Event at
Crossword, Hyderabad, *Sakshi Newspaper*

"Sharing the feelings that the devotees experience at these places is what makes it adorable."

— Mr. J.A. Chowdary, former STPI Director, during the
Book Reading Event at Crossword, Hyderabad
— *Vaartha Newspaper*

Krishna

A Journey through the Lands & Legends of Krishna

DEV PRASAD

JAICO PUBLISHING HOUSE

Ahmedabad Bangalore Bhopal Bhubaneswar Chennai
Delhi Hyderabad Kolkata Lucknow Mumbai

Published by Jaico Publishing House
A-2 Jash Chambers, 7-A Sir Phirozshah Mehta Road
Fort, Mumbai - 400 001
jaicopub@jaicobooks.com
www.jaicobooks.com

KRISHNA: A JOURNEY THROUGH
THE LANDS & LEGENDS OF KRISHNA
ISBN 978-81-8495-170-7

First Jaico Impression: 2010
Sixth Jaico Impression: 2015

Printed by
Repro India Limited
Plot No. 50/2, T.T.C. MIDC Industrial Area
Mahape, Navi Mumbai - 400 710

Contents

...

Contents

Foreword

•••

I have great pleasure in writing this Foreword to *Krishna: A Journey through the Lands & Legends of Krishna* because it is a special book. It is a travelogue, but a travelogue with a difference. The reader dwells simultaneously in two periods — the present as well as the distant times of Krishna and Radha. We are in the present as we accompany the author on his travels and visits to holy places that have witnessed Lord Krishna's appearance on Earth. But the story of Lord Krishna and Radha, takes us back centuries — probably more than 25 centuries.

The traveller's journey is vividly presented. We learn about the approach to every spot and building he visits. We see the palace, temple, and holy buildings as he sees it; we enter the structure and see the idols and pictures on the walls. Dev Prasad has an eye for detail and can simultaneously and accurately convey even the ambience of the place. Thus, we see the very colours of the idols, their height, the material the idols are made of, and he even tells us on which side of Lord Krishna's idol Radha's idol is placed! He is right by our side, giving us historical details of the places we see. Throughout the book, the passages in italics are those that present legendary lore as it took place.

Embedded in history and legend is a moving love story. At the centre of it all is Lord Krishna, one of the most fascinating figures in world mythology. With Him is His Divine Consort, Radha, Herself an elusive figure. Whose daughter was She? Was Her father a king? Was She older than Lord Krishna? What was

xiii

the nature of Her relationship with Krishna — entirely platonic, or more intimate? Why did She not go to Mathura even after Krishna had killed Kansa? Did She meet Krishna again after He left Brij Bhoomi? If yes, where? None of these, or other similar questions can be answered with any degree of finality. But here She is in Dev Prasad's book, the Beloved of the Lord. We see Her with the Lord again and again, singing and dancing devotedly, a gopi who has come to pervade Krishna's world as no one else ever had. They are a Divine Couple, but Their love is strikingly human, with petty lover's quarrels and pleasant reconciliations.

The climax is reached in the Radha-Krishna *baithak*, when Krishna offers to make Her the Queen of Mathura. Until this episode, She has been more or less a gopi loved by Krishna, just a presence in Brij Bhoomi. But here, She becomes an individual, gentle but firm, with remarkable insight into Her own character; She knows where She will fit in and where She will be an unhappy stranger. This last meeting is human, deeply moving, and dignified. How insightful and moving are Her words — "I am an innocent and uneducated milkmaid. What will I do in Mathura... I have been brought up in the open spaces of Barsana. I like to run and play around in the open fields. I would not like to be confined to the walls of a palace. I want to be a free bird and not live in a golden cage."

Uddhav's visit to the gopis is singularly appropriate as the conclusion of the Krishna-Radha love story, for the two lovers are divine yet human. The Krishna-Radha story provokes delight and mild regret — even the Divine Couple could not influence events so as to enable Them to be happy. The story humanises the work.

The book has much to offer different types of readers — even to one who is not a tourist, or is only an armchair tourist. The tourist gets all the information he needs to make the best of his journey. On the one hand it is a professional tourist guidebook offering details about the approach to a temple, *sarovar* (lake), or other holy places, what to see, the facilities available and what to guard against. It is also a journey to an enchanting past. History or legend, the verifiable details and stories of Krishna and Radha's love are blended here, so the thoughtful visitor has much to ponder about. The book gains authenticity by the fact that it is written by an engineer who has himself visited each one of the temples, *sarovars*, and other places mentioned in the book. The language is simple and lucid. The author seems to be chatting with the reader, sharing his own experiences, as a friend might do.

I congratulate Dev Prasad on the excellent book he has written. This is his first book and I hope he will write more books to delight the reader.

L.S. Seshagiri Rao,

Eminent writer in English and Kannada, Retd. Professor, Bangalore University.

Preface

...

India. A land of Gods and Goddesses. There are hundreds of Gods and Goddesses worshipped in India everyday by a billion people. If you count the different incarnations and forms that each God and Goddess takes, then their number may cross a thousand! The most colourful personality among Them all is Lord Krishna. As kids, we all read all about Lord Krishna. Some of the most popular stories are those about Krishna breaking pots and stealing butter and curds from His neighbourhood, showing the entire cosmos to His foster mother Yashoda in His tiny mouth, hiding the gopis' clothes while they were bathing, killing numerous demons during His childhood and showing His Viraat Swaroop to Arjuna. Each time I read these stories, I was fascinated. I had heard and read so much about Brij Bhoomi, the land where Krishna was born and had spent His childhood. Mathura, the holy city where Krishna was born and the surrounding towns of Vrindavan, Gokul, Mahavan, Baledo, Raval, Barsana, Nandagaon and Madhuvan were all my favourite daydream haunts. I longed to visit these places. My heart also longed to visit Dwarka, the only city in India which is a part of the Char Dham and also a Sapta Puri. This was the city where Krishna had spent the major part of His life as Dwarkadheesh, the Emperor of Dwarka, not to forget the holy town of Kurukshetra where the famous battle between the Pandavas and Kauravas took place, and the spot where Lord Krishna unveiled His pearls of wisdom in the form of the holy *Bhagavad Gita* and showed His Original Form to Arjuna. I also wanted to visit the places near Somnath where Lord Krishna and Lord Balarama shed Their mortal bodies and proceeded towards Their Holy Abode, Vaikunta.

My original intention was to just visit the holy places in Brij Bhoomi. Writing a book had never crossed my mind. However, during my first trip to Brij Bhoomi, I was enchanted by what I saw. The forests where He, Lord Balarama, and Their cowherd friends, had played everyday. The houses in Gokul and Vrindavan that Krishna used to stealthily enter to steal butter and curds. The *sarovars* (lakes) beside which Krishna spent His time in the company of His divine consort Radha. The countless ghats, bordering the Yamuna, each carrying a fascinating tale. The Goverdhan Hill that Lord Krishna had lifted with His tiny finger to humble the ego of Lord Indra, the King of the Gods. The holy river Yamuna, where Lord Krishna battled with the poisonous serpent Kaliya and danced on him. The holy Yamuna which was blessed by the touch of Lord Krishna's lotus feet. I automatically began to take notes of whatever I saw. I also spoke to many people to understand the legends and stories associated with each place.

After my return, I decided to pen my experiences in the form of a travelogue. I realised that though most of the people know about quite a few incidents that had happened during Krishna's lifetime, there were numerous stories that hardly anyone was aware of. Most of the people are aware of the Krishna Janmasthan (birthplace of Lord Krishna) in Mathura, the ISKCON Temple at Vrindavan and the sacred hill at Goverdhan. The more discerning tourist is probably aware of a few more famous Vrindavan temples like Rangaji, Banke Bihari, and Govind Dev temples. However, the many stories associated with Lord Krishna take you on a fascinating journey of *Goloka* on earth. More than the places themselves, it is the legend surrounding each place that is fascinating. For example, how many people are aware that there are two towns claiming to be the real Gokul? How many are aware of the captivating story of Radha Kund where Radha and Krishna competed with each other to create sacred tanks? Or the Brahmanda Ghat at Mahavan where Lord Krishna, as an Infant, showed the entire cosmos to His mother Yashoda? Or the heart-breaking incident at Mor Kutir in Barsana where Radha leaves Krishna? Or Kusum Sarovar where Uddhav was given a lesson in true devotion by the illiterate gopis and led to his being born again as a creeper? Or Akroor Ghat where Lord Krishna and Lord Balarama showed Their original forms as Lord Vishnu and Lord Sheshanag to a confused Akroor? Or the fascinating stories at Imli Tala, Kesi Ghat, Manasi Ganga, Brahma Kund, the various temples and *kunds* of Brij Bhoomi?

I had the good fortune to visit all these places. I realised that because of very little awareness the tourists would visit only the famous places like Krishna Janmasthan and other such places. I hardly saw any tourists at places like Man Sarovar, Akroor Ghat, Brahmanda Ghat, and other such places where astonishing events had taken place 5000 years ago. I thought to myself, why restrict my book to a mere travelogue? Why not add the legends too? With this I began to conceptualise the form the book would ultimately take.

I had started to pen my experiences in all these places, along with the legends associated with them. This is when I realised that Brij Bhoomi played host to only a small portion of Lord Krishna's life. Lord Krishna was on this planet for 125 years and He stayed in Brij Bhoomi for only 28 years. He spent the rest of His life in Dwarka. I had also read that He left this material world and went back to His Holy Abode Vaikunta after witnessing His Yadava clan annihilate themselves in a midnight carnage at a place located near Somnath in Gujarat. So Dwarka and Somnath were added to my itinerary! When people heard of my plans, they advised me, "A book on Lord Krishna without narrating the famous incident at Kurukshetra where the Lord narrates the *Bhagavad Gita* to Arjuna? You should write about Kurukshetra too!" So the book takes the reader through a journey that starts in the dusty towns and forests of Brij Bhoomi (Uttar Pradesh), then proceeds to the coastal town of Dwarka (Gujarat), traverses to Kurukshetra (Haryana), and finally culminates in Somnath (Gujarat).

The first challenge in writing this was the question that kept cropping up in my mind, should I order the places according to the sequence of events during the lifetime of Lord Krishna, or should it be ordered as a travel itinerary? After considerable debate, I decided that it would be best to have a combination of both and try to keep both orders intact. The only places where I had to compromise were Mathura and Kusum Sarovar. Since Krishna was born in Mathura but grew up in Gokul, Vrindavan, and Nandagaon, only to return later to Mathura to slay His maternal uncle Kansa, I too had to follow the same path and ended up describing various temples in Mathura in two places in the book. Similarly, I have described the Uddhav incident at Kusum Sarovar along with other divine spots of Goverdhan because of its proximity to Goverdhan town. However, in keeping with the flow of Lord Krishna's story, it should have come after Krishna's return to Mathura. Except for these departures, I have tried my best to retain the sequence of places the same as they figure during the lifetime of Lord Krishna.

The next challenge was how to narrate the story and also talk about the history of these places. After a lot of thought, I decided to interweave the two. I have described each place that I visited and also blended it with the legends. I wanted to give readers a visual treat so that they would *experience* the legends and feel that they were witnessing it. I have made a conscious effort to write all the legends in italics and have used the present tense. I have also written these passages using only the first person or the second person in an effort to make the readers feel as if they are witnessing what happened thousands of years ago.

The narration of each town starts off with a verse from the *Bhagavad Gita*, which is appropriate to the events surrounding that town.

Writing a biography of a living person is relatively simple. You meet many persons and conduct numerous interviews and record the conversations which you can capture in the form of a book. But, how do you write the story of a personality born 5000 years ago? Someone whose exact date and place of birth are not known. A person whose departure from the planet is equally mysterious. A person whom you have never seen in flesh and blood. A person about whom you can never verify facts. A person who also happens to be the eighth incarnation of Lord Vishnu and revered as the Supreme Lord by a billion people! Someone who is known by a thousand names in different parts of India — Krishna, Kanha, Kanhaiya, Govinda, Gopala, Parthasarathy, Vasudeva, Murlidhara, Madhusudhana, and Keshava, to name a few.

I gathered information for my book by reading various reference books, browsing websites, personally visiting all the places described in the book and talking to many knowledgeable people, including a few local guides. Though I managed to collect a plethora of information, the flip side was that I got multiple versions of stories and sometimes, even contradictory stories. It has been my endeavour to present the different versions and leave it to the reader to decide which one is authentic. There were a few places like Indra Kund and Airavata Kund where even the locals were either not aware of its exact location, or the legend associated with it. In such cases, authentication becomes a major challenge.

Since I decided to write about only those towns that were directly witness to the pastimes of Lord Krishna and the places whose sands were sanctified by the touch of His lotus feet, I have not mentioned three famous pilgrimage places that are dear to His devotees, namely Udupi, Guruvayoor, and Jagannath Puri since, as per my understanding, Lord Krishna never visited them. This omission should not be seen as belittling the greatness of these three places.

I hope this book helps you become aware of the various places and legends associated with Lord Krishna and also appreciate the glories of the Supreme Lord better.

I am grateful to Prof. L.S. Seshagiri Rao who went through the script and offered valuable suggestions. His guidance throughout the execution of the project has been invaluable to me.

1

Who is Lord Krishna?

...

People believe that Lord Krishna is the eighth incarnation of Lord Vishnu. They also believe that He was the only *Poorna Avatar* (complete incarnation) of Lord Vishnu among His ten incarnations. A *Poorna Avatar* means that He was the same as Lord Vishnu Himself. In other words, Lord Krishna had all the powers that Lord Vishnu has. This is probably why, it is only in this incarnation of Lord Vishnu, that He can be seen using His divine Sudarshan *Chakra* (Discus), *Shanka* (Conch) and flying on His vehicle, Garuda. There are many who consider Him to be the Supreme Lord and more powerful than Lord Brahma and Lord Shiva. There are others who consider Him to be on par with Lord Brahma and Lord Shiva. There are a few who do not believe Him to be the Supreme Lord. They say that He was a righteous prince who fought for *Dharma* (righteousness), an excellent statesman and a diplomat par excellence, but nothing beyond that.

There are many questions about Lord Krishna starting right from His date and place of birth. Was He born in 3000 BC? Or was it 1000 BC? It is always difficult to know the exact date of birth of someone born a few thousands of years ago, but can the difference be as high as 2000 years? Was He born in present day Mathura? Or was Mathura as described in the scriptures a different place? In present day Mathura, there is another place about a kilometre from the famous Krishna Janmasthan (birth place of Lord Krishna) which claims to be the 'real spot' where Lord Krishna was born. As those aware of the story know, on the

1

eventful rainy night when Lord Krishna was born in the prison cell in Mathura, His father Vasudev took Him to Gokul to protect Him from the evil Kansa. Here too, there is a confusion. There are two towns near Mathura which claim to be the 'real' Gokul, the place where Lord Krishna and Lord Balarama spent Their childhood. One of them is present day Gokul, which has the advantage of having the same name as the place mentioned in the Scriptures. The other is an adjacent town, Mahavan, which is a couple of kilometres from this town and claims to be the 'real' Gokul! So, what do we have now? Each town has its own Nanda Bhavan where Nanda Maharaj is supposed to have lived with Yashoda, Rohini, Krishna, and Balarama. Each place has its own share of tourist spots where the demons Putana, Trinavarta, and others were killed. Each flaunts the divine spot where the Supreme Lord showed the entire cosmos in His mouth to Yashoda.

Any discussion on Krishna would be incomplete without talking about His divine consort Radha. Since time immemorial, people have been trying to figure out what relationship this Divine Couple shared. This is linked to another pertinent question — who is Radha? There are many people who believe that Radha is an incarnation of the Goddess of Fortune, Goddess Lakshmi. Since Goddess Lakshmi is the wife of Lord Vishnu, they believe that Radha married Lord Krishna. They believe that She was His wife, albeit for a very brief period, before he left the dusty villages of Brij to go back to Mathura. There are others who believe that Radha was a *Rishi* (sage) in Her previous birth and because of the blessings of Lord Vishnu was born as Radha, His consort. These people believe that Radha and Krishna shared a platonic relationship. According to them, the relationship between the divine couple was that of God and devotee. There are many who believe Radha and Krishna were divine soul mates who shared Their joys and sorrows together during Lord Krishna's stay in Brij Bhoomi. There are some who believe Radha to be a *part of* Krishna, *an expansion*. According to them, Radha and Krishna are two individuals from the same soul. The analogy they use is that of the sun and sunshine. One comes from the other and you can't have one without the other. The same can be said of Radha and Krishna. What makes this relationship even more unusual is the fact that Radha was older than Krishna. Again, the difference in the age between the two is not clearly known. There are some who believe Radha was older than Krishna by only a few months. There are some who think She was older by one full year. There are a few who believe the difference to be as high as five years. There is also a mystery surrounding the identity of the man She married. Some believe She was engaged to another cowherd, even before She met Krishna. There are others who say that She was already married to another cowherd when she first met Krishna. There are a few who believe that though She was engaged to another cowherd, She broke off that engagement and married Krishna. There are others who say that though She broke off Her engagement and spent Her time with Krishna, She didn't marry Him. The 'other cowherd' in question? Well, here too, there is no consensus! Some believe his name to be Ayyan and others say it was Abhimanyu (not to be confused with Arjuna's son with the same name). In fact, there are a few who say that Ayyan (Abhimanyu?) was not a cowherd but served in the army of Kansa! The profession of Radha's father Vrishabhanu is equally uncertain. Some believe he was an ordinary cowherd. Others believe he was a king of a part of Brij Bhoomi.

One more mystery surrounding Radha is the fact that there is no explicit mention about Her in the ancient text *Srimad Bhagavatam*. There is an implicit reference about Her but you won't find Her name anywhere. One of the earliest texts that mentioned Her by name is the legendary poem *Geet Govind* scripted by the famous poet Jayadeva. However, some people believe that Sage Shuka deliberately avoided taking Her name while narrating *Srimad Bhagavatam* to King Parikshit. They believe that Shuka was Radha's pet parrot in one of his earlier births and that he had such love and respect for Her that had he uttered Her name he would have swooned for six months.

There are different versions regarding when Krishna first met Radha and also the location of Their first meeting. According to one version, He was still an infant, swaying in a cradle when Radha came from Barsana with Her family to Nanda Rai's house in Gokul. However, another version says that when Krishna was a three year old boy, he was dragging the grinder mortar tied to His back, and Radha met Him then for the first time. This happened in front of the two trees that He had just uprooted, to give liberation to Nalakuvara and Manigriva and release them from a curse.

If the location of their first meeting is uncertain, so is the venue of Their last meeting. The most popular belief is that Krishna met Radha for the last time in Brij Bhoomi before He and Balarama accompanied Akroor to Mathura. A second version says that They met for the last time in Kurukshetra, when They came with Their respective families to bathe in the sacred Samantapanchaka tank after a solar eclipse. A third version states that Radha, along with Her gopi friends, came to Dwarka to meet Krishna for the last time. It is believed that They bathed at Gopi Sarovar, after which, They gave up Their mortal bodies and their souls achieved liberation.

People ask why Radha and Krishna separated. Why did Krishna not return from Mathura and go back to Radha? Why did He make Her wait forever? The truth perhaps is that, Krishna indeed wanted to come back and take Radha with Him to Mathura. He wanted to make her the Queen of Mathura. However, Radha was reluctant. She believed that the Kanha whom She loved was a carefree cowherd of Vrindavan. She felt that this Kanha would be very different from Prince Krishna of Mathura. She loved playing in the fields and forests of Nandagaon and Barsana. She did not want to be confined within the palaces of Mathura. She knew she would miss the open spaces of Barsana. So it was Radha who was against going to Mathura to stay with Krishna. Others believe that since Radha and Krishna are part of the same Supreme Lord, there is no question of separation. It is just a question of one soul in two bodies.

There are differences of opinion regarding the location of Dwarka where Lord Krishna spent the last 97 years of His life. Most people believe that ancient Dwarka, where Lord Krishna lived, is the same as present day Dwarka. However, there are others who believe that ancient Dwarka was close to the current location of Dwarka, but not the same. They believe that ancient Dwarka was hit by a tsunami and was submerged in the Arabian Sea. There is also a view that combines both these theories and states that ancient Dwarka where Lord Krishna lived is a combination of what is present day Dwarka and also the submerged portions of the great city that have been found during recent excavations. There are a few who believe that none of this is true. They say that the ancient city of Dwarka is nowhere near the present Dwarka on the western tip of Gujarat. They are convinced that the ancient Dwarka was in the current district of Junagadh, on the southern tip of Gujarat. Their logic is simple. It is a well known fact that during the end of His stay on earth, Lord Krishna advised His Yadavas to visit the holy place Prabhas Patan which is located near Somnath. The Yadava men went to Prabhas Patan and performed all religious rituals during the day. However, as night fell, they began to drink and soon got intoxicated. In their inebriated state, they began to abuse each other and killed each other. Towards the end of this midnight carnage, Lord Krishna and Lord Balarama left for Their Holy Abode, Vaikunta. The moot question raised by many people is, if Lord Krishna advised His men to visit Prabhas Patan which is near Somnath, shouldn't Dwarka also be somewhere close to Somnath in Junagadh? If Lord Krishna wanted His men to visit a few holy places, why would he ask them to travel 250 km, the distance between the current towns of Dwarka and Somnath? During those days of bullock carts and horse carriages, it would have taken them a few days to cover that distance. Based on this logic, they stick to their theory that the ancient Dwarka was near Somnath.

Though there are different versions of the story, the most popular one believes that a major part of erstwhile Dwarka city is now submerged in the Arabian Sea and the remaining part is the current Dwarka town. The original Dwarka city extended up to Bet Dwarka in the north, Okha in the south, and Pindara in the east. The portions between Bet Dwarka and Okha now lie under the Arabian Sea and the only way to commute between the two places is by ferry. It is believed that Dwarka's submergence in the Arabian Sea coincided with the departure of Lord Krishna to His Holy Abode Vaikunta which also marked the beginning of Kali Yuga.

The Archaeological Society of India (ASI) have conducted many explorations and confirmed the existence of this holy city.

The Marine Archaeology Unit (MAU) of the National Institute of Oceanography also conducted underwater studies in 1983 in the coastal waters of Dwarka under the guidance and supervision of the world renowned Marine Archeologist Dr. S.R. Rao.

Between 1983 and 1990, the township of Dwarka was discovered and found to be extending to more than half a kilometre from the shore. At Bet Dwarka, the team found a wall, 560 metres long, visible on the shore itself. Dating the pottery found there gave them the date of the civilisation — 528 B.C. They also unearthed a *mudra* (seal) which was an important clue confirming the existence of Lord Krishna's city because the *Mahabharata* refers to the fact that Lord Krishna wanted every citizen to carry some sort of identity (*mudra*). The township was built in six sectors along the banks of a river. It was also noticed that the layout of Dwarka city, as described in the holy books matched with the findings of the lost city discovered by the team led by Dr. Rao.

There are many who have challenged the veracity of the episode of the Yadavas killing one another and Krishna departing to His Heavenly Abode at the end of the carnage. They have called it purely fictitious and a figment of imagination. Their logic is that Lord Krishna was the Supreme Lord and omnipotent. How could He and His men succumb to the curse of a mere mortal Gandhari, at the end of the Kurukshetra war, which led to the bloody destruction of the Yadava dynasty? Could He not have averted this? However, the believers in the authenticity of this gory episode have an answer to this. They believe that Lord Krishna was aware through His divine omniscience that the Yadavas would be intoxicated with power and would cease to walk on the path of righteousness a few years after the Kurukshetra war. The only solution would be to end their dynasty through self-destruction. Gandhari was a mere tool in His scheme of things. That's probably why, Lord Krishna, much to the astonishment of the onlookers, smiled even as Gandhari abused and hurled her venomous curse on Lord Krishna and His Yadava dynasty. He was merely using her as a tool and she was only obeying His command. Lord Krishna had the highest regard for women. He wanted to show the world that before a pious and righteous woman, even the Supreme Lord has to bow.

If you think that Dwarka and Somnath have lots of unanswered questions, then Kurukshetra is not far behind. The date of the famous Kurukshetra battle has been debated over the years. The date ranges from 150 B.C. to 3138 B.C. and each date has been computed with considerable justification. There are also different versions regarding the total number of verses in the *Bhagavad Gita* that Lord Krishna preached to Arjuna at Kurukshetra, ranging from 700 to 745.

The debates continue...

There are these and other interesting questions about Lord Krishna and His life in this book, but I am chiefly interested in describing the places that I visited and the legends associated with each of them. It has been my humble effort to take the readers to the different sacred places in India where Lord Krishna spent a major part of His life.

2

Brij Bhoomi

...

Brij Bhoomi is where Lord Krishna performed several amazing acts 5000 years ago. It covers an area of 2325 sq. km. It extends from Banchari in the north to Agra in the south. The Brij Bhoomi consists of 12 forests (*vanas*) and 24 groves (*upavanas*) and all of them are considered places of pilgrimage. Each place is of historical significance and associated with various incidents that took place in Lord Krishna's life.

Mathura is considered to be the 'heart' of Brij Bhoomi, since it is at the centre and also happens to be the birthplace of Lord Krishna. The important towns to the east of Mathura are Raval, Baldeo, Gokul, and Mahavan which are located on the other side of River Yamuna. Adjacent, and to the north of Mathura, is the temple town of Vrindavan. On the other side of Mathura is Madhuvan. To the west of Mathura are Radha Kund and Goverdhan. To the northwest are Barsana and Nandagaon. The River Yamuna flows through the heart of Brij Bhoomi. There are many who consider Yamuna to be more sacred than Ganga because Lord Krishna sanctified Yamuna during His childhood days by playing and swimming in it.

Brij Bhoomi narrates the eternal love tale between Radha and Krishna. People here believe that you can reach Krishna only through Radha. This could be the reason why Radha is held in very high esteem in the Brij region. It is probably the most commonly used word by the man on the street. The word 'Radhe' has different meanings, depending on the context! If you are travelling through the narrow lanes of Vrindavan in a cycle-rickshaw, the driver may loudly say 'Radhe! Radhe!' to the passers-by who are blocking him. When two people meet, they greet each other with a cheerful 'Radhe! Radhe!' When the same two depart, they bid farewell with 'Radhe! Radhe!' When someone arrives at your doorstep, don't be surprised if they enquire 'Radhe? Radhe?' I realised that the holy name 'Radhe' stands for 'excuse me', 'hello', 'goodbye', 'is anyone there?' and probably has many more meanings! There are numerous places in Brij Bhoomi that are witness to the eternal friendship between Radha and Krishna. As you walk through the lanes of the dusty towns or cut across the fields, you can feel Their divine presence. They seem to be present everywhere.

Every year, during the month of Shravana, to commemorate the birth of Lord Krishna, Brij Parikrama is held along with colourful celebrations. Thousands of devotees, from all over India, come to Brij Bhoomi and perform the sacred Parikrama, which encompasses the 12 forests, 24 groves, River Yamuna, Goverdhan Hill and all the important towns associated with the life and times of Lord Krishna.

The 12 forests are Bahulavan, Bhadravan, Bilvan, Bhandiravan, Kamyavan, Khadiravan, Kumudavan, Lohavan, Madhuvan, Mahavan, Talavan, and Vrindavan. The 24 groves are Gokul, Govardhan, Barsana, Nandagram, Sanket, Paramadra, Aring, Sessai, Mat, Uchagram, Kelvan, Sri Kund, Gandharvavan, Parsoli, Bilchhu, Bacchavan, Adibadri, Karahla, Ajnokh, Pisaya, Kokilavan, Dadhigram, Kotvan, and Raval.

Vishram Ghat in Mathura is the starting point of the Brij Parikrama. The devotees bathe in Yamuna at Vishram Ghat and commence their Parikrama. Many of them perform the entire Brij Parikrama barefoot.

3

Mathura

...

"*Yada yada hi dharmasya glanir bhavati bharatha,
Abhyuthanam adharmasya tadaathmanam srijamyaham*"

("Whenever there is a decline in righteousness, and a rise in
unrighteousness, at that time, I descend Myself, Oh descendant of
Bharata.")

(*Bhagavad Gita* 4.7)

Mathura is one of the holiest places in India since it is the
birthplace of Lord Krishna. Brij Bhoomi is where Lord Krishna
spent His childhood and Mathura is the biggest town in Brij
Bhoomi. It is approximately 150 km to the south-east of Delhi,
on the Delhi-Agra Highway. Mathura is located at 27.28⁰ N
latitude and 77.41⁰E longitude.

The drive to Mathura from Delhi takes about five hours. I had
been advised by many travellers to start off early in the morning
from Delhi, to avoid the heavy traffic at Faridabad, enroute
Mathura. Since Faridabad is an industrial town, it is best to cross
the Delhi-Haryana border before nine in the morning. The traffic
begins to build up after that. I suggested to my driver Ashwani
that we leave Delhi at around seven in the morning. He said that
though it was a good idea to leave early to beat the 'office traffic',
it would be quite a challenge to drive when visibility was poor, due
to the thick fog that engulfs the entire city during the winter. I
told Ashwani, "Don't worry! We are visiting the holy land of Lord
Krishna. He will find a way out."

Ashwani replied, "I admire your optimism, but let me warn you that visibility has been less than one metre during the past one week. It would be foolhardy to venture out in such conditions."

I replied, "Let us get ready by seven a.m. and then take the final call."

Ashwani nodded and headed off to his sleeping bag.

The next morning heralded a pleasant surprise. The fog that had engulfed the entire city, from evening till late morning, during the past one week, had suddenly vanished completely!

Ashwani, who was cleaning the car when I came out of the hotel building, was all smiles, "Saab! You were right. Lord Krishna has taken care of the fog!"

We hastened at a speed of 80 miles an hour in the air-conditioned Toyota Qualis I had hired for the trip. The entire atmosphere was crystal clear and there was absolutely no hangover of the week-long fog. It was just unbelievable! Or should I say, knowing the kind ways of the Lord, this was not really unbelievable for the believer, but just a re-confirmation of the presence and potency of the Mighty Lord and His way of beckoning us to His Holy Abode in such a hassle-free way.

Since we had started quite early, we didn't get stuck at Faridabad. Traffic was building up, but there were no signs of any traffic jam yet. What was impressive about the highway was that it was a four-lane highway, with absolutely no potholes. The median in the middle of the road was adorned with grass and shrubs all along the highway.

We continued our journey and reached Mathura by noon. I had booked a room in Hotel Radha Ashok. This was probably the best hotel in Mathura, though it is a bit expensive by Mathura standards. However, the location and ambience of this hotel is very good. It was not located in the crowded and narrow bylanes of Mathura town, but in a quiet spot, away from the hustle and bustle. Just a couple of miles before we reached Mathura town, we noticed a narrow quiet road to our left. We took that road and within half a mile, we found Hotel Radha Ashok on our right.

The receptionist welcomed us with a warm smile and asked the hotel boy to take us to our room. The room was very impressive, with all the modern amenities that one would generally find in a five-star hotel in a big city. Since most of the temples in Mathura were closed in the afternoon, we decided to have our lunch and then commence our spiritual journey into the holy town of Mathura.

After lunch, we drove towards Mathura town. We took the Delhi-Agra Highway and after a couple of kilometres, took a left turn. As soon as we turned, we were surrounded by no fewer than 20 guides. The guides at Mathura are quite aggressive compared to their counterparts at other famous tourist destinations in the country. They insist or rather *threaten* to escort you to all the temples in the vicinity! Each person insists that he is not a guide but a Brijwasi brahmin student, who desperately needs money to finance his education, even if he looks more than 50 years old! We had been cautioned at Hotel Radha Ashok, not to hire any of these non-Government approved guides. However, avoiding them was proving to be a big challenge. They kept insisting on taking us to Krishna Janmasthan. I told them that I wanted to visit Kansa Qila. They walked away with a look of disbelief on their face. Looking at our car registration number, it was obvious to them that we had come from Delhi. Had we driven for five hours just to see Kansa Qila, they left wondering!

KANSA QILA

Kansa Qila means Kansa's fort. This is the place from where the tyrant king, Kansa, ruled Mathura and harassed its residents 5000 years ago. It is believed that the fort, which is in ruins today, was built by Raja Mansingh of Jaipur on the exact location where Kansa had built his

Kansa Qila

palace. An observatory was built here later by Maharaja Sawai Jai Singh of Ajmer, who was very fond of astronomy.

This fort is on a small hillock and not very easily accessible by road. We drove halfway up the hillock and then had to walk the rest of the way on a narrow dusty path to reach the fort. There were hardly any visitors here. The entire fort was in ruins. Whatever was left, was not taken care of. No wonder the local guides were shocked when I told them that I wanted to visit Kansa Qila!

Path leading to the ruined fort

When I reached atop the hillock, I could see only the remains of a ruined fort. What might have been beautiful gardens a few centuries ago are now reduced to unkempt grasslands, with grass and weeds growing everywhere. As I gazed at the ruined fort, I could visualise the beautiful palace that stood in its place thousands of years ago. A palace that was home to the King of Mathura.

Ugrasena is the King of Mathura. He is held in high regard by his subjects, since he is known as a just ruler. He treats saints and sages with great respect and dignity. There is hardly any crime in his kingdom. Women and children lead a very safe life. It is not unusual to see women walk alone in the city in the middle of the night. Trade is also flourishing. There is hardly any sign of poverty in the kingdom.

However, all this is now slowly changing. Ugrasena's son, Kansa is growing up. As he is growing in years, so is he in wickedness. In his previous birth, Kansa was born as Kalanemi and had been killed by Lord Vishnu's incarnation, Lord Rama. Kansa continued his demonic behaviour in this birth as well. He has total disregard for saints and sages. He and his friends love to harass sages when they are performing yagnas and pujas. The kingdom, which was once regarded as a safe haven for women and children, is no longer so. There is crime everywhere. People are killed for materialistic gains. Travellers are no longer safe from dacoits. King Ugrasena is helpless, since his son Kansa is beginning to gain wield a strong influence over his army.

Inspite of his cruel and wicked nature, Kansa has a soft corner for one person he dearly adores. It is his cousin, Devaki, daughter of Devaka. He treats his cousin as his own sister. He is happy that she is getting married to his good friend, Prince Vasudev.

The wedding of Devaki and Vasudev has just concluded. As is the custom in traditional marriages, Devaki must leave her house and go with Vasudev to start a new life. Kansa feels sad that his sister will be by his side only for a few more minutes and after that, she will be gone from Mathura. He is unable to bear the pangs of separation. He wonders what to do. Suddenly, he gets an idea. He tells Vasudev, "Oh Vasudev! I have a request."

Vasudev says, "Kansa, please tell me your wish."

Kansa says, "Devaki is my beloved sister. She will soon leave this kingdom. I want to spend as much time as possible with her. Can I accompany you and Devaki in your chariot to your kingdom? This way, I will be able to spend some more time with her. I will return to Mathura once you reach your kingdom."

Vasudev hugs Kansa and says, "Dear friend! Please come with us. You need not return once we reach my kingdom. You are most welcome to stay as our guest, for as long as you wish."

Devaki and Vasudev bid farewell to all their friends and relatives in Mathura. They mount the royal chariot, waiting to take them home. Kansa also joins them. The royal chariot is decorated with flowers and precious gems. It has seats made of soft satin cushions. They make themselves comfortable in the chariot. Together the three of them speed towards the outskirts of Mathura. Many residents of Mathura do not want to leave their beloved daughter so soon. They all accompany the chariot in a long procession. There is happiness and joy everywhere. All the birds are singing along with the soft melodies played by the royal orchestra.

The procession has covered a few miles. Suddenly the atmosphere begins to change. The birds stop singing and dark clouds gather. There is darkness everywhere. Everyone is surprised at this sudden change. Vasudev realises *that this is not a good omen. He is right.*

Suddenly they hear a loud voice from the Heavens, "Oh Kansa! You fool! You are escorting your beloved sister to her kingdom, but you don't know that she will give birth to eight sons and her eighth son is destined to kill you." Kansa is stunned when he hears this. He loves his sister so much. How could she give birth to someone who could kill him? How could she do this to him? Hot-headed that he is, he decides that the best thing would be to kill her immediately. He draws his sword and is about to kill Devaki on the spot. However, Vasudev realises his brother-in-law's evil intentions, and rushes towards him. He falls at Kansa's feet and says, "Oh Kansa! Devaki is your beloved sister. I am your good friend. How can you think of killing her, just because of the voice we heard?"

Kansa roars, "I am not taking any chances Vasudev."

He pushes Vasudev aside and swings his sword over Devaki.

Vasudev realises that Kansa is determined to kill Devaki. He shouts, "Wait Kansa. I have an idea."

Kansa puts his sword down and asks, "Tell me what is on your mind?"

Vasudev says, "I promise to hand over the eighth child to you. Since you are destined to be killed by the eighth one, why should you kill Devaki and the first seven?"

Kansa thinks this over and replies, "I will imprison you. I will take the eighth child and kill him. However, do not cheat me. If I notice that you are lying, or cheating me then I will kill both of you instantaneously."

Vasudev comforts him, "Oh Kansa! I am the most righteous among kings. I am the most truthful among noblemen. I would die rather than lie or cheat a friend."

Kansa too is aware of this. He knows that his friend Vasudev would rather die than lie. He sheaths his sword and shouts at his guards, "Take them away! Throw them into the prison!"

The chariot and the accompanying procession turn back and head towards Mathura. The news of Devaki and Vasudev being taken as captives soon reaches everyone in the kingdom. Kansa reaches his palace. He sees King Ugrasena waiting at the entrance. The King looks grim. He thunders, "Kansa! How dare you do this? How can you imprison Devaki and Vasudev? They are newly-wed and they deserve to be in the palace and not in the cold cells."

Kansa says, *"Devaki's eighth son is destined to kill me. Vasudev has promised to hand him over to me. I have imprisoned them because I want them to stay under my watchful eyes."*

Ugrasena is seething with anger. He shouts at his guards, *"Guards! Arrest my son Kansa. Throw him into the prison."*

None of his guards move. Ugrasena is shocked. He repeats his command. There is still no response from any of them.

He shouts, *"Didn't you hear me? Arrest him!"*

Kansa laughs wickedly, *"My father! You are so naïve! None of them work for you any more. They now work for me."*

He turns towards his guards and instructs them, *"Arrest my father. Throw him into the prison. I am now the King of Mathura!"*

The guards rush towards a stunned Ugrasena and holding him by his shoulders, lead him away to prison.

The news of King Ugrasena's arrest and Kansa taking over as king reaches the streets of Mathura. The people shiver with fear. They realise that the kingdom will now become even more unsafe for women and children. They sense crime increasing everywhere. Saints and sages are assassinated by Kansa and his men. Trouble is brewing everywhere. The saints pray to Almighty God to protect them. All the Gods and Goddesses witness these diabolic events on Earth. They know that there is only one Person who can save Earth from this catastrophe. They rush to Vaikunta, the Holy Abode of Lord Vishnu. Lord Vishnu is resting, with His eyes closed, on the giant serpent Lord Sheshanag. Goddess Lakshmi is sitting near His feet.

The Gods and Goddesses bow to Lord Vishnu and Goddess Lakshmi and plead, *"Oh Lord! Oh Narayana! We have been witnessing the most shocking events on Earth. There is crime everywhere. Righteousness has lost its place. Sages are being assassinated everyday. Kansa is a tyrannical king. He and his men are torturing the people. It has become hell on Earth for the poor denizens. Please protect them."*

Lord Vishnu opens His eyes and smiles, *"Whenever Dharma and Righteousness are destroyed, I incarnate and go to Earth and protect the people. Please do not worry. Go back to your Abode. I will soon take birth as the eighth Son of Devaki and Vasudev and kill Kansa."* The Gods and Goddesses, relieved at hearing this, bow once again to Lord Vishnu and return to Their Abode.

KRISHNA JANMASTHAN TEMPLE

Entrance of Krishna Janmasthan Temple

Krishna Janmasthan is the most important temple in Brij Bhoomi. As the name indicates, this is the very spot where Lord Krishna was born 5000 years ago. The temple is located in the heart of the city. For security reasons, private vehicles are not allowed inside the premises of the Krishna Janmasthan Temple. In fact, no vehicle can be parked within 500 metres of the temple's premises. We parked our car in a small field nearby, which is also a parking lot.

As soon as I got off the car I was surrounded by no less than 50 guides. Each one of them insisted on taking me to Krishna Janmasthan. There seemed to be lots of confusion among them regarding the timings of the temple. Some of them promised to escort me to the temple right away and show me all the spots that breathed the holy 5000 year old history. The rest of them argued that the temple was closed for lunch and would open only after 3 p.m. They offered to escort me from Mathura to Gokul and take me around the temples of Gokul.

As the two groups were busy locked in a heated argument, I stealthily managed to escape and made my way towards the Krishna Janmasthan Temple. As I stepped on to the main road, where the famous temple stood, I saw a police barricade that prevented all vehicles from entering the road. The only way to approach the temple was on foot. Small gift shops were lined up on either side of the road. It was amazing to see that although every shop sold similar items, all of them seemed to be doing very good business. All of them sold various souvenirs of Radha and Krishna — idols, cassettes, DVDs, CDs, T-shirts, books, and posters. I was told at the entrance that the temple was closed and would open only at 3 p.m. I still had about 30 minutes and so I went around the colourful shops near the temple premises.

Sri Krishna Janmasthan Temple is a few metres above the ground — almost like as if it were on a small hillock. As I reached the huge gates at the main entrance heavily armed security guards welcomed me. After a thorough frisking by the 'bomb detector' wielding policemen, I was allowed to walk up the ramp. When I reached the top of the ramp, I saw a huge open courtyard. Huge and open-air courtyards seem to be a hallmark of most of the ancient temples in North India.

The original temple was built by Vajranabha and later re-built by Vikramaditya. The original idol was 15 feet tall and made of gold and precious gems. Mahmud Ghazni ransacked the temple and desecrated the idols. It is believed that this temple was destroyed and rebuilt 17 times. The final assault was by Aurangzeb.

Currently, the Sri Krishna Janmasthan Temple complex houses many temples. At the left corner of the courtyard is the Keshav Dev Temple. The idols are on the left hand side of the temple. In the middle of the sanctum sanctorum, is a huge idol of Lord Krishna, made of white marble. Below this idol are smaller idols of Krishna, Radha, and Balarama.

Behind the Keshav Dev Temple is the Giriraja Temple. There is a black idol of Lord Krishna here. Like in many other Krishna temples in north India, this idol also has only the face of the Supreme Lord and not the full figure. As I proceeded, I came across the Yogamaya Temple.

To the right of the courtyard, after I climbed a few steps, I came across the biggest temple in the complex. This is also the most crowded. The main deities in this temple are Radha and Krishna. Both idols are made of white marble. Krishna is to the left of Radha. Below these huge idols is a smaller pair of Radha-Krishna idols. There is also a black idol (only the face) of Krishna to the right.

To the left of the main sanctum sanctorum is a counter where *pedas* (a sweet made from sugar and milk) was sold. I bought 250 grams of these and gave it to the priest. The priest took the packet of *pedas* from me and went close to the Radha-Krishna idols. He performed a *puja* and returned a few minutes later with the *peda* packet. He gave it back to me (it had become God's *prasada* after the *puja*) and a garland of marigold flowers.

As I performed the parikrama of the main deities in the sanctum sanctorum, I saw huge pictures depicting the *Dasha Avataras* (ten incarnations) of Lord Vishnu. To the left of the sanctum sanctorum is a small room that houses idols of Jagannath, Balarama, and Subhadra, reminiscent of Jagannath Puri. To the right is another similar small room that houses the idols of Rama, Sita, and Lakshmana. Right opposite, is an idol of Lord Hanuman, ever waiting to serve His Lord. Next to this, is a small room, with a Shiva Linga called Keshaveshwar. The Shiva Linga is enclosed in a cage-like structure. Opposite this is another room that houses the idol of Goddess Durga.

Between this temple and the Keshav Dev temple is the main and most important temple, though not the biggest. I desperately wanted to see this one since this is the actual birth spot of Lord Krishna. Next to the Keshav Dev temple, is a narrow, inconspicuous looking entrance leading to a passage that finally leads to a dimly lit small room. This narrow passage is the prison passage leading to the small room that was a prison cell 5000 years ago, where Kansa had imprisoned Devaki and Vasudev. On the right side of the room is an elevated platform that has a slab that marks the exact birth spot of Lord Krishna. There are various paintings and pictures adorning the wall above the raised platform. To the left is a painting depicting Lord Shiva bowing to Lord Vishnu. On the right is a painting of Lord Brahma paying obeisance to Lord Vishnu. In the centre is a picture of Devaki and Vasudev getting a glimpse of the Supreme Lord in the prison cell. Below this is a picture of Vasudev carrying an Infant Krishna in a small basket, across the River Yamuna that was in spate, on the rainy night when the Supreme Lord descended on this planet. There is also a picture of Lord Krishna, four-armed like Lord Vishnu. On the raised platform I saw an idol of Lord Krishna on a slab of stone. I found numerous devotees bowing and touching this sacred slab with reverence.

Above the raised platform, I found verses of *Garbha Stuti* painted on the walls. These were the holy verses sung by Lord Brahma and Lord Shiva in praise of Lord Vishnu. Since these verses were addressed to the womb of Devaki when she was carrying the foetus of Lord Vishnu, they are known as *Garbha Stuti* (verses for the foetus).

To the right of the raised platform, is a beautiful verse written in Hindi:

"Jinke dono haath Bansuri se shobha paarhe hai, Sri Ango ki kanthi nutan megh ke samaan shyam hai, saavale ang par pitambar sushobith ho raha hai, laal hote pakke huve bimbafal ki sushma chine lethe hai, sundar mukh Poornima ke Chandrama ko bhi lajith kar raha hai, aur netra praful kamal ke samaan manohar pratit hothe hai, un Bhagwan Sri Krishna ke siva doosra koi bhi parama tatva hai yeh mein nahi jaantha"

(He whose Hands are adorned with the flute, whose fresh limbs and body are like dark blue clouds, He whose dark body is adorned with golden clothes, whose red lips are like a ripened fruit, whose beautiful face can even put to shame the beautiful full moon, whose eyes are as beautiful as a lotus, I can't imagine this Supreme Lord to be anyone but Lord Krishna).

Though this room is quite small and dark, almost like the prison that it was thousands of years ago, you can't find a holier place than this in the country since it marks the exact birth place of Lord Krishna, when Lord Vishnu descended to earth in His eighth *avatara* (incarnation).

Devaki and Vasudev are thrown into the prison cell. Kansa has instructed his men to chain their hands and feet although the couple have been locked in a cell that is heavily fortified.

Devaki weeps and wonders that instead of being in the comforts of the beautiful palace along with my husband Vasudev, here she is, sitting on a cold and damp prison. Instead of soft cushions on her bed, she has a bare floor. She felt sorry for Vasudev. What crime had he committed? If he had not married her then he would not have been in such a sorry state. Vasudev, as if reading her mind, consoles his wife and asks her to spend her time thinking of the Supreme Lord instead of brooding over the recent events over which they have little control.

A few months pass by. Devaki gives birth to a beautiful male child. Sage

Narada goes to the court of king Kansa.

Kansa asks, "Oh Narada! What brings you here?"

Sage Narada smiles, "I heard Devaki has given birth to her first child."

Kansa nods his head, "Yes but it is the first child so I have nothing to worry. I am destined to be killed by her eighth child and Vasudev has promised to hand over his eighth child to me."

Sage Narada laughs, "Oh Kansa! You are so naïve! Which is the first child and which is the eighth child depends on the way you count. If you count in the forward direction then the first born is the first child. However, if you count in the backward direction then the last born is the first child. So it depends on the way you count."

Kansa glares at Sage Narada. He has got him confused.

He asks Narada, "What do you mean by this? What are you trying to say?"

Narada laughs, "Oh King! All that I am trying to do is caution you. You cannot assume that the last son will be the eighth son," And saying this, Sage Narada departs.

Kansa is in a fix. How can he know which of the eight sons is destined to kill him? Another wicked idea takes shape. He decides to kill all the children.

Kansa enters the prison cell where Devaki and Vasudev have been watching their first child.

He asks Devaki, "Where is your son? Hand him over to me."

Devaki pleads, "Oh Brother! We have promised to give our eighth son to you. Why do you need our first born?"

Kansa, with a wicked gleam in his eyes, says, "It depends on the way you count. I am not sure who the eighth son is. I will kill all of them."

Kansa snatches the infant from the hands of a wailing Devaki and flings the infant on the hard stone of the prison walls. The newborn is instantly killed. The blood splashes on the white prison clothes of Devaki and Vasudev. They are heartbroken. Devaki weeps inconsolably. Kansa leaves the room with a triumphant look on his face.

The years roll by. Devaki gives birth to five more sons. Each time a child is born, the security guards report the cries of a wailing child to Kansa.

Kansa wastes no time. He goes inside the prison cell and throws the newly born child against the hard prison ground. This way, the first six sons are killed by the evil Kansa on the day they are born.

Devaki is once again pregnant. She is expecting her seventh son. Lord Vishnu remembers the promise He had given to His serpent king Lord Sheshanag in Their previous incarnation. Lord Vishnu and Lord Sheshanag had taken birth as Lord Rama and Lord Lakshmana during Treta Yuga. Towards the end of Their incarnations, Lord Sheshanag had requested Lord Vishnu, "Oh My Supreme Lord! In this incarnation, I was Your younger brother and because of this I had to face many dilemmas. One of them led to the abduction of Sita Devi. In My next incarnation, I do not want to face such dilemmas as a younger brother. Please make Me Your elder brother."

Lord Vishnu had smiled and blessed Him, "You got an opportunity to serve Me since You were the younger One. I would like to serve You in Our next incarnation. I will be born as Your younger Brother. Let Your wish come true."

Lord Vishnu knows the time has come for Lord Sheshanag to be born as the seventh son of Devaki so that He can take birth subsequently, as His younger Brother, the eighth Son of Devaki. He asks Lord Sheshanag to enter the body of the embryo that is growing in Devaki's womb. Lord Sheshanag follows Lord Vishnu's instructions. Lord Vishnu now calls Goddess Yogamaya.

Yogamaya bows before Lord Vishnu and asks Him, "Oh Supreme Lord! What made You remember Me? How can I serve You?"

Lord Vishnu says, "Oh Goddess! Lord Sheshanag has entered the foetus that is in Devaki's womb. If He is born to Devaki then His life would be in danger. Please transfer the foetus from Devaki's womb to Rohini's womb."

Goddess Yogamaya bows to Lord Vishnu and says, "As You wish, Oh Lord!"

Rohini is Vasudev's first wife. Vasudev had sent her to Gokul for her safety when he was imprisoned at Mathura. She is staying with Nanda Rai and his wife Yashoda.

Rohini is sleeping. She sees a bright glow in her dream. The glow of light slowly becomes bigger and brighter. She sees Goddess Yogamaya standing at the end of the light. Goddess Yogamaya says, "Oh Rohini! You will soon become pregnant. You will give birth to a handsome and strong baby boy."

Rohini, who is childless, hears this with a mixed reaction. She is happy that she will become a mother soon. However, she is worried about what society will say. Her husband Vasudev has sent her to Gokul for safety. She is staying with Nanda. What will the people think? Won't they suspect that she has an illicit relationship with Nanda?

She expresses this concern to Goddess Yogamaya.

The Goddess pacifies her, "Don't worry, My child. Please do not worry about who the father of the Child is. It is none other than your husband Vasudev himself. I will also ensure that the people of Gokul do not suspect that you have been having an illicit relationship with Nanda."

Saying thus, Goddess Yogamaya disappears. She now appears in the dream of Nanda Rai and informs him, "Oh Nanda! Rohini is soon going to give birth to a Boy. The father of her Child is none other than her husband, Vasudev. However, since she has been staying with you, the people of Gokul may suspect that she has been having an illicit relationship with you. Luckily, many people in this village are unaware that she is staying with you. Tomorrow, I want you to officially 'bring' Rohini from Mathura to Gokul. People will think that she conceived in Mathura and has now come to stay with you."

Nanda Rai bows to Goddess Yogamaya. Goddess Yogamaya transfers the foetus from Devaki's womb to Rohini's womb.

It is early morning. The first rays of the sun enter the prison cell through the windows. Devaki wakes up in her prison cell in Mathura. She suddenly notices that her belly is looking flat. She is shocked and screams. Vasudev wakes up.

He asks her, "Devaki! What's the matter?"

Devaki is weeping. She sobs, "Oh Lord! I have had a miscarriage. I have lost my foetus."

Vasudev also notices her flat belly. He realises that there must have been some kind of divine intervention, but he is unable to figure out what has happened.

The news of Devaki's miscarriage soon reaches Kansa. He immediately suspects foul play. He rushes to the prison cell where he has imprisoned Devaki and Vasudev.

He shouts, "Devaki! Where have you hidden your infant? Don't try to cheat me. I know you have hidden your baby!"

Devaki continues to sob and ignores his presence. Kansa is now fuming. He pulls out his sword and says, "I had enough of this! I am going to kill both of you."

Lord Sheshanag, using His divine vision, realises that His parents need protection from Kansa. He multiplies Himself into thousands of serpents and enters the prison cell where Devaki and Vasudev are held captive. The army of serpents attacks Kansa. They begin to spew venom at him. Kansa is stunned. From where did so many serpents enter the prison cell suddenly? He drops his sword and rushes out of the prison to the safe confines of his palace. The serpents are invisible to Devaki and Vasudev so they are puzzled at Kansa's behaviour. They wonder why he looked so scared and ran away.

In the meanwhile, Rohini gives birth to a strong handsome Boy, He is none other than the incarnation of Lord Sheshanag Himself. Since Goddess Yogamaya had extracted Him from the womb of Devaki and transferred Him to the womb of Rohini, He is also known as 'Sankarshana' which means, 'one who is extracted'.

Vasudev was Sage Kashyap in his previous birth. His present wives Devaki and Rohini were Aditi and Kadru (Kashyap's wives) in their previous birth. Aditi had given birth to Vishnu's Vamana Avatara in that birth. So the Supreme Lord wanted Kadru (who had given birth to serpents in that birth) to give birth to Seshanag in this birth as Balarama. This is another reason why Rohini got the privilege of being Balarama's mother. This is apart from the consideration of safety, since Devaki's sons were being killed by Kansa in Mathura.

Lord Vishnu realises that the time is now ripe for Him to descend to the earth.

He instructs Goddess Yogamaya, "Oh Goddess! I want you to take birth at Nanda Rai's house as Yashoda's daughter. I will take birth as Devaki's Son. Please instruct Vasudev to take me to Gokul to Nanda's house and exchange the babies and carry You to Mathura."

Goddess Yogamaya bows and says, "As You wish My Supreme Lord!"

Saying this, She enters the womb of Yashoda in Gokul.

The exact year of Lord Krishna's birth is quite controversial. Many believe that, as per the Gregorian calendar, it was on July 19, 3227 BC.

Tonight is the eighth night of the waning moon in the Hindu month of Shravana. The star is Rohini Nakshatra. The trees are swaying as the gentle wind blows across Brij Bhoomi. The birds are chirping and flowers are spreading their fragrance everywhere. The stars are twinkling in the sky. Suddenly there is peace and goodness everywhere, as Lord Vishnu descends to the earth. All the Gods and Goddesses come from Heaven to watch this divine spectacle. They bow before the Supreme Lord and adorn His path with celestial flowers.

Lord Vishnu enters the prison cell of Vasudev and Devaki who are sleeping. There is a bright glow in their cell. They wake up and see the Supreme Lord before them. Lord Vishnu displays His four-armed form. The Sudarshana Chakra, Conch, Mace, and Lotus adorn His hands. The Kaustubha gem decorates His neck. His body has the beautiful bluish complexion like dark clouds. Devaki and Vasudev are stunned to see the Almighty is His omnipotent form. They fall at the lotus feet of the Supreme Lord and seek His Blessings.

Lord Vishnu blesses them, "Oh Vasudev and Devaki! Please get up. I have come to take birth as your eighth Son. In your previous birth, you had performed the most severe penances and I was pleased with you and had asked you to seek a boon. You had desired that I should be born as your Child. I want to fulfil your desire."

Devaki weeps with joy. She says, "Oh Lord! I am indeed supremely blessed to become the mother of the Lord of the three worlds. However, I want to have You as my infant. I want to enjoy motherhood. In Your current four-armed form, I will end up worshipping You. I will not be able to enjoy motherhood. Please take birth as a normal infant."

Lord Vishnu smiles, "Oh Devaki! As you wish. I will be born as a normal infant from your womb. You will forget My visit to your prison cell in this form. You will forget that you have given birth to the Supreme Lord. You will treat Me the way any normal mother would treat her son. You will experience joys and pains experienced by any normal parent."

Saying this, He enters the womb of Devaki. Goddess Yogamaya using Her divine powers, makes Vasudev and Devaki forget Lord Vishnu's visit to their prison cell. She also makes them forget that they will soon become parents of the Supreme Lord.

Lord Vishnu is born in the form of a handsome Child. Goddess Yogamaya awakens Vasudev and tells him, "Oh Vasudev! Devaki has given birth to your eighth Son. He is not safe here. Please take Him to Gokul. Go to your cousin Nanda Rai's residence. Nanda's wife Yashoda has given birth *to a baby. I command you to exchange the babies and get Yashoda's baby here."*

Vasudev says, "I can't do this since my hands and legs are chained and there are guards all around the cell."

Goddess Yogamaya smiles, "Do not worry. I will take care of that."

The moment She utters this, a miracle happens. The chains tied to Vasudev's hands and legs break open. All the prison doors begin to open by themselves. The security guards fall asleep.

There are multiple doors that lead to the exit. All the doors are open. Vasudev picks up the divine Child and walks out of the prison.

KRISHNA JANMASTHAN TEMPLE — THE *OTHER* DIVINE LOCATION

As in the case of many other important historic places, a controversy surrounds the exact birthplace of Lord Krishna in Mathura. There are a few people who believe that Lord Krishna was not born at the famous Krishna Janmasthan Temple that I had just visited. They believe that He was born in another place, close to the

Krishna Janmasthan - second location

famous Krishna Janmasthan. I was curious and decided to visit that place too. This place is about 500 metres to the north of Potara Kund. A dilapidated signboard near Potara Kund led me to this temple.

The temple was not on the main road but in one of the quiet, dusty bylanes so I almost missed it. It was an inconspicuous looking building. Had I not seen the signboard, I could have mistaken it for someone's residence. This temple is also known as Yogamaya Temple since Vasudev had brought Yogamaya here

Idols of Vasudev, Krishna and Devaki

from Gokul. As I entered inside the premises, I saw a small courtyard. To my left was the main altar. It had white idols of Vasudev, Devaki, and a black idol of four-armed Krishna. As I walked further ahead, I came to the Yogamaya Temple which had a white idol of Goddess Yogamaya. The temple was in a dilapidated state and did not have many visitors. Apart from the priest, I did not see anyone around.

POTARA KUND

Side view of Potara Kund

As I proceeded about 500 metres to the left of Krishna Janmasthan, I saw Potara Kund. *Potara* means 'diapers'. It is believed that when Lord Krishna was born that rainy night, his clothes were washed in this *kund*. This *kund* was dry and tall grass grew everywhere. There were many steps on all four sides of the *kund* that led to the centre that contained water from the times of Krishna.

DWARKADHEESH TEMPLE

The Dwarkadheesh Temple is located quite close to Vishram Ghat which is on the banks of River Yamuna. This temple was built in 1815 by a wealthy devotee, Seth Gokuldas Parikh. He was the treasurer of the state of Gwalior. The temple is in the middle of a busy and narrow street. It was impossible to drive our car on this road so we parked the car near one of the ghats near Yamuna and walked to this temple. There were lots of small shops on either side of the road.

Dwarkadheesh Temple

As I stood in front of the temple on the main road, I saw a flight of steps. These led me to a huge courtyard. There were a few more steps in the courtyard that led me to the main temple. In the courtyard, I saw lots of devotees sitting on huge cloth mats. They were totally immersed in singing and chanting. Many of them were playing cymbals. All around the courtyard, I noticed many pictures and paintings. The inscriptions on the walls were in Hindi and Gujarati that serve as a gentle reminder to the visitors that Lord Krishna, as Dwarkadheesh, resided for many decades at Dwarka, in Gujarat. Near the sanctum sanctorum, there were 12 cream-coloured pillars decorated with green flower petals. These 12 pillars held a huge dome at the centre. I saw beautiful paintings, depicting the wonderful pastimes of Krishna, adorning the dome.

When I reached the temple, I found that the view of the sanctum sanctorum was blocked by a curtain. Suddenly, the flashlights facing the curtain lit up. Seeing this, the devotees, sensed that the curtain would be drawn back. They immediately stood up and rushed towards the sanctum sanctorum. Chants of 'Dwarkadheesh Ki Jai' filled the cool winter air. The idol of Lord

Krishna was worth beholding. Made of black marble, the face was so expressive that it looked as if the divine Lord Himself was standing there! There was also a beautiful idol of Goddess Rukmini, the incarnation of Goddess Lakshmi, by His side. One very striking feature was the red *tilak* applied on the forehead of Dwarkadheesh. In the dimly lit room, it flashed like a string of red rubies adorning His forehead.

Dwarkadheesh Temple is quite unique in many ways, compared to the other Krishna temples in Brij Bhoomi. In most of the temples in Brij Bhoomi, we see the two-armed Krishna, with his legs criss-crossed, playing His flute. However, in this temple, Lord Krishna is in His four-armed form, as is the case in most of the Krishna temples in Dwarka, Gujarat. After viewing the deity, I performed parikrama. I noticed one more unusual feature in this temple. Instead of applying red *kumkum* to decorate the walls, as is the case in some of the temples, the priest had applied cow dung on the walls. It served as a reminder that Lord Krishna is Lord Govinda, the 'Protector of Cows'. The devotees who visited this temple were predominantly Gujaratis so I felt I was in some town in Gujarat, and not in the heart of Brij Bhoomi.

4

Mahavan

...

*"Paritranaya sadhunam vinashaya cha dushkrutham,
Dharma sansthapanarthaya sambhavami yuge yuge"*

("To save the pious people and eliminate the evil and to re-establish righteousness and principles firmly, I appear millennium after millennium.")

(Bhagavad Gita 4.8)

About 15 km south-east of Mathura, close to the banks of the sacred River Yamuna, lie the twin towns Gokul and Mahavan. Gokul and Mahavan two kilometres apart. In order to reach these towns, I had to take the road from Mathura to Agra. After travelling for around 12 km, I took the road to the left which led me to these twin towns. While travelling to Mahavan, I had to cross the Yamuna. I saw the exact spot where Vasudev crossed the Yamuna, carrying Lord Krishna.

The whole of Mathura is reverberating to the sounds of loud thunder. The sky is frequently illuminated with lightning. Vasudev, is carrying the divine Infant, and has managed to safely reach the banks of the Yamuna. Inspite of the torrential rains, he does not face any hurdles on the muddy road. There are pools of water everywhere but he manages to avoid falling into them.

He thinks happily, "How lucky I am! First, the chains opened and then the doors! I was also fortunate that the prison guards were sleeping. My Son is safe. I will ask one of the boatmen to take me to Gokul where I can leave

31

Him at Nanda's house for safe keeping."

Alas, his joy is short-lived.

As he approaches the banks of the river Yamuna, he finds the river in full spate. It resembles a ferocious ocean rather than a calm river. The waves of the angry river are beating against the hard rocks. He looks around for a boatman who can ferry him across the river to the other side. Alas! There is not a single boatman in the vicinity.

Vasudev thinks that he could row a boat himself and reach the other side of the river. He looks around and cries in despair, "Alas, I do not see any boats too. Oh Lord! What do I do now?"

He decides to wait for a few minutes to see if the rains subside. However, the rains increase. They begin to lash out with greater rigour. Vasudev is at loss for ideas.

Finally, he thinks that the only option for him is to carry his Son and cross the river himself.

He lifts the basket that holds the Supreme Lord and begins to cross the river. As he walks a few metres into the river, he notices the water level slowly, but steadily, increasing. The water which was knee-deep has now become waist-deep. It is rising further continuously.

He realises that the level of the water is too high for him to carry the basket in his hands. He decides to carry it on his head.

Saying this, he puts the basket on his head and continues his journey across the Yamuna. Lord Sheshanag, resting in Vaikunta, thinks His Lord is in trouble. He sees His Lord getting drenched in the heavy rains. Vasudev is holding the basket containing His Lord on his head. The basket is completely exposed to the incessant rains.

Sheshanag decides to protect His Lord immediately.

Within a flash, He is in the River Yamuna. He spots Vasudev walking in the river, carrying a basket on his head. He swims behind Vasudev and lifts up His hood. The hood rests above the basket, thus protecting the Infant from getting drenched in the rain. All the Gods gather in the Heavens and look towards Earth to watch this divine spectacle of Vasudev crossing the ferocious Yamuna on a dark, rainy night with only thunder and lightning for company. The mighty Sheshanag is protecting His Master with His mighty Hood. Some of the Gods are smiling at Sheshanag's naivety! Does the Supreme Lord need any protection? He who protects us all is being offered protection!

The River Goddess, Yamuna, realises that the Infant being carried by Vasudev is no ordinary being, but the Incarnation of Lord Vishnu. She bows her head and says, "Oh Supreme Lord! I am indeed blessed today by Your divine presence. I have been so lucky to have the good fortune to see You today. It is my privilege that Vasudev decided to choose me as the means for Your divine journey."

The Supreme Lord opens His lotus shaped eyes and peers down from the basket and smiles at Her.

Goddess Yamuna continues, "Oh Supreme Lord! Please allow me to touch Your lotus feet in reverence." Suddenly a huge wave lifts itself from the surface of the river and rises to the basket. It gently touches the lotus feet of the divine Child. The Supreme Lord lifts His tiny right hand and blesses Goddess Yamuna.

Goddess Yamuna, her head still bowed in reverence, pleads, "Oh Lord! Though I consider myself fortunate that You chose a journey across the river, I also feel sad that the journey has been very short. You will be reaching Gokul within a few minutes. Please do not abandon me so soon. Your divine body would no longer be touching and blessing me. I have a request to You, My Lord!"

The Supreme Lord, known for His benevolence towards His devotees asks, "Oh Goddess! Please tell Me Your desire. I will fulfil it."

Goddess Yamuna says, "Oh Lord! I want You to spend more time with Me. I want You to play in my waters. Every minute that You spend here, I would be that much more blessed. Please promise to visit Me frequently and play with Me."

The Supreme Lord smiles and says, "As You wish."

Vasudev has now reached the other side of the river safely. The rains have stopped. He lowers the basket, expecting to see a drenched Child huddled in the basket. He is amazed to find that his Child is completely dry. There is not a drop of water anywhere on His divine body. Vasudev is totally oblivious of the fact that Lord Sheshanag had protected his divine Son.

He sighs happily, "Tonight is a night of miracles and this is just one more of them!"

Krishna, in order to keep up His promise to Goddess Yamuna, spent a major part of His childhood, playing and frolicking with His friends, in the Yamuna.

There seems to be some confusion as to where exactly Vasudev secretly brought Krishna when he left Him in the care of Yashoda and Nandarai. The residents of Mahavan believe that the original town of Gokul stood at Mahavan but it was destroyed by the tyrant king Mahmud Ghazni and his barbaric army at the beginning of the 11th century. Many centuries later, the town was re-built but under a different name, Mahavan. However, the people of the current Gokul believe that theirs is the 'real' Gokul. Mahavan is known as Old Gokul and the current Gokul as New Gokul.

Sri Chaitanya Mahaprabhu believed that many of the places where Lord Krishna performed His miracles, which are described in the holy scriptures as being Gokul, are mainly found in Mahavan (Old Gokul). Therefore his followers, the Gaudiya Vaishnavas, often just visit Mahavan (Old Gokul) and do not visit New Gokul. Gokul attained importance during the time of the famous Vaishnava saint, Vallabhacharya (1479-1531) when it became a major centre of the Vallabhacharya cult.

Mahavan is an ancient dusty town, two kilometres south of Gokul. Most of the temples are located close to each other, on a small hillock. Next to the hillock is a big field that serves as a huge parking area. As I walked up the hillock, I saw many temples on either side of the road.

YOGAMAYA TEMPLE

After I walked a few metres on the hillock, I noticed a narrow lane to my right. There was a very old and dilapidated signboard that said that this lane was the one that Vasudev used when he brought Lord Krishna from Mathura on that eventful rainy night when the Supreme Lord descended on this planet.

As I turned right and walked down this path, I saw a temple right ahead. This was the Yogamaya Temple. Some say this is the birthplace of Balarama and some believe this to be the birthplace of Yogamaya. This is a quiet place and not many visitors come here.

Inside the temple, is an idol of Yashoda on the right and that of Nanda Rai on the left. At the centre is an idol of Yogamaya. At the back is a black idol of Balarama. In front of Yogamaya is an idol of Krishna playing His flute. The idols look very colourful adorned in red clothes. This is one of those rare temples where the idol of Lord Balarama is bigger than that of Lord Krishna. The reason for giving

Vasudev entered Gokul town via these lanes

prominence to Lord Balarama could be the fact that this happens to be His birthplace.

Vasudev has reached Gokul. He walks stealthily through the bylanes of the town and reaches Nanda's house. He steps inside and goes into the room where Yashoda is sleeping.

Yashoda has just given birth to a baby Girl. The Girl is no ordinary Child. She is Goddess Yogamaya. She is sleeping next to Her mother, Yashoda. Vasudev enters Yashoda's room. He has been instructed by Goddess Yogamaya to leave his Son in Yashoda's room and take Yashoda's Child with him back to Mathura. Recollecting this, he walks towards Yashoda's bed. He leaves his Child next to her. He picks up her Daughter and puts Her in his basket and leaves the house silently. Vasudev's departure is as silent as his arrival. No one in Nanda's household, including Yashoda herself, has seen his arrival. Nor has anyone seen him swapping the two Children.

Vasudev once more walks to the banks of River Yamuna. He crosses the river to reach the opposite bank. He retraces his steps to the Mathura prison. As soon as he steps into his prison cell, the prison doors close. He removes the divine Child from his basket and places Her next to his sleeping wife. Within a few seconds, the chains bind them up again. The security guards wake up from their deep slumber.

Goddess Yogamaya stands before Vasudev.

Vasudev, with folded hands, bows to her and says, "Oh Goddess! I have completed all the tasks according to Your command. Please tell me what should I do next?"

Goddess Yogamaya smiles and blesses him, "Oh Vasudev! I have heard so much about your courage. Today I was fortunate enough to witness it. You have successfully completed all the tasks. I know that you are absolutely truthful. If Kansa asks you what has happened tonight then you will narrate all the incidents that you witnessed. This would cause harm to your newborn Child. Keeping your Son's safety in mind, I want you to forget all that you have seen, heard and done tonight. You will not be obliged to tell Kansa the truth since you yourself will not remember it."

Vasudev bows to Goddess Yogamaya and says, "As You wish, Oh Goddess!"

Goddess Yogamaya, using Her divine powers makes Vasudev forget all that has happened this eventful night. She blesses Vasudev and leaves his prison cell.

Suddenly, the infant Girl begins to cry. This alerts not only Devaki but also the security guards. They realise that Devaki has delivered her eighth Child. Everyone in Mathura has been waiting for the arrival of the eighth Child since He is destined to kill Kansa. The security guards run to Emperor Kansa's palace. They had been given special privileges to enter his room at any time of the day or night if they are carrying the news of the birth of Devaki's children. Hearing their footsteps, Kansa, spending sleepless nights, springs from his bed. The security guards convey the news of the birth of the eighth Child of Devaki.

Kansa is very keen to have a look at his future assassinator. He rushes immediately to the prison where Devaki and Vasudev are captive.

He enters the prison cell that houses Devaki and Vasudev.

He looks at them angrily and asks, "Where is your eighth Child? Where is the Boy who is destined to kill me? Hand Him over to me immediately."

He looks around impatiently and finds an Infant sleeping next to Devaki.

Devaki gets up and falls at Kansa's feet. She pleads, "Oh Brother! I have given birth to a baby Girl. Look at Her innocent face and tell me if She can ever be destined to kill you. Please spare Her life."

Kansa is stunned hearing this. A girl! How is this possible?

He screams, "I have been cheated! Someone is playing around with me! The prediction was that Devaki would give birth to a boy. How has she given birth to a girl?"

He looks around for an answer. There is silence in the room.

He roars, "I do not care if you have given birth to a boy or a girl. I do not want to take chances. I am going to kill Her right away."

Devaki wails, "Oh dear brother! Stop! Please don't kill an innocent girl."

Kansa does not listen to her screams. He tries to fling the Child on the hard ground. However, on a night of miracles, there is one more. The Infant escapes from his clutches and soars into the dark sky. She stops in mid-air and changes into Her real Self as Goddess Yogamaya, with eight arms and is seated on a tiger. One of the hands holds the divine Discus and the other holds the Conch. She also holds a Sword, Club, and Lotus in her other arms. She is decorated with garlands made of celestial flowers, dressed in bright red garments and Her neck is adorned with gems and jewels. She is surrounded by celestial beings who are worshipping Her. There is an aura of bright light surrounding Her. Kansa is blinded by the bright light and unable to look at her.

She looks at Kansa and laughs mockingly at him, "You fool! How dare you try to kill Me? You cannot kill Me. The Person who is destined to kill you has been born already. He is safe somewhere else, far away from your clutches." Saying this, the Goddess laughs once again and vanishes.

Kansa is looking at his empty hands, He is stunned at the turn of events. He realises that his attempt to kill all Sons of Devaki has failed. Devaki and Vasudev, who watch the proceedings, are equally stunned. They know that a miracle has happened but do not know anything beyond that. Kansa glares at them and storms out of the prison cell.

Yogamaya is considered to be an incarnation of Goddess Durga. She played an important role in Krishna's life. It is believed that She was instrumental in transferring Balarama from the womb of Devaki to the womb of Rohini. Later, when Krishna was born, she put the prison guards to sleep and removed the shackles from Vasudev's legs which enabled him to leave the prison in Mathura and go to Gokul. Yogamaya was born to Yashoda on the same night as Krishna. When Vasudev reached, Nanda's house, he exchanged Krishna with Yogamaya and took the latter to Mathura. When Kansa tried to kill Yogamaya, She slipped from his hands and soared into the sky. She took Her original form of Goddess Durga and mocked Kansa for failing to kill Devaki's eighth Child. It is also believed that She played a vital role when Lord Krishna performed His lilas with the gopis and Radha. Due to these legends, people in Brij Bhoomi revere Yogamaya as much as Radha and Krishna. Almost every town in Brij Bhoomi has atleast one temple dedicated to Yogamaya.

PUTANA TEMPLE

Infant Krishna on top of the dead demoness

After visiting Yogamaya Temple, I returned to the main road of the hillock. As I proceeded straight and walked up the hill, on my left, I came across a temple that marked the spot where the demoness Putana was killed by Lord Krishna. This was the Putana Temple. This temple had a huge yellow idol of Putana, lying 'dead' on the floor. Infant Lord Krishna was crawling on top of her.

I asked the priest, "Is it not strange to find a temple built in memory of a demoness?"

The priest laughed, "You should not perceive it that way. This temple has been built to narrate the story of the victory of good over evil."

Kansa is stunned by the recent turn of events. He narrates what Goddess Yogamaya told him, to his court. He tells them how a mere Child has escaped his deathly clutches and vanished into thin air.

He asks his loyal ministers, "Tell me what to do now? My Killer has already taken birth. How do I find Him? He has been hidden somewhere by Vasudev."

One of his ministers advises Him, "Oh King! I have an idea. Please instruct your men to kill all newly born infants in your kingdom."

Kansa closes his eyes and thinks for a moment. His lips curve into a wicked smile.

He calls his security guards and instructs them, "I want you to split into different groups. Each group shall travel in a different direction. You will go from house to house and search for infants born during the past two months. Any infant less than two months old should be put to death immediately."

The security guards bow and depart. During the next few days, they carry out the King's orders. They go from house to house. They enter and snatch the newly born infants from their wailing mothers and put them to death. They do not care for the pleas or wails from the parents of the newly born infants. They are bent upon carrying out the king's heinous orders.

Kansa keeps getting reports on the number of killings carried out each day. However, he is still feeling uneasy. He fears the Person destined to kill him is still alive. He has also been getting reports from his spies that Vasudev has left his eighth Child in Gokul, in the house of Nanda Rai.

Kansa decides to use the services of the demon Putana to kill the Child. Putana is summoned.

She asks him, "Oh Mighty King! Please tell me why you have called me. How can I help you?"

Kansa tells her, "It has been destined that I am to be killed by the eighth Son of Vasudev and Devaki. I have heard that Vasudev secretly took his Child away from Mathura and kept Him in the safe custody of Yashoda and Nanda Rai in Gokul. I want you to go to Gokul to Nanda Rai's house and kill that Infant."

Putana bows her head and replies, "As you wish, my Lord. Let me go to Gokul right away."

Putana transforms herself into a beautiful woman and comes to Nanda Rai's house at Gokul. She introduces herself, "I am a pious brahmin's wife and I have come to see the Child. I will bless the Child with longevity. I will breast-feed your child since my milk has the power to give strength to newborn infants."

Yashoda gives the Child to her. Putana takes the Child to another room and closes the door behind her. She sits on the ground and begins to feed Krishna poisoned milk. Krishna realises that this is no ordinary woman but *a demon in disguise. He also realises that He is being poisoned. He bites her and immediately, Putana transforms back into her original form. She lets out a loud scream and falls dead on the ground. The entire town reverberates with her screams.*

Nanda Rai, Yashoda and their neighbours hear the loud noise of Putana screaming one minute and a loud thud of her crashing to the ground the next. They think a thunderbolt has fallen! They break open the door and rush inside. The family and villagers panic.

They notice a huge, ugly, dead demoness lying on the ground and Krishna sitting on her abdomen and playing with a mischievous look in His eyes.

Yashoda faints but quickly recovers. She hugs Krishna and asks Him if He is safe, without realising that He is the Supreme Lord.

Since Putana has been killed by Lord Krishna, she achieves moksha (freedom from the repeated cycle of births and deaths) and her soul commences its journey towards Heaven.

Putana, in her previous birth, was Ratnamala, the daughter of King Bali. Lord Vishnu, in His Vamana Avatara, arrived at the spot where King Bali was performing 'Homa'. Seeing the radiating body of Lord Vamana, Ratnamala desired that she should have Lord Vishnu as her Child in her next birth and be able to breast-feed him like any mother feeds her infant.

Vamana discerns what is going on her mind and He Blesses her, "May your wish come true."

Later, when Vamana crushes Bali with His foot, she gets upset and says that if she gets a Son like Him then she will mix poison in her milk. So during the incarnation of Lord Krishna, both her wishes are fulfilled. She breast-feeds Him like any mother and also gets an opportunity to mix poison in her milk. Lord Krishna remembers this incident and hence He forgives her. Since she is killed by Lord Krishna, she achieves liberation and her soul rises to Heaven.

The legend of this temple came as an eye-opener to me. The Supreme Lord is all merciful and He forgives even those who have tried to kill Him. A person who has tried to kill the Infant ends up getting moksha.

TRINAVARTA TEMPLE (LAKSHMI NARAYAN TEMPLE)

As I walked up the hill past the Putana Temple, on my left was the spot where the demon Trinavarta was killed by Krishna. A temple has been built here known as the Trinavarta Temple. It is also known as the Lakshmi Narayan Temple. It has white idols of Narayan and His consort Lakshmi. Lord Vishnu is in His four-armed form, serving as a gentle reminder to the devotees that Lord Vishnu and Lord Krishna are one and the same.

Idols of Lakshmi and Narayan

Kansa is worried and depressed. Inspite of his consistent efforts and that of his well-wishers and friends, he is not able to harm Krishna. He had pinned his hopes on Putana. She is dead.

He sits all alone, deep in his thoughts. One of his friends comes to visit him. Seeing his friend in a forlorn state, he asks him, "Oh mighty king! Please tell me why you are so worried." Kansa explains to him the problem and the cause of his worries.

His friend laughs, "Oh Kansa! Don't be so depressed. I have a solution for your worries."

Kansa's eyes light up. He looks up and asks, "Is it? What solution do you have?"

His friend says, "I have a demon friend here named Trinavarta. He can kill the Infant within no time."

Kansa asks him, "Where is your friend? I do not see him."

His friend says, "Oh Kansa, please go near your palace window and look outside. You can see him."

Kansa looks out of his palace window. He sees the green coloured typhoon demon Trinavarta in the form of a whirlwind. He asks Trinavarta to show him his powers, which he displays, causing lots of destruction.

Kansa is impressed with this demon and his prowess.

He looks at his friend and says, "Thanks a lot, my friend. I am sure Trinavarta can do the job. Please ask him to go to Gokul immediately and kill Nanda Rai's Son."

Trinavarta goes to Gokul. When he reaches the quiet town, he turns into a whirlwind and causes a lot of destruction. Since he is invisible, no one knows what is happening. Soon, he reaches Nanda Rai's house. He sees Infant Krishna playing alone in the courtyard. He looks around and finds no one protecting the Child. He lifts Krishna and carries Him off. He soars higher and higher in the sky. Since the whirlwind has created a great dust storm, there is poor visibility everywhere. Initially, both Yashoda and Nanda Rai are unable to see what is happening. As the dust settles, suddenly they see Trinavarta, in the form of a whirlwind lifting Krishna. They are aghast. They come out of their house, running and screaming.

Neighbours and passers-by are bewildered. In the meanwhile, unknown to the villagers watching and standing below, a big fight ensues in the high skies between Krishna and Trinavarta. Both try to strangle each other. Who can match the Supreme Lord? Though Trinavarta tries his best to strangle the divine Child, he is no match to Lord Krishna who strangles him to death. As Trinavarta dies, he drops Krishna from a great height but nothing happens to Krishna as He lands safely on the hard ground. When Yashoda and Nanda Rai rush to the spot, they are thrilled to see Him safe. They hug Him and thank the Lord for saving their Son.

The atmosphere in and around the temple is very serene and quiet. Forget a whirlwind or a typhoon, there are no signs of even a gentle breeze to shake the leaves of the trees there. After all, Trinavarta, the whirlwind, was dead!

YASHODA BHAVAN

Proceeding further, I reached the top of the hillock. I noticed a big courtyard, which housed many buildings, each one a temple in its own right. As I looked straight ahead, I saw Yashoda Bhavan. Next to it was the biggest building, Nanda Bhavan, which housed the Chatti Palana Temple. To the left was the Balarama Revathi Temple.

Yashoda Bhavan, as the name suggests, is the place where Yashoda resided. As is the case in many temples in Brij Bhoomi, here too, the devotees are not allowed to stand. They say it is disrespectful to stand. I was asked to sit in front of the idols. Only after I sat down, the curtain was drawn aside, showing me the deities of Krishna, Balarama, Yogamaya, Yashoda, and Nanda.

Idols of Krishna, Balarama, Yogamaya, Yashoda, and Nanda.

At the extreme left is a black idol of Lord Krishna. Next to it is the idol of Nanda. To the right are idols of Balarama and Yashoda. In the extreme right corner is the idol of Yogamaya. Surprisingly, the idol of Balarama is black, a colour that is normally associated with Krishna. In front of these idols, an idol of Infant Krishna is kept in a cradle. The devotees are allowed to swing the cradle. One more salient feature of this temple is that the devotees are allowed to enter the sanctum sanctorum and touch the idols.

Lord Shiva has a strong desire to see Lord Vishnu as the Infant Krishna. He disguises Himself as a brahmin to see Krishna at Nanda Rai's house in Gokul.

He stands outside Yashoda Bhavan and starts singing praises of Lord Vishnu, asking Krishna to show Himself to Him.

An old woman, who is passing by, sees Him. She thinks He is a poor brahmin begging for alms.

She tells Lord Shiva, "There seems to be no one inside this house, so please come to my house. I will give You alms."

Lord Shiva smiles and replies, "I cannot come with you because I take alms only from the house that I have Myself approached. Otherwise I would prefer to remain hungry."

The old lady says, "It is an insult to me and my village if a brahmin has to remain hungry and go back empty-handed so I will go inside and check."

She finds Yashoda inside and informs her about the waiting brahmin. Yashoda takes a plate containing rice and other food items and places a necklace on top of the heap, as 'Dakshina'. She comes out and apologises to Him for the delay, since she was bathing and dressing up the Infant.

She keeps the plate before Lord Shiva and says, "Oh Holy brahmin, please take the contents of this plate."

Lord Shiva looks at the contents of Yashoda's plate. He looks towards the heavens and asks, "Oh Lord! Why are You testing Me like this? I pray to You to present Yourself instead of making Yashoda come with such alms!"

He tells Yashoda, "Please bring your Infant. I would like to see Him."

Yashoda refuses, "Oh brahmin, I cannot bring Him outside because the Infant just had His bath, He will catch a cold."

She says this because she suspects the brahmin's honesty. When the brahmin keeps insisting that she get the Infant out, Yashoda tells Him, "In the past, many people have come here disguised as saints and tried to kill my Son. So I have stopped trusting people who come here just to see my Son."

At that time, Goddess Yogamaya comes disguised as an old woman. She is able to recognise the brahmin. She asks Yashoda to show the Child to Him.

Yashoda tells the brahmin, "Oh brahmin! I will bring the Child outside only on one condition. You can see Him, however I would not like You to touch Him since I am scared."

The brahmin agrees. Yashoda goes inside and brings Lord Krishna in her arms and asks the brahmin to bless the Child. The brahmin has tears of joy in His eyes and weeps in ecstasy.

He bows before the divine Child and says, "Oh Lord Vishnu, I would like to touch Your divine feet from where rises the Ganga that I take on My head."

Saying this, Lord Shiva comes out of the brahmin's body and touches Krishna's feet. Yashoda is unable to see this since Lord Shiva's divine form is invisible to her. Once Lord Shiva has seen and touched Lord Krishna, he feels elated and returns into the body of the brahmin. He thanks Yashoda and leaves the scene as quickly as He had come. Goddess Yogamaya realises who the brahmin is so She bows and touches with Her head the spot where Lord Shiva had stood. She asks Nanda Rai and Yashoda also to touch the ground that Lord Shiva had stood on. When they ask why, She tells them the true *identity of the brahmin. Then She Herself vanishes.*

NANDA BHAVAN (CHAURASI KHAMBHA MANDIR)

Nanda Bhavan

This is the main and the most famous temple in Mahavan. The biggest building in the courtyard, this is the place where Krishna grew up and spent His first three years with His foster parents Nandarai and Yashoda. The walls of this yellow-coloured building have lots of paintings that depict the pastimes of Krishna. Since this was the residence of Nanda Rai, it is known as Nanda Bhavan. It is also known as Chaurasi Khambha (84 pillars) Temple since there are 84 pillars inside the temple. It is believed that there are 84,00,000 species of life in this material world. Each of these pillars is said to symbolise 1,00,000 species, thus representing all the life in the universe.

This temple has surprisingly huge idols. At the centre is a huge idol of Balarama. The idol of Nanda Maharaja is on the left and that of Yashoda's on the right. In a cradle below, is the idol of Infant Krishna. As in the case of Yashoda Bhavan, here too, the priests allowed the devotees to swing the Infant Lord Krishna's cradle.

The news of Putana's and Trinavarta's deaths has reached Kansa. He is a tormented man. He had pinned all his hopes on these messengers of death. He was sure they would be able to kill Krishna. They had failed. He begins to ponder what he should do next.

He thunders, "Is there no one in my court who can take up the challenge to kill the Child?" At that time, Shakatasura lands in his court and says, "I will kill the Child."

Shakatasura is invisible. Kansa is unable to make out who is speaking.

Kansa looks all around and asks, "Who is there? Who is speaking?"

Shakatasura replies to him, "It is your friend Shakatasura. Many years ago, I had a very strong body and was very proud of it. I went to a sage's hermitage and started uprooting all the trees. The sage, cursed me saying that since I was so proud of my body, I would lose my physical form. I asked him for forgiveness. The sage said that he could not revoke the curse but could ensure that in the Dwapara Yuga, I would get Moksha."

Kansa says, "I want you to go to Gokul and kill Nandarai's Son."

Shakatasura promises him, "I will kill the Child before sunrise tomorrow."

Saying so, Shakatasura proceeds towards Gokul.

Krishna is lying in a cradle in the courtyard. He spots the invisible Shakatasura through his divine vision, though no one else is able to see him. The invisible asura takes the form of a cart and hurtles towards the cradle to crush the Child. With all his might, he tries to crush the cradle but nothing happens. Shakatasura attacks the cradle again and again, but in vain. Krishna knows that this is no ordinary cart and it is a demon in disguise. He kicks the cart with His small legs. This sends the cart high in the air and after a few turns and twists in the air, it falls and breaks. Everyone comes out hearing the loud crash. They find the cart broken into a thousand pieces and Krishna smiling at them. Shakatasura dies immediately. As promised by the sage who had cursed him, He gets moksha the moment Lord Krishna's body touches him. His soul begins its journey towards the Heavens.

Nanda Rai asks, "Who threw the cart so high in the air?"

The maids, who had watched this divine spectacle, tell him, "Oh Sir! Your Son kicked the cart and that sent the cart soaring high in the air."

Nanda Rai says, "I am unable to understand how a small Child can do that. Let me go and consult Shandilya Muni on how to protect my Son from such frequent evil incidents."

He carries Krishna with him to meet the holy sage.

CHATTI-PALANA TEMPLE

I spent a considerable amount of time trying to locate the Chatti-Palana Temple. The books and tourist guides that I had read had mentioned that this temple was within this temple complex. The only temples that I could see were Yashoda Bhavan, Nanda Bhavan, and Revathi Balarama Temple. There was no sign of another temple building within these premises. Imagine my surprise when I discovered that the Chatti-Palana Temple was located within Nanda Bhavan itself!

On the sixth day after the birth of Lord Krishna, the Chatti Puja was performed here, hence the name Chatti-Palana. This temple has no idols. It has a huge painting on the wall. The painting depicts Yashoda holding Krishna and Rohini holding Balarama. Some believe that this section of Nanda Bhavan was a cowshed where the naming ceremony for Balarama and Krishna took place on the sixth day (hence the name 'Chatti'). Others believe that the actual location of the cowshed is a few metres away from Nanda Bhavan and the painting here only depicts the naming ceremony event.

Nanda Rai reaches Shandilya Muni's hermitage and waits till the holy saint completes his morning prayers. He bows before Shandilya Muni and asks him, "Oh Saint! Please tell me why there are so many attempts to harm the Child? Please advise me how I can protect Him."

The Sage laughs and says, "No one can harm the Child since He is the Supreme God. He protects the whole universe. No one needs to protect Him."

He bows before the Lord and prays to Him, seeking His blessings. Nanda is puzzled and confused.

Shandilya replies, "I would like you to perform the naming ceremony for both the children. Please ensure that you keep it a low-key event. Kansa and his men are killing all the infants born in the past few months. If he comes to know that there are two children who were born here recently, then he will send his men here and kill the babies."

Nanda Rai is shocked to hear this. He nods his head in agreement.

Shandilya Muni continues, "I would advise you to perform the ceremony in the cowshed."

Nanda Rai is shocked and asks, "Cowshed?"

Shandilya smiles, "Yes. Cowshed. No one other than you, Yashoda and Rohini should be aware of this ceremony."

Nanda Rai says innocently, "I was planning to invite the entire town to come and bless my children. If I perform this in a cowshed with only Yashoda and Rohini, who will come and bless my children?"

Shandilya smiles once again and says to himself, his children are none other than the Supreme Lord and Sheshanag! Whose blessings do They need?

He does not reveal his thoughts but just says, "Today, safety is of prime importance, more important than even blessings. Please do not make this a grand event otherwise the news will spread to Mathura and Kansa and his men will land here. They are capable of butchering your kids."

Nanda shudders at the thought and immediately agrees.

He asks Shandilya, "Oh Holy One! Please tell me. Who is the right person to officiate at the naming ceremony?"

Shandilya Muni says, "The best person for this is Garga Muni. Please contact him immediately."

Shandilya, through his divine powers, was aware that the two Babies were the children of Devaki and Vasudev. He had suggested Garga Muni's name since he was Vasudev's 'Kul-Guru'.

Nanda says, "I will do as you advise. I know that whatever advice you give me is in the best interests of my Children."

Saying this, Nanda Rai leaves Shandilya Muni's hermitage.

Nanda Rai reaches home. He tells Yashoda and Rohini about his discussions with Shandilya Muni. They listen with mixed feelings. They are glad that the Children's naming ceremony will be performed soon. However, like Nanda Rai, they too feel sad that they have been asked to perform this in a cowshed.

Soon after this Nanda departs for Garga Muni's ashram.

Garga Muni has just finished his prayers when Nanda reaches his ashram. Nanda Rai falls at his feet and seeks his blessings.

Garga Muni blesses him and asks, "Please tell me what brings you here?"

Nanda Rai narrates his visit to Shandilya Muni's Ashram.

And then he says, "Oh Learned Saint! You are the most honoured of all sages. My Children and I would be blessed to have you perform the naming ceremony."

Garga Muni knows that the Children are the avataras of Lord Vishnu and Lord Seshanag. He says, "It is I who am blessed to be performing this act. The Almighty has granted me this privilege and I am thankful."

Nanda Rai looks puzzled since he is unable to comprehend Garga Muni's words.

Garga Muni decides on the exact date and time for the ceremony and tells Nanda about it.

Nanda bows and says, "Oh Holy Saint! I look forward to your visit."

Saying this, he takes leave and proceeds back to his town.

The namakarna (naming ceremony) day dawns.

Garga Muni arrives at Gokul unobserved. He has informed Nanda that he will not come to his house. He would come directly to the cowshed instead.

Nanda goes to the cowshed accompanied by Yashoda and Rohini. Yashoda and Rohini bring the Babies there. Everything is ready for the puja and the naming ceremony. Soon Garga Muni arrives.

Nanda, Yashoda, and Rohini pay obeisance to Garga Muni. Garga Muni lifts his right hand and blesses all of them.

Garga Muni asks Nanda, "Where are the Babies?"

Nanda points towards the cradles lying on a haystack. Garga Muni goes to the cradles. He finds the Babies cheerfully smiling at him.

Like Shandilya Muni, Garga Muni also recognises that They are Divine Children. He realises that Rohini's Son is the Lord Sheshanag himself and Yashoda's Son is none other than Lord Vishnu.

Garga Muni folds his hands respectfully and pays obeisance to both of them.

He thinks, how fortunate I am to be seeing the Supreme Lord and Seshanag with my own eyes! How lucky I am that I have been asked to come and perform this ceremony.

Soon, the naming ceremony starts. Garga Muni chants the hymns and the names of the various Gods and Goddesses. He pours holy water, ghee, and offerings into the sacrificial fire.

Garga Muni picks up the fairer and older of the two Babies.

He says, "This child will grow up to be the strongest among men. He will have the strength of a thousand elephants. Because of His strength ('Bala'), I will name him Balarama."

Since Garga Muni is aware that this Baby has been moved from one womb to another, he also names him 'Sankarshana'.

He puts Balarama back into the cradle. Now he picks up the darker and younger One. He says, 'He is Krishna, the dark and handsome One. His beautiful blue body resembles the dark clouds. He is Shyam Sundar, the handsome dark coloured One."

Nanda Rai is delighted. He repeats the names, "Balarama! Krishna! Balarama! Krishna! Lovely names for these lovely Boys!"

Yashoda and Rohini are also delighted. They hug the babies.

The ceremony is over.

Nanda, Yashoda, and Rohini once again bow to Garga Muni. He blesses all of them and departs. Nanda, Yashoda, and Rohini quietly retreat along with Balarama and Krishna in their arms.

Nanda says happily, "I am glad everything went off well, as planned. No one noticed Garga Muni. No one was witness to the naming ceremony at the cowshed. No one knows a thing. My Children are as safe as ever!"

Little did he realise that he could not have been farther from the truth!

The fact was that Garga Muni had been followed throughout his journey to Gokul by Kansa's spies. They saw him open the cowshed door and enter. Another set of Kansa's spies had seen Nanda, Yashoda and Rohini arrive at the cow shed a few minutes before Garga Muni. They had also seen Yashoda and Rohini carrying their babies in their arms. Kansa's spies hid themselves a little distance away from the cowshed. They did not know what was going on inside. They noticed Garga Muni leave after sometime. A few moments later, the others followed. Garga Muni went back to his village. The rest went back to Nanda Rai's house. Kansa's men followed them back to Nanda Rai's house. Later they galloped back to Mathura.

Next morning, they met Kansa in his court and broke the news. Kansa heard the whole story and is livid.

He thunders, "Can anyone tell me what is going on? Why has Garga Muni stealthily gone to Gokul? What happened in the cowshed?"

His Kul Guru says, "Oh King! I am sure that Garga Muni has gone to Gokul to perform the namakarna of Nanda's children."

Kansa says to him, "I find the whole event highly suspicious. Why is everything done in such a secretive manner? Why should Garga Muni go all the way to Gokul? Nanda could have found someone else in Gokul to do the job."

His Kul Guru replies, "Garga Muni is the 'Kul Guru' of Vasudev, so it is very clear now that the children whom Nanda is fostering are, in reality, the children of Vasudev."

REVATHI-BALARAMA TEMPLE

Next to the Nanda Bhavan Temple complex, near the entrance, on the left is the Revathi-Balarama Temple. The temple has idols of Balarama and Revathi at the centre. To the left of Balarama is the idol of His father, Vasudev. To the right of Revathi is the idol of Rohini, the foster mother of Bala-rama. In front of these idols, is a cradle with the idol of Infant Krishna. As in Yashoda

Revathi-Balarama Temple

Bhavan, here too I was allowed to touch all the idols and swing Lord Krishna's cradle. The bright red clothes of the idols gave the proceedings a festive look.

PATALA DEVI TEMPLE

As I came out of the courtyard of Nanda Bhavan and descended the hillock, within a few metres to my left I saw an underground temple. This is the Patala Devi Temple. I had to descend about 20 steps to reach the temple entrance. As I stepped inside, I saw many idols, each depicting a different form of Goddess Durga. The main deity is Goddess Yogamaya who is an incarnation of Goddess Durga. She was sitting on a tiger, holding a sword and a Chakra in Her two right hands. In Her two left arms, She held a Conch and a Club. Her bright red dress was adorned with fine gold embroidery. Peacock feathers were placed

51

Patala Devi Temple

on either side of the idol.

On the opposite side was the idol of Maha Gauri Durga. Between these two, on the left wall, were seven idols, all different forms of Goddess Durga - Kaal Yaatri Durga, Kaal Yaayni Durga, Skanda Durga, Kushmanda Durga, Chandraganta Durga, Brahmacharini Durga, and Shail Putri Durga

UTKHAL (GRINDING MORTAR)

I descended the hillock and went back to the car park. Ashwani did not want to visit the temples so he was waiting for me at the car park. Our car sped towards the outskirts of the dusty town. The next halt was Utkhal, which is located a kilometre away, to the left of the hillock. This place was so inconspicuous that I would have missed it had I not been watchful. It is a small temple housed in a huge compound, on the right side of the road. There is an old signboard that says 'Sri Utkhal Bandhan Ashram'. Utkhal means grinding mortar and Bandhan means tied. This is the place where Krishna, while tied to the grinding mortar, had liberated Nalakuvara and Manigriva, the two sons of Kubera, the treasurer of the Gods, by knocking down the two Arjuna trees. This is also the place where the 'Damodara incident' took place.

As I entered the compound, to my left I saw a small open room with no doors. There was a painting on the wall that depicts Lord Krishna, in His Infant form, pulling the Grinding Mortar and in the process, splitting the two Arjuna trees. Nalakuvara and Manigriva, having been freed from the curse, are coming out of the trees and saluting and seeking the blessings of the Divine Lord. In front of the painting is an ancient grinding mortar believed to be the same one that Yashoda had used to tie her mischievous Child 5000 years ago. To the right is an ancient tree that is supposed to be a part of the Arjuna tree that Lord Krishna broke. The footprints of Krishna can be seen here.

Yashoda finishes feeding Krishna. She gets up and becomes busy with her chores. Krishna begins to cry. Yashoda returns and says to him, "I finished feeding You just now. What do You want now?"

Krishna says, "Please give me some butter. I am hungry."

Yashoda refuses, saying she has just fed Him. She returns to her work.

Krishna is very angry He sees a pot full of butter suspended from the ceiling. The pot is too high for Him. He climbs on the grinding mortar lying nearby. However, He is still unable to reach the pot. He gets angry and decides to break the pot. He takes a stone and aims at the pot. His aim is perfect and in a flash, the pot breaks. The butter falls on the floor and Krishna takes lumps of butter in His small hands and begins to eat. Hearing the noise of a pot breaking, Yashoda comes out running. She sees the entire room in a mess. There is butter lying all over the floor along with broken pieces of the earthen pot.

Yashoda picks up a stick and runs towards Krishna. She catches Him with great difficulty. She says, "You have used the grinding mortar to climb and You have broken the pot. I will teach You a lesson. I am going to tie You to the same grinding mortar. Let me see what You will do."

Saying this, she tries to tie Him with a rope to the mortar. She keeps tying Him but the rope is always short. She begins to wonder what kind of miracle this is. She does not realise that the Supreme Lord can not be tied with a few feet of rope! Yashoda feels tired and begins to sweat. She fetches more and more rope but they all prove insufficient. With her hand on her head, she shakes her head in despair.

Seeing this, Krishna feels sorry for His mother. He now allows Himself to be tied. Yashoda decides to go to the river with her friends for a bath. Krishna begins to walk along with the grinding mortar behind Him. He comes out into the open courtyard. He walks wherever He pleases, dragging the grinding mortar tied to His back. Suddenly He stands still and views the open courtyard. He sees two twin Arjuna trees at one end of the courtyard. He goes towards them. He walks in between the two Arjuna trees. Since He is small He is able to pass between the trees. However, the grinding mortar, tied to His back is stuck between the two trees. Krishna is unable to move. He heaves at the stone and pulls it with all His might. The trees fall and the grinding mortar is freed. Krishna is once again able to move freely. However a miracle happens! Behold! When the two trees fall to the ground, two shining divine personages emerge, one from each tree. They both fall at Lord Krishna's feet and seek His blessings.

They say in unison, "Oh Lord Krishna! You are the Supreme Controller of the three worlds. It is our good fortune that we got a chance to see You. We are thankful to Narada for having opened our eyes and cursing us. It has helped us realise our true self. We will give up all materialistic comforts and spend the rest of our lives chanting Your holy names."

Krishna smiles, "Since You have realised your folly and decided to lead a virtuous life, I promise to lift you back from this materialistic world to My Abode, Vaikunta."

Saying this, Krishna blesses them and they depart to Vaikunta in their divine forms.

The two personages who had emerged from the trees were Nalakuvara and Manigriva, the sons of Lord Kubera. They had once behaved in a very rude and arrogant manner in the presence of Sage Narada. He had cursed them to fall from Heaven to the Earth. He also cursed them, "You two are very proud of your youth and handsome bodies. May you lose them and become trees."

Both Nalakuvara and Manigriva had realised their folly. They fell at the feet of Sage Narada and begged for forgiveness, "Please forgive us, O Holy One! Please forgive our immature words and behaviour. Please recall your curse."

Narada said, "I cannot lift a curse once it is uttered. However, since you are now repentant, I will help you. You will become Arjuna trees and live in a courtyard in the village of Gokul. Lord Vishnu will incarnate as a Human during the Dwapara Yuga. He will free you with His touch."

Nalakuvara and Manigriva bowed to Narada. Instantly, they turned into Arjuna trees and landed in Gokul, awaiting the arrival of the Supreme Lord who would free them.

Now they were free once again. They got back their youthful bodies. They started chanting the holy names of the Supreme Lord and went to Vaikunta.

The grinding mortar played a key role in this divine incident. After this incident, Lord Krishna was also known as Damodara.

Dama means 'ropes' and Udara means 'abdomen', so Damodara means 'one who was bound by a rope around the abdomen'.

Proceeding right ahead, on the other side of the compound, is another temple. There is a white idol of Radha on the right and a black idol of Krishna to the left. To the right of Radha is another white idol, Yamuna. To the extreme right is a silver idol of Lalitha, one of Radha's friends. To the left of Krishna is a silver idol of Vishaka, another friend. To the extreme left there is another idol of Krishna, playing His flute. Next to this temple is a goshala that houses many cows. There is also a small hut where a few families stay. They take care of the goshala.

On the opposite side of the road, facing Utkhal is the Nanda Rai well on a small hillock. It is believed that Nanda Rai used to fetch drinking water from this well.

BRAHMANDA GHAT

Driving past Utkhal, after a few kilometres, we came across the banks of River Yamuna. On the right is the Brahmanda Ghat. This is the very place where the Lord of the Universe showed the entire cosmos in His mouth to Yashoda. Since Lord Krishna had shown Yashoda the entire cosmos (Brahmanda) at this spot, this place is known as Brahmanda Ghat.

Brahmanda Ghat

Yashoda wants to have a bath. She does not want to leave her Infant Krishna alone in the house since He is very mischievous. She takes Him also along with her to the bathing ghat on the banks of River Yamuna. She walks to the bathing ghat along with her friends. Her friends have also brought their kids with them.

The ladies leave their kids on the banks of the river and step into the

55

waters. They bathe while the kids play nearby.

Suddenly, one of the kids notices Krishna eating mud. He asks Him to stop but Krishna does not listen to him. He and a few other kids rush towards where the women are bathing. The kids shout, "Yashoda Maiya! Krishna is eating mud. We have asked to him to stop eating but He does not listen to any of us."

Yashoda is frustrated on having to listen to such complaints everyday from her friends. She finishes her bath quickly and rushes out. She meets Balarama and asks Him, "Did you see Krishna? What is he doing? Your friends told me that Krishna is eating mud. Is it true?"

Balarama nods His head, "Yes. What you heard is true."

In her wet clothes, Yashoda rushes to the spot where she had left Krishna.

She spots Krishna sitting and playing all alone.

Yashoda asks, "Krishna what are you doing?"

Krishna replies, "Maiya! I am playing."

Yashoda says angrily, "Don't lie. I know what you are upto. All the kids ran to me and told me that You have been eating mud."

Krishna asks innocently, "Why would I do such a thing? They are lying Maiya."

Yashoda says, "Even Your Brother Balarama told me that You are eating mud."

Krishna smiles at her, "Even He is lying."

Yashoda is still angry. She does not believe Him.

She tells Him, "Oh! So all of them are lying, are they? Let me see for myself. Open Your mouth immediately."

Krishna smiles, "As you say, Maiya. See for yourself."

Krishna opens His small mouth. Yashoda is amazed. She does not see any mud. Instead, what she sees stuns her. She sees the entire universe in His mouth. She sees the planets, the stars. She sees the sun and the moon. Her small Infant transforms Himself into the Lord of the Universe, Lord Vishnu. The Supreme Lord shows His four-armed form and His Viraat Swaroop (Cosmic Form) and she becomes the first human to see Him. In Him, she sees all other Gods and Goddesses. She sees fire. She sees water. She sees the tallest mountains and the deepest oceans. She sees Brij Bhoomi,

River Yamuna, her house, and even herself! The Viraat Swaroop of Lord Krishna has no beginning and no end. She realises her Child is no ordinary Child but the Supreme Lord as an Infant.

Lord Krishna realises that Yashoda will never be able to treat Him as a mother would normally treat her son. She would instead worship Him like a devotee. She would stop enjoying her role as a normal mother, unlike the other women of Gokul.

Realising this, He tells her, "I will make you forget whatever you have seen now."

Krishna closes His eyes and thinks of Yogamaya.

Yogamaya arrives and says, "Oh Supreme Lord! What is your command?"

Krishna replies, "Please make Yashoda forget whatever she saw. I do not want her to know who I am. I want her to think of Me as her Child so that she can enjoy the pleasures of a normal mother. I do not want to snatch away her motherhood."

Yogamaya obeys.

To the right of Brahmanda Ghat is the River Yamuna and to the left is the temple. The temple, which houses idols of Radha and Krishna, has many paintings depicting several incidents that took place during Krishna's times and one of them depicts this divine incident. I noticed many vendors selling small balls made of mud. These balls symbolise the divine incident when Krishna ate mud and showed the cosmos to His mother.

RAMAN RETI

Raman Reti is a place on the outskirts of Mahavan, on the way to Gokul. This is the place where Krishna and Balarama played with Their friends and turned somersaults on the sands, hence the name Reti which means 'sand'. I saw a lot of white sand here, especially within the temple premises.

Inside the huge courtyard, on the right, were three temples. The first one was a small temple of Lord Shiva. The next one was a small temple of the Nava Graha. The third one was the main temple which is snow-white in colour.

The main temple had two pairs of Radha-Krishna idols. The

Raman Reti

big pair was on the left and the small pair on the right. On the right were idols of two saints — Sri Chandraji Maharaj and Sri Gopalji. On the left were two more idols of Sri Harinamdasji and Sri Brajanandaji. To the extreme left was an idol of Lord Hanuman. The entire temple was made of white marble. The walls around the temple had huge paintings, depicting the pastimes of Lord Krishna, which can be seen while performing the temple parikrama. The temple had a beautiful inner courtyard where I saw many sadhus sitting and singing melodious bhajans, the glories of Lord Krishna. The singing was so melodious and enchanting that I didn't feel like leaving. I was tempted to say goodbye to Bengaluru and settle down here! The outer courtyard was surrounded on all four sides by small huts that were ashrams for these sadhus. I could spot lots of deer in and around the temple premises.

The white sand here is considered very holy since Krishna and Balarama played on them. I noticed many devotees performing parikrama of the temples by rolling on these sands. They hoped to get blessed by the touch of the same holy sand that had touched the bodies of Krishna and Balarama.

Krishna and Balarama are playing with Their cowherd friends. They are all rolling over each other on the white sand. After playing for a long time in the hot sun, They begin to feel thirsty and hungry. Since they consider Krishna as their leader, they ask Him what they should do.

Krishna advises them, "I can see many brahmins performing homa and puja. Let us go and ask them for food." Krishna who is lying on the white sand gets up and walks towards the brahmins. Balarama and the other cowherds too get up and follow Him. Krishna approaches the brahmins and says, "Oh Holy Ones! We are feeling hungry and thirsty. Can you please give us something to eat and drink?"

The brahmins are so engrossed in performing the rituals that they take no notice of Him. Balarama repeats Krishna's request. The brahmins are still engrossed in their rituals. They do not take any notice of the young cowherds who are pleading for food. The cowherds are disappointed. Unable to bear the thirst and hunger any longer, some of them begin to cry.

Krishna says, "Please do not worry, My friends. Let us walk on this white sand for a short distance. I can smell the aroma of good food. I am sure the wives of these brahmins must be close, cooking food for their husbands."

Krishna walks ahead, followed by Balarama and His cowherd friends. As Krishna has predicted, soon they see the brahmin ladies cooking food for their husbands.

Krishna approaches them and says, "We have been playing for a long time under the hot sun so we are thirsty and hungry. Can you please give us some food?"

The ladies recognise who Krishna and Balarama are. They bring all the cooked food and offer it to Krishna, Balarama, and Their cowherd friends. They bow before the divine Children and say, "Oh Lord of the Universe! We are blessed to have You Two visit us. We are doubly blessed that You Two will eat our food."

Lord Krishna, with a mischievous smile on His lips, says, "Oh brahmin ladies! You have cooked this food for your husbands. Won't they get upset to find that you have distributed the food to Us?"

One of the ladies replies, "Oh Supreme Lord! We can cook once more for them. We get an opportunity to serve them daily, but we do not get an opportunity to serve You like this."

Krishna knows the devotion of these brahmin ladies. He does not want to test them. However, He wants to show to His cowherd friends the essence of true devotion to the Lord. He is merely using these women to do so.

He continues, "Oh brahmin ladies! I am sure that your husbands need the food that you have cooked to offer it to the Gods as Nivediya (the first offerings that are given to the God at the end of the puja before it is eaten by the mortals.) Will you not be polluting the Nivediya by offering this to Us before your husbands offer it to the Gods?"

The ladies, weeping with joy, prostrate before Krishna and Balarama. They touch Their feet and seek Their Blessings.

One of them says, "You are the Supreme Lord. Can we ever have a better opportunity of offering Nivediya than this? Our husbands are foolish that they did not recognise You. They are busy performing their rituals and have missed such a great opportunity to serve You Both in person and seek Your Blessings."

Lord Krishna and Lord Balarama bless the brahmin ladies. They, along with Their cowherd friends eat the food that has been offered to Them.

Lord Krishna tells His friends, "It is not enough just being learned and educated. Look at the brahmin men. All of them are so well versed in all the holy scriptures and holy verses. They perform numerous puja, homa, and penances but their arrogance has covered their eyes and they fail to recognise Us. Their wives are not educated. They are well versed only in simple household chores. However they know what true bhakti (devotion) is. Their simplicity has enabled them to recognise and serve Us. I do not care for any rituals. For me, bhakti is of prime importance."

As I left this place, I could still smell the aroma of the food cooked by the brahmin wives lingering on. I wish I could have seen the cowherds too!

5

Gokul

...

"*No mam pashyati sarvatra sarvam cha mayi pashyati,
Tasyaham na pranashyami sa cha me na pranashyati*"

("Whoever sees Me present in all beings and all beings existing within Me, I am never lost to him and he is never lost to Me.")

(*Bhagavad Gita* 6.30)

Gokul is located 15 km to the south-east of Mathura. Gokul, for many, is the 'real' Gokul, where Krishna was secretly raised by Yashoda and Nandarai. However, there are others who believe that Mahavan is the 'real' Gokul where Krishna lived. There are many locations here that are connected with Infant Krishna's growing up days. The similarity with Mahavan was so striking that I began to wonder which of the two the 'real Gokul' was! Gokul is located at 27.45° N latitude and 77.72° E longitude.

We travelled on the Mathura-Agra highway, in the direction of Gokul. Within a few minutes, we crossed the River Yamuna. We knew that we would be reaching Gokul soon. Suddenly, we saw a signboard indicating a left turn for Gokul. The signboard indicated that Gokul was around three kilometres away. When we took the left turn, we saw lots of young men standing on the road. Some of them were frantically waving at us, using both their hands. I told my driver that there might be a roadblock ahead, so these men were cautioning us to avoid taking the road ahead. My driver laughed at my innocence. He said that they were also guides who wanted to force themselves upon hapless tourists. He was right. Within a few seconds our car reached the human barricade. Each man insisted that he was 'not a guide, but a Brijwasi brahmin student' performing this task to further his education. The guides at Gokul are as aggressive as their counterparts in Mathura. I refused to enlist any of them. One of them was enterprising enough to climb our Toyota Qualis and hang onto the footboard. My driver accelerated, hoping that he would get scared and drop off. However, he did not realise that these men have nerves of steel. As my driver accelerated and kept turning on the winding roads, the guide hung on to the car, swaying his body in the same direction as the car to prevent his fall.

After a couple of kilometres, I asked my driver to stop the car and told him, "Let us hire him. Any person, with this level of perseverance to guide us, must be a true devotee of Lord Krishna. Let him take us around Gokul."

Ashwani waved his hand and the guide happily jumped into the car.

The guide told us that there were a few salient features of this holy town. No meat, alcohol, and eggs are sold here. People believe that crows don't stay in this town at night and they will die if they do so.

Surprisingly, there are more than 2000 Gujarati families staying here. Most of the shops carry signboards both in Hindi and Gujarati. I felt as if I was in a small town in Gujarat and not Uttar Pradesh!

As I entered Gokul town, I passed through a huge gate known as Gokul Dwar. After passing through it, I saw a *goshala* (cowshed) to my right. It is believed that the secret naming ceremony of Lord Balarama and Lord Krishna was performed by Garga Muni in this very *goshala*. On the right is a road known as Makhan Chor Galli. It is believed that Krishna would walk through these lanes and enter the houses of various villagers and steal the butter and distribute it to His friends. The gopis would be upset on finding their butter and curds stolen everyday. They even complained to Yashoda a few times about the pranks Krishna and His friends would play.

Yashoda is sitting inside her house. She is surrounded by many gopis who are also residents of Gokul. All of them have come to meet her with the sole purpose of complaining against her mischievous Kanha.

One lady says, "Sister Yashoda! Your Son comes to my house every day. He stealthily enters my house through the back door. He walks into the storeroom and opens the earthern pots and dips His hands inside and takes scoops of butter. I can hear the jingle of His anklets and know that He has arrived. Immediately, I run to the storeroom but He runs away very swiftly. I am unable to catch Him."

Says another, "Sister Yashoda, Kanha enters my storeroom through one of the windows. He steals butter and curds from the earthern pots. As soon as He hears me approaching, He leaps out of the window."

Says the third lady, "As if His coming and stealing was not bad enough, these days He brings His friends too. Yesterday I had gone to the ghat to bathe. When I returned, I found your Son along with all the village boys sitting inside eating butter and curds."

Says the fourth, "He is not only a thief but also a very naughty Child. He came to my house too, to steal butter. I keep the butter in an earthern pot that is hung from the ceiling. Since He was not able to reach it, He took a stone and threw it at the pot. The pot broke and the entire floor was covered with butter. Do you know what I saw when I went inside the storeroom? Your Son was sitting on the floor eating the butter!"

Says the fifth one, "Your Son also invites all the monkeys of Gokul and distributes butter and curds to them!"

All these complaints sound familiar to Yashoda since she has experienced them too! She is unable to bear this any longer. However, she wants to protect her Son against these tirades.

She screams, "Stop! Stop complaining! See Him playing outside, just watch Him."

Saying this she points at the courtyard outside. All the women peer outside. They see Krishna running around on His small legs. He is clapping and laughing along with His friends.

Yashoda says, "Look at Him. He looks so sweet. He looks so innocent. He is such a nice Child. Do you really believe He plays such pranks?"

All the gopis watch Krishna for a few minutes. They agree that He indeed is a very sweet Child. They begin to forget all the thefts. They lose their anger. As they watch Him running around on His small legs and hear the sweet melodious sound of the anklets on His feet, their heart is filled with joy and love for this Divine Child.

Suddenly, one of the ladies comes out of the trance and replies, "Oh Yashoda! This is not the first time. Each time when we come and complain, you tell us that your Son looks so sweet and innocent that he can't be the thief. In the past, we believed you and went back. Not this time. Now we are going to catch Him and punish Him."

Saying this, all the gopis rush out of Yashoda's house to catch Kanha and His friends.

As I stood and watched the lane intently, I felt as if one of the house gates had opened. I saw two small kids running out. One was dark, and wore golden clothes and the Other was fair and wore dark blue clothes. Their faces were smeared with curds. They were clutching lumps of butter in their tiny hands. Twenty gopis were chasing them with sticks. Was it real? Or was I imagining it?

NANDA YASHODA BHAVAN

Similar to Mahavan, this town too boasts of a Nanda Yashoda Bhavan. This is the house where Krishna was left in the custody of Yashoda and Nanda. When I entered the premises, on the left side of Nanda Yashoda Bhavan, I found a small play area with lot of sand. This is the place where Lord Krishna played as an Infant and also showed the world some of His miracles.

Entrance of Nanda Yashoda Bhavan

An old lady is selling fruits. She goes from house to house but no one buys any fruits from her, inspite of her selling them at a very low cost. She reaches Krishna's house and calls out "Please come out and buy some fruits."

She Prays to the Supreme Lord, "Oh Lord! I have roamed around the entire village but no one has bought any fruits from me. Am I destined not to sell even one? If this is what the Lord wishes then let it be so. If it is destined, then I will remain hungry."

The Supreme Lord is very benevolent towards His devotees. Hearing her prayers, Lord Krishna, who is playing on the sand, comes to her and asks, "Oh Lady! Please tell me who you are?"

She replies, "I am a fruit seller. No one has bought any fruits from me today. Please ask Your mother if she will buy some from me."

The Lord smiles, "Can I buy a few?"

The lady replies, "You may buy if You are willing to pay the price that I ask."

The divine Child innocently says, "Oh Lady! I am a small boy. I do not know what you mean by 'price'. What do you mean by that?"

The old lady replies, "Let me explain. I will give You some fruits. You must give me something in return. It is that simple. Understood?"

Krishna smiles, "Yes! I have understood. You give me the fruits first."

The old lady asks Him, "How many fruits do You want?"

Krishna says, "I want all the fruits that you have."

The old lady is thrilled. Since morning, she has been struggling to find a single customer. Finally she has found one who wants to buy her entire stock!

She hands over all the fruits to Krishna. The Infant manages to take all of them in His small hands.

She looks at Krishna and says, "Now please give me something in return."

Krishna says, "I will give My love to you."

Saying this, He sits on her lap.

The old lady laughs, "How am I going to fill my stomach with Your love? I want something that I can use to fill my stomach."

Krishna says, "Please wait here. I will get you lots of grains."

Saying this, He rushes inside. He dips His hand inside a container containing food grains. He removes a handful and walks out of the room. Since His fist is very small, He is not able to carry all the grains with Him. He drops most of the grains on the way and by the time He reaches the old lady, He has only a few grains left in His hand.

He says, "Here! Take these! I have brought some grains for you. Please take them and fill your stomach."

The old lady is disappointed. She has handed over her entire stock to this Child but He has given her only a handful of grains in return.

She thinks, this innocent Child does not know how many grains He must give me in return of the fruits that I gave Him. However, ever since He sat on my lap to display His love and affection, a strange ecstasy fills my heart. I do not have any desire left in me. I feel so contented and happy though I do not know the reason.

She takes the handful of grains that the Child standing in front of her is holding. She puts the grains in her basket and covers the basket with a dirty piece of cloth and leaves the courtyard. She returns home with mixed feelings. She is disappointed that she has got only a handful of grains in return for a basketful of fruits. However, she is also feeling quite contented. She feels as if all her desires have been fulfilled.

She reaches her home. She puts the basket down on the ground and removes the cloth covering the basket. She gets the biggest surprise of her life! Her entire basket is filled with jewels and precious gems! A handful of grains has been converted into a basket full of gems! Who else but the Supreme Lord could have done that? She realises that the young boy whom she had just met was no ordinary child but God Himself!

As I walked past the main arch, I reached the main entrance of Nanda Bhavan. Inside, on the left, is an idol of Lord Shiva. It is believed that when Krishna was consistently attacked by various demons, His mother Yashoda felt scared and was concerned about the safety of her Infant. She prayed to Lord Shiva and asked Him to protect her Son from demons, without realising that her Son was an Incarnation of Lord Vishnu, the Protector of the whole Universe! Lord Shiva, hearing Yashoda's innocent pleas, agreed and promised to stay in the form of an idol at the entrance of Nanda Bhavan.

Right opposite the idol of Lord Shiva, is a small room known as the Putana Moksha room. This is the room where the demoness Putana tried to poison Krishna but was killed in the bargain. Since she was killed by the Supreme Lord, she attained *moksha* immediately. There is a huge statue of Putana lying on the floor with Infant Krishna crawling on her body. This reminded me of Putana Temple in Mahavan, which narrated the same story.

Inside Nanda Bhavan is a room filled with different idols. At the centre is a huge idol of Balarama, with a snake hood rising above him — a reminder to devotees that Balarama is an incarnation of the Lord Seshanag. To the left is an idol of Nanda and to the right is that of Yashoda. In front of these are the idols of Krishna, Balarama, and Revathi on the left. On the right are idols of Krishna and Yogamaya. Yogamaya is an incarnation of Goddess Durga and here She is mounted on a tiger, like Goddess Durga. In front of all these idols is a cradle with an idol of Infant Krishna in it. The way these idols have been set up resembles that in Mahavan. Devotees are allowed to swing this cradle and receive the blessings of the Supreme Lord. The priest opens and closes the curtain every few minutes. The people here believe that the curtain needs to be closed every few minutes to feed Infant Krishna. One striking feature of this temple is the fact that the idol of Balarama is bigger and more prominent than that of Krishna. One more noteworthy feature is the fact that the idol of Balarama is black and a peacock feather adorns it, which we normally associate with Krishna.

By the time I came out of Nanda Bhavan, the guide realised that I was spending too much time for his comfort. He felt he was better off chasing tourists who would spend just five minutes at each temple and still pay him the same amount. He collected ten rupees from me and hastily excused himself, saying he had to rush to complete some personal errands!

YASHODA GHAT

Yashoda Ghat in Gokul is equivalent to the Brahmanda Ghat in Mahavan. Just as people in Mahavan believe that Lord Krishna showed the whole Universe to His mother Yashoda at Brahmanda Ghat, people at Gokul believe that this divine incident took place here in Gokul. This serene ghat is on the banks of Yamuna where

Yashoda Ghat

lots of devotees take a holy dip. As in any ghat, this one too has many long steps that lead down to the river. The many huge trees that surround this ghat provides shade to the tourists. If you are tired and need respite from the hot sun then you have come to the right place.

6

Raval

...

"*atra tam budhi samyogam labhate paurva dehikam,*
Yatate cha tato bhuyah samsidhau kurunandan"

("On taking such a birth, he regains the divine spiritualism of
his previous birth and through that he tries to make further
progress to achieve perfection Oh! Son of Kuru dynasty.")

(*Bhagavad Gita* 6.43)

Raval is around 10 km to the south-east of Mathura, one
kilometre off the main road. This is also on the eastern side of
the Yamuna. This small place is very famous since it is the
birthplace of Lord Krishna's divine consort, Radha. There are
some who think that Radha was born and brought up in Barsana.
There are others who believe that She was born in Raval, but
spent Her childhood in Barsana. Raval is a small town, much
smaller than Mahavan and Gokul. The visitors to this town
primarily come to visit the Radha Rani Janmasthan Temple.

RADHA RANI JANMASTHAN TEMPLE

The most famous place in Raval is the Radha Rani Janmasthan
Temple. The temple is in an isolated place, away from the hustle
and bustle of the small dusty village. There are lots of trees near
the temple. The shade from these trees provides respite from the
scorching heat of the afternoon sun. It is believed that the palace
of Vrishabhanu stood at this location.

Radha Krishna Tree

The Radha Rani Temple is a huge temple made of white marble. The entire courtyard is also made of pure white marble. The wooden doorway is decorated with silver plated arches. This temple has two pairs of idols of Radha and Krishna, kept on a raised podium. The bigger pair of idols are behind the smaller pair. Krishna, in his style so typical of Brij Bhoomi, is playing His flute.

The priest there was an educated person who had served in the Indian Army for many years before he had retired. He welcomed me warmly and performed the *Mangala Arati* of the idols. After the *Mangala Arati*, he took a saffron cloth and put it on the idols of Radha and Krishna. I felt blessed when he placed the cloth on my shoulder. He also gifted us a huge plate of sweets.

From the terrace of the first floor, I could see a huge pond nearby. This was the same pond where Vrishabhanu found Radha sitting on a lotus.

Lord Vishnu is resting in His Holy Abode Vaikunta. He realises the time has come for Radha to be born on Earth. However, She is hesitant. Lord Vishnu asks Her for the reason.

She replies, "Oh Lord! I want to be born on earth as Your consort. How can I be born when You are still in Vaikunta?"

Lord Vishnu replies, "I will take birth on Earth in a few years. However You are destined to be born before Me."

She replies, "I will take birth on one condition."

Lord Vishnu says, "Please tell Me. I will fulfil any of Your conditions."

She says, "I do not want to see the world without having seen You. Therefore, I will keep My eyes closed. I will open My eyes only when I see You."

Lord Vishnu smiles and agrees to Her condition.

King Vrishabhanu is returning from River Yamuna, after his daily bath. On the way, he comes across a pond in the middle of which, is a huge golden lotus. He is awe-struck. He has never seen such a huge lotus and that too a golden one. He gets into the pond and walks towards the lotus. He notices a small baby sitting in the middle of the flower. The girl is smiling at him. He feels Her smile is radiating more light than the sun. He realises that She must be some Divine Child. He lifts the girl from the lotus and looks questioningly towards Heaven.

Lord Brahma descends from Heaven. King Vrishabhanu prostrates before Him and seeks His blessings.

He asks Lord Brahma, "O Lord! Please tell me who this Divine Child is?"

Lord Brahma replies, "In your previous birth, you and your wife had performed severe penance and austerities. When I asked you for a boon, you had wished to have a daughter who would be the beloved of Lord Vishnu. Take this Girl with you. She is your Daughter. She will be the consort of the eighth incarnation of Lord Vishnu who will appear on the planet in a few years from now."

King Vrishabhanu is thrilled. He lifts the Girl and carries her home. She is known as Radha, Radhika and even Radha Rani, the Queen of Brij Bhoomi. He and his wife had been childless till then, so they are very happy to have a Child whom they can call their own. They pamper her and take very good care of their darling Radha. However, they also feel sad that she is born with Her eyes closed. They assume She is blind and so they frequently pray to the Supreme Lord to restore Her eyesight.

Radha is five years old.

Narada meets Vrishabhanu and informs him, "Nanda Rai and Yashoda of Gokul are parents of a beautiful Infant, Krishna. Please invite all of Them to your house."

Vrishabhanu follows Narada's instructions. He invites Nanda Rai, Yashoda, Rohini, Krishna and Balarama to his house for lunch. Nanda Rai arrives with his family to Vrishabhanu's house. Vrishabhanu and his wife warmly welcome Nanda Rai and his family. Nanda Rai asks Vrishabhanu, "Where is your lovely Daughter?"

Vrishabhanu calls out, "Radha! Look who has come to meet You."

Radha comes out to meet Nanda Rai and his family. She senses the divine presence of Lord Vishnu's incarnate, Lord Krishna, in the room. As per Her wish, She opens Her eyes and the first person She sees is Her consort, Lord Krishna.

On the opposite side of the temple is a huge garden. This garden is believed to be 5000 years old and was originally the garden of Radha Rani. As I entered this garden, I saw a beige-coloured temple at the centre. This had idols of Radha and Krishna, sitting on a swing. To the left of this temple was a strange sight. There were two trees, completely entwined! One tree was black, representing Krishna and the other tree was white, representing Radha. These are popularly known as Radha-Krishna trees.

7

Baldeo

...

"*Anantaschasmi naganam varuno yadasamaham,*
Pitrunam aryama chasmi yamah samyamatam aham"

("Among the Nagas (a type of serpent), I am the Serpent God
Ananta and among the aquatics, I am Varuna, the God of
aquatics. Among the ancestors, I am Aryama and among the
controllers of death, I am Lord Yama, the God of Death.")

(*Bhagavad Gita* 10.29)

Baldeo is a small town approximately 20 km south-east of
Mathura, around seven kilometres from Mahavan. The famous
temple of Lord Balarama, also known as Baldeo and Dauji, is in
this town. It is believed that Lord Balarama, also known as
Baldeo, used to rule here. This is how the town got its name.
Baldeo is located at 27.42^0 N latitude and 77.82^0E longitude.

BALARAMA TEMPLE

Vehicles are not allowed near the temple complex. Ashwani had
to park far away from the temple and I walked the distance through
the narrow bylanes of this holy town. The temple has a huge
courtyard. When I reached the temple, the huge main gate was
closed. I waited for a long time for it to open, but there was no
sign of anyone coming to open the gates. Suddenly, I noticed many
devotees walking across the other side of the row of gift shops. I
followed them and noticed that there was one more gate to the
right of the main gate, which was open and all the devotees entered

Balarama Temple

the temple premises through this gate.

The deities here are Balarama and His wife, Revathi. The deity of Balarama is black and that of Revathi is white. Since Revathi's idol is placed on the side of the altar, it can be viewed only from the opposite side and not from the front. The deity of Balarama was installed by Vajranabha and is one of the biggest idols in Brij Bhoomi.

The cream-coloured walls surrounding the entire courtyard has dark blue inscriptions in Sanskrit and Hindi. The entire floor of the courtyard is made of white stones and marble. Initially, there were very few devotees and the place was very quiet. Suddenly, lots of devotees arrived and they began to sing songs related to Lord Balarama (Baldeo). The quiet atmosphere suddenly became festive.

KSHIR SAGARA KUND (BALBHADRA KUND)

Kshir Sagara Kund

Next to the Balarama Temple is the Kshir Sagara Kund, also known as Balbhadra Kund. It is known as Kshir Sagara Kund because it is believed that this *kund* was built by Brij people who filled it with milk from 1,00,000 cows as an offering to Lord Balarama. Kshir Sagara means sea of milk. This *kund* is also known as

Balbhadra Kund since this is the tank where the original idol of Lord Balarama was found. The idol was lost for a long time but one night Saint Gokulnath had a dream and a divine voice told him that he would find the idol of Balarama in this sacred tank. The next morning, Saint Gokulnath found the idol of Balarama at the very spot indicated to him in the dream.

8

Vrindavan

...

"*edeshu yagneshu tapahasu chaiva daneshu yat punya phalam pradishtam,*
Atyeti tatsarvam idam viditva yogi param sthanamupaiti chadyam"

("Anyone who accepts the path of devotional service will achieve the same results as those from studying the Vedas, performing sacrifices, austerities and charitable work. By performing devotional services, the devotee surpasses all these and reaches the abode of the Supreme Lord.")

(*Bhagavad Gita* 8.28)

Vrindavan is about 15 km from Mathura. It is believed that during the era of Lord Krishna, this place was a forest filled with Tulsi plants. Tulsi is also known as *Vrinda*; hence this town was named *Vrindavan* which means 'a forest of Tulsi plants'. Vrindavan is located at 27.58° N latitude and 77.7°E longitude.

It is believed that Nanda Rai felt that Gokul was a very dangerous place to live in because Krishna had been attacked by various demons like Putana, Trinavarta, and Shakatasura. He decided that it would be safer to move to Vrindavan to escape the wrath of Kansa and his allies.

Nanda Rai is sitting with his fellow villagers and friends. He announces, "Yashoda and I do not want to stay in Gokul any longer."

His friends are shocked. They ask him, "Oh Chieftain of Gokul! Please tell us the reason for this decision."

Nanda Rai replies, "As you are all aware, ever since the birth of my Son Krishna, there have been innumerable attempts to kill Him. Demons have come here in all shapes and forms. I want to go to a different town. I hope they will not trouble us then."

The villagers try to make him change his decision. They plead with him, "Oh Nandaraiji! You are the chieftain of our town. You are our king. We all worship you. If you leave us like this, we will become orphans. Please change your decision."

Nanda Rai continues, "One demoness came and tried to poison Him by feeding Him poisonous milk. Later, another demon, in the form of whirlwind, tried to kidnap Him. One more demon hid himself inside a cart and tried to crush my Infant. How do you expect us to continue to stay in such an unsafe town?"

The villagers ask him, "Please tell us where you plan to go."

Nanda Rai replies, "I plan to go and stay at Vrindavan. I do not want to stay in the eastern part of River Yamuna. Let me stay for some time on the other side of the river. I hope the demons will stop harassing us."

Many villagers cry out, "Oh Nanda Rai! We too want to accompany you. Please take us with you."

Nanda Rai says, "Tomorrow morning, as the sun rises, we will leave in our bullock carts. We will carry all our belongings with us, including our cattle. Whoever wants to join us, is free to do so. Whoever wants to stay back in Gokul, is free to stay back. If you plan to come with us then please go home and start packing your belongings."

Nanda Rai spends the rest of the day helping Yashoda pack.

It is morning. Nanda Rai has loaded all his bullock carts with household items. Accompanied by Yashoda, Rohini, Balarama, and Krishna, he leaves Gokul. Hundreds of Gokul residents follow suit. They too decide to start a new life at Vrindavan. The caravan slowly leaves Gokul and soon crosses River Yamuna. River Yamuna sees Lord Krishna and Lord Balarama in the caravan. She bows before Them and seeks Their Blessings. By noon, Nanda Rai, accompanied by his family and fellow villagers, reaches Vrindavan.

Though Mathura is a bigger city and has the Krishna Janmasthan (birthplace of Lord Krishna) located in the heart of the city, it was the smaller town, Vrindavan, that stole my heart. It is believed that Vrindavan alone has over 5000 temples! There are several sacred spots here that are associated with glorious incidents from Krishna's life. Every day, hundreds of devotees go around the entire temple town. This is known as Vrindavan Parikrama. The parikrama is around 15 km and would take a day to complete. People walk bare feet. The dusty path that is used for this parikrama is known as parikrama path and is quite well known to the locals. While performing Vrindavan Parikrama, many of the important temples, ghats, and other sacred spots are visited. A visit to the famous Loi Bazaar is a must. There are small shops on either side of the road. The shops sell different items, the common thread among them being Lord Krishna — pictures, paintings, idols, key chains, gift articles, flutes, CDs, DVDs. There are many shops that sell milk-based products since curds, milk, buttermilk, and butter are available here in abundance.

Vrindavan is one of the most important places for followers of Lord Krishna, especially those who follow Gaudiya Vaishnavism traditions. Any visit to this temple town is incomplete without knowing about Lord Chaitanya Mahaprabhu, Nityananda Prabhu, and the six Goswamis.

The Gaudiya Vaishnavism, which is prevalent in Vrindavan and many eastern states of India, was founded by Sri Chaitanya Mahaprabhu. Sri Chaitanya Mahaprabhu was born in Mayapur, in the eastern part of India on the evening of February 18, 1486. He was born to a poor brahmin couple, Jagannath Mishra, and Sachi Devi. He is considered as the combined incarnation of Lord Krishna and Radha and because of His golden complexion, He is also known as *Gaura Hari*, which means the golden complexioned Lord Hari (Lord Vishnu). He took *sanyasa* at an early age and travelled throughout the country, visiting holy places. He spread the glories of Lord Krishna through *sankirtans* (congregational chanting) of the holy chant 'Hare Rama Hare Rama Rama Rama Hare Hare, Hare Krishna Hare Krishna Krishna Krishna Hare Hare'. The brahmins objected to this, saying that this holy mantra should be chanted only by brahmins and not by everyone. Lord Chaitanya realised that the anger of the brahmins was gaining momentum. He felt it would be better to devote His time in performing devotional duties rather than fighting brahmins. He pacified the brahmins by interchanging the two sentences and forming a new Mahamantra 'Hare Krishna Hare Krishna Krishna Krishna Hare Hare, Hare Rama Hare Rama Rama Rama Hare Hare'. He told the people that the best way to reach God and attain *moksha* in the Kaliyuga is through constant chanting of the Mahamantra.

Lord Nityananda is considered to be the prime associate and main disciple of Chaitanya Mahaprabhu. He is also considered to be the incarnation of Lord Balarama and is known as Nitai. The names of Chaitanya Mahaprabhu and Nityananda Prabhu are always taken together as Nitai-Gauranga (Nitai = Nityananda Prabhu, Gauranga = Chaitanya Mahaprabhu) and are considered to be inseparable. They are also the two principal architects of Gauda Vaishnavism. Nityananda Prabhu was born in the year 1474 to a brahmin couple Hadai Ojha and Padmavati in a village named Ekachakra in Bengal. He spent his first 12 years in Ekachakra leading an ordinary life. However, at the age of 13, he was asked to accompany a saint, Lakshmipathi Tirtha, to various holy places in the country. People who attended his *sankirtans* were astonished by his level of devotion and love towards the Supreme Lord. They concluded that he was no ordinary saint but an incarnation of Lord Seshanag (Lord Balarama). Nityananda Prabhu met Chaitanya Mahaprabhu in Nadia in the year 1506. It is believed that both were filled with great ecstasy on meeting each other and the witnesses commemorated this episode by building a Gaura-Nityananda Temple in Nadia. After this, Nityananda Prabhu became a staunch devotee of Lord Chaitanya and both of Them spread the message of God through Their teachings.

Lord Chaitanya realised the importance of Brij Bhoomi where Lord Krishna and Radha had spent their childhood. He was aware that during the past few centuries, many holy places had been lost and forgotten. People had become too busy chasing material comforts to think of these spiritual places. Lord Chaitanya felt sad. He wanted to revive the lost glories of Brij Bhoomi by rediscovering the holy places associated with the Supreme Lord's pastimes. He spent many years at Vrindavan which is considered the 'heart' of Brij Bhoomi by the Gaudiya Vaishnavas. He realised that He would need the help of many of his ardent followers to spread the holy message of the Supreme Lord. He took the assistance of the 'Six Goswamis of Vrindavan' to accomplish this. They were Sri Sanatana Goswami, Sri Rupa Goswami, Sri Jiva Goswami, Sri Raghunatha Das Goswami, Sri Raghunatha Bhatta Goswami, and Sri Gopala Bhatta Goswami. The Six Goswamis were staunch followers of Lord Chaitanya Mahaprabhu and spread his teachings to the entire nation.

Sri Rupa and Sri Sanatana were brothers born to a Saraswat Brahmin couple in Karnataka who later migrated to Bengal. Sri Sanatana Goswami is believed to be the reincarnation of Sanata Kumar, one of the four Kumars, sons of Brahma who had cursed Jaya and Vijaya, the door-keepers of Vaikunta to be born as Asuras for not allowing them to meet Lord Vishnu when they went to Vaikunta. Both Sri Rupa and Sri Sanatana were working as government servants during the regime of the Muslim king Hussaiñ Shah in Bengal. They came in contact with Lord Chaitanya Mahaprabhu and became His devotees. Lord Chaitanya asked the brothers to go to Vrindavan and spread the glories of Lord Krishna. Both Rupa and Sanatana immediately gave up their government jobs and headed to Vrindavan. They stayed there for the rest of their lives, rediscovering many of Lord Krishna's places, spreading the name of the Lord through their teachings and writings. Sri Sanatana is associated with rediscovering and commencing the worship of the Radha Madan Mohan Deities at Radha Madan Mohan Temple. Sri Rupa Goswami discovered the lost idol of Lord Govinda, which he installed and worshipped at the Radha Govind Dev Temple.

Sri Jiva Goswami was not only the nephew of Sri Sanatana Goswami and Sri Rupa Goswami, but also their brightest student. After their death, Jiva Goswami became the most respected Goswami in Vrindavan. He wrote thousands of Sanskrit verses based on the philosophy of Lord Chaitanya Mahaprabhu. He started the worship at Radha Damodhar Temple. He also played an important role in restoring the glory of Radha Kund and Shyam Kund. Both Radha Kund and Shyam Kund were lost for thousands of years and they were rediscovered by Lord Chaitanya Mahaprabhu. However, it was Jiva Goswami who is credited with restoring them to their lost glory.

Sri Raghunatha Das Goswami was born in a rich man's family but he had an aversion to materialistic comforts. He was fascinated by the pastimes of Lord Krishna and ran away from home to join Lord Chaitanya Mahaprabhu at Jagannath Puri. Later, he moved to Brij Bhoomi and stayed for 40 years at Radha Kund and Shyam Kund, spreading the teachings of Lord Chaitanya Mahaprabhu and Lord Krishna. It is believed that the Goverdhan Shilas (stones) that are seen near Radha Kund and Shyam Kund were brought 500 years ago by Sri Raghunatha Das Goswami and he worshipped them daily after bathing at Radha Kund and Shyam Kund.

Sri Raghunatha Bhatta Goswami is believed to be an incarnation of one of the gopi friends of Radha. Though he was not a prolific writer like Sri Jiva Goswami, he was a very good singer. Thousands of people would flock to listen to his deeply moving *sankirtans* and *Srimad Bhagvatam* glorifying Lord Krishna. He stayed for 45 years in Vrindavan and was a close friend of Sri Rupa Goswami. He was also associated with Radha Govind Dev Temple where he would daily recite the holy verses of *Srimad Bhagvatam*.

Sri Gopala Bhatta Goswami was a disciple of Lord Chaitanya Mahaprabhu and came to Vrindavan on His advice. He is also believed to be an incarnation of one of the gopi friends of Radha. He found 12 Saligramas in the river while bathing, one of which later turned into the beautiful Radharaman idol. This idol is worshipped in the Radha Raman Temple. He stayed for 45 years in Vrindavan teaching and spreading the message of the Supreme Lord. He was a staunch follower of Lord Chaitanya Mahaprabhu and began to miss His presence in Vrindavan; so he took His *asana* (seat) and cloth and kept them in Vrindavan where he worshipped them daily. These items are still kept at the Radha Raman Temple.

Vajranabha was the great grandson of Krishna. He was the son of Aniruddha and Usha. Aniruddha, in turn, was the son of Pradhyumna, who was son of Krishna and Rukmini. After the disappearance of Krishna and Balarama from earth and with the onset of Kaliyuga, people began to indulge in materialistic comforts, forgetting the glorious days of Krishna and Balarama.

Vajranabha decided to build temples to bring back the awareness of these Gods among the people. He had never seen Krishna and Balarama so he sculpted the idols based on the description that he heard from his mother Usha. Since he was not sure of his creation, he decided to make three idols of Lord Krishna and asked Usha to choose the idol that resembled the Lord. Usha told him that the first idol resembled Krishna from the feet to the navel (this idol was installed at the Radha Madan Mohan Temple). She told him that the second idol resembled Krishna from the navel to neck (this idol was installed at the Radha Gopinath Temple). The third idol resembled the face of Krishna (this idol was installed at the Radha Govind Dev Temple). It is believed that if a devotee sees all the three idols on the same day then he will attain *moksha*.

SRI KRISHNA BALARAMA TEMPLE (ISKCON)

The Sri Krishna Balarama Temple is located at the entrance of the holy city of Vrindavan. It is believed that Krishna and Balarama used to come to this part of Vrindavan with their cowherd friends and cattle for grazing. This is known as *Go-charana lila*. This temple was built by ISKCON and is one of the biggest, cleanest, and most beautiful temples in

Entrance of ISKCON Temple

Vrindavan. His divine Grace A.C. Bhaktivedanta Swami Prabhupada established this temple in 1976 on Ram Navami.

The temple complex has many buildings, each built with beautiful white marble. As I entered the main gate, I saw two huge stairways on either side of the main building. I took the stairs on the right, which led me to a room at the top. This room had huge black and white photographs depicting different incidents from Srila Prabhupada's life and his teachings.

The building on the left houses the s*amadhi* of Swami Prabhupada. This is where his body was laid to rest when he passed away in 1977. His house has been turned into a museum. There is a beautiful black statue of Swami Prabhupada at the centre of the *samadhi* chamber. His body was placed directly below the statue.

Outside this room, there were stairs that took me to another room at the top. This room had many sculptures made of black stone with framed inscriptions in black on a golden background. All inscriptions were related to the qualities of a spiritual master. The top room and the *samadhi* room below share a common ceiling so from the top room, when I peered down, I could see the *samadhi* below.

As I walked past these two buildings, I came across a huge brown gate with a huge bell hanging at the top. Walking past this huge gate, I found myself inside a big inner courtyard. On the left, there was a food stall that served *prasada* and to my right, I saw a book stall that sold all the books published by ISKCON and a gift shop that sold articles like T-shirts, pictures, key chains and many gift articles — all centred around Lord Krishna.

Idols of Radha and Shyamsundar

In front of these shops is an open courtyard. On the other side, there are three altars. The first altar on the left has white idols of Chaitanya Maha-prabhu and Nityananda, popularly known as Gaura and Nitai. In front of these idols are idols of Srila Prabhupada on the left and Srila Bhaktisiddhanta Goswami on the right. The centre altar has a black idol of Krishna and a white idol of Balarama. A small Tulsi plant is kept right at the front. The altar on the right has a white idol of Radha and a black idol of Shyamsundara (Krishna). There are also idols of Radha's *sakhis,* Lalitha and Vishaka, fanning Radha and Krishna.

To the left of the courtyard, there is a statue of Srila Prabhupada. Along the walls of the courtyard are paintings that reminded me of the murals in Ajanta caves. Srila Prabhupada had encouraged the devotees to sing and dance while chanting the holy names of the Lord and I could see his legacy alive even today. I saw numerous devotees singing and dancing in the courtyard. Chants of 'Hare Krishna Hare Krishna Krishna Krishna Hare Hare Hare Rama Hare Rama Rama Rama Hare Hare' filled the air. One striking feature of this temple complex is the high level of cleanliness. It is definitely one of the cleanest temples in Vrindavan.

SRI RADHA VRINDAVAN CHANDRA TEMPLE

This temple is the latest entrant in the temple town. Like the 'older' ISKCON Temple, this is also located on the outskirts of the town. As we drove from Mathura, a few kilometres before we reached Vrindavan town, we saw this temple on our left. It is situated before the ISKCON Temple. Though this temple has been built by ISKCON Bangalore, it is not known as the

Sri Radha Vrindavan Chandra Temple

ISKCON Temple, probably because Vrindavan already has one ISKCON Temple. This one is known as Sri Radha Vrindavan Chandra Temple and also as The Krishna Heritage Consortium. Some of the locals also call it Akshaya Patra Temple. The Akshaya

Patra scheme is aimed at providing mid-day meals to poor school children studying in the nearby areas. This scheme was started by ISKCON at Bangalore and became a great success. Based on its resounding success in Bangalore, ISKCON decided to replicate this scheme in other states too. In Vrindavan, this temple is the centre for the Akshaya Patra scheme.

The temple is a beautiful sand-coloured circular building that looks like a huge lotus in bloom. It reminded me of the lotus feet of Lord Krishna. The ground floor of the building has a huge kitchen that prepares food under the Akshaya Patra scheme. Visitors are allowed inside only after they don special aprons and headgear. The size of the vessels was astonishing! They were gigantic because the authorities have to cater to the hungry mouths of thousands of school children. There was also one huge chapatti-making machine. One of the temple *prabhus* (the term used for the priests here) was kind enough to show us around.

·The altar was on the first floor of the building. There was a huge central area where the devotees sat and chanted the holy names. A circular dome ceiling adorned the temple. Towards the far end, I saw the most beautiful idols of Radha and Krishna, housed in a golden *mantapa* (pedestal). They were white and looked resplendent in their beautiful dresses. The mantapa was surrounded by a pink arch-like structure. In front of these huge marble idols, small brass idols of Radha and Krishna were placed. The altar had a wooden door with idols of Garuda and Hanuman carved on it. On either side of the altar was a beautiful painting of a peacock, adorned with coloured glass pieces.

Outside the temple, on the right is an amphitheatre. Next to the amphitheatre, an ISKCON official was distributing *khichdi* as Krishna *prasada*. It was prepared using *desi ghee* (processed butter) and tasted awesome. The temple premises have a huge car park area and also have lots of free space for kids to play.

VARAHA GHAT

The Varaha Ghat is located quite close to Gautama Rishi Ashram, near ISKCON Sri Krishna Balarama Temple. Years ago, the Yamuna used to flow close by so there was a ghat here.

However, the Yamuna has now drifted away a few kilometres and so there is no ghat here. I was unaware of this and so spent considerable time looking for the ghat. I had instructed my driver to drive close to the Yamuna, hoping to find this ghat. There seemed to be no trace of it. I had heard that it was quite close to ISKCON and near the 'starting point' of the Vrindavan Parikrama path. So after a futile search, I instructed my driver to turn back and head towards the 'starting point' of Vrindavan Parikrama. The locals also didn't know the location of this place, in spite of its wonderful divine history. I noticed my guide Mathuresh pronouncing the place as *Baraha* instead of *Varaha*. It occurred to me that maybe I should ask the locals for 'Baraha Ghat' instead of 'Varaha Ghat'! The ploy worked well and very soon we reached Varaha Ghat! I saw a few signboards in Hindi proclaiming that the area was Baraha Ghat.

When I managed to locate Varaha Ghat after a long search, I was thrilled since I felt that the major task of hunt was over and locating the Varaha Temple would be just a matter of minutes. However, it was not so. It was a pity that in spite of spending considerable time I was unable to locate this temple. Incidentally, this was the only temple in the entire Brij Bhoomi that I had been unable to locate inspite of my best efforts.

Varaha was the third avatara of Lord Vishnu. Lord Vishnu took the form of a ferocious boar Varaha to kill the demon Hiranyaksha and rescue the world. This ghat is known as Varaha Ghat because Lord Krishna showed His Varaha Form to the gopis at this place.

The gopis, along with Radha, come to meet Krishna on the banks of the River Yamuna. Krishna has arrived here ahead of the gopis. Krishna decides to play a trick on them. He hides Himself in the bushes near by. After some time, Radha arrives at the river bank with Her friends. Krishna is nowhere to be seen. She soon becomes impatient and calls out for Him. Krishna comes out from the bushes, however not in His usual form of a young boy. He wants to have some fun with the gopis and Radha and so He appears in the Varaha Avatara. When the gopis and Radha see this, they shriek. What stands in front of them is not a young boy with whom they have played earlier, but a huge Boar roaring and displaying mighty weapons in Its mighty arms. They see the Boar controlling the entire Universe. All the stars and planets are revolving around the Boar. The entire cosmos is at Its mercy. This sight is too much for the naïve and innocent village bred gopis. They expected to see a handsome Lad and not a ferocious looking Boar surrounded by the entire cosmos. They pray to Krishna and ask Him, "Oh Kanha! Please come in the form that has charmed us all these years."

Lord Krishna, who always listens to His devotees, immediately takes His form of a young cowherd and stands before them. The gopis and Radha are thrilled to see Him in His 'normal' form.

It is quite ironical that the innocent gopis preferred to see their Kanha as a cowherd rather than see Him in His divine Form that millions would have died to see! There is a Varaha Temple here to commemorate this incident. Though I could not locate this temple, I have read that this temple has idols of Radha, Krishna, and Varaha.

KALIYA GHAT

Kadamba Tree at Kaliya Ghat

I was on the Parikrama Path. As I passed Varaha Ghat and walked ahead a few metres, I came across Kaliya Ghat on the right side. As in the case of Varaha Ghat, here too, the Yamuna does not flow close by any longer. Thousands of years ago, at Kaliya Ghat, the river used to flow next to the Kadamba tree that enabled Lord Krishna to jump into the river. However, the river has drifted away. Thankfully, I did not have much trouble locating this place.

This is the very spot where Lord Krishna jumped from the Kadamba tree into River Yamuna and fought with the serpent Kaliya.

Krishna is playing with His friends on the banks of the river Yamuna. The ball falls into the Yamuna. None of the cowherd boys is ready to enter the Yamuna because they fear the poisonous Kaliya.

Krishna says, "I will jump into the river and bring back the ball."

He is cautioned by all the villagers not to jump in since a deadly poisonous serpent Kaliya, dwells in the Yamuna. However, Krishna does not listen to them. He jumps from a nearby tree and dives deep within the Yamuna. He meets the wives of Kaliya who ask Him to leave. However, Krishna does not agree. In the meanwhile, Kaliya, who is asleep, wakes up.

The wives of Kaliya plead with Him, "Please escape from this place. Our husband has woken up. He will kill You."

Krishna laughs and says, "I do not need any protection. It is your husband who actually needs protection."

Kaliya gets very angry and demands to know who has disturbed his sleep. Poison begins to froth from his mouth. In the meanwhile, all the agitated villagers come to the banks of the Yamuna to see what has happened to Krishna.

Kaliya asks Krishna, "Who are You?"

Krishna replies, "I am the Destroyer of all evils. I will spare you if you surrender and seek forgiveness."

Arrogant Kaliya laughs, "It will be You who will be running for mercy."

Krishna repeatedly cautions him but Kaliya does not listen. A grim fight ensues. Kaliya tries his best to attack Krishna with his poisonous fangs, however all this has no effect on the Supreme Lord. Though he spews poison at Krishna, he is unable to overcome Him. A big fight ensues. Lord Krishna, though a small Boy, has the strength of the Mighty Lord and He subdues Kaliya.

Then Krishna mounts Kaliya and begins to dance. Kaliya lifts his hood out of the water and comes to the surface and the villagers are astonished to see Krishna dancing on the deadly Kaliya. All the villagers had been crying, thinking something terrible has happened to Krishna. However they are thrilled to witness this divine spectacle. Krishna dances on Kaliya, all the Gods descend from Heaven and bow before Him.

Kaliya's wives bow before Lord Krishna and plead, "Oh Supreme One! Our husband was foolish that he did not recognise you. His arrogance blinded his senses which made him fight You. Please forgive and free him."

Kaliya too asks for forgiveness. He bows before Krishna and says, "Oh Supreme Lord, because of my arrogance I could not realise who You are. Please forgive me."

Krishna tells him, "I shall forgive you only on one condition."

Kaliya says, "Oh Lord, please tell me what Your wish is. I will obey."

Krishna says, "You must leave the Yamuna and not harass the people staying on its banks."

Kaliya agrees.

Lord Krishna releases Kaliya, who falls at His lotus feet and begs for forgiveness.

Krishna commands him, "Kaliya! You left Ramanaka Island to escape getting killed by Garuda. You can return safely because Garuda will not eat you once He sees My footprints on your hood."

Kaliya and his wives once again worship and bow before Lord Krishna and leave the Yamuna. The holy river becomes free from poison. This news reaches Kansa and he begins to realise that Lord Krishna is no ordinary Child but may be an avatar of Lord Vishnu. Who else could take on and humble the powerful Kaliya with such ease?

A temple has been built to commemorate this incident. The temple has a white idol of Balarama at the centre. This idol is flanked by two black idols. They are the two wives of Kaliya. Behind the idol of Lord Balarama is a big black idol of the serpent Kaliya. On top of the serpent is a black idol of Lord Krishna playing His flute. Lord Krishna is seen dancing on the evil serpent Kaliya, after vanquishing him.

To the left of this temple is a huge Kadamba tree. It is believed that this ancient tree is the same Kadamba tree from where Lord Krishna took a plunge into the Yamuna to confront Kaliya.

RADHA MADAN MOHAN TEMPLE

Radha Mohan Temple is located close to Kaliya Ghat. On the Parikrama Path, this temple is also on the right side, off the main road. There are two Radha Madan Mohan Temples, adjacent to each other. I had to walk on a ramped path to reach the old temple. The red imposing tower of the old temple can be seen from afar.

It is believed that after Lord Krishna humbled the mighty Kaliya in Yamuna river, He rested on this hillock. Since He was drenched with the water of Yamuna, He began to feel cold. At that time, 12 suns (known as Dwadasha Aditya) came here and gave their warmth to their Lord. Hence this hillock is known as Dwadasha Aditya Tila (hillock of the 12 suns). Due to this heat, Lord Krishna began to sweat and the *sarovar* formed due to His perspiration is known as Praskandara Sarovar (lake formed due to perspiration)

Radha Madan Mohan Temple

The Radha Madan Mohan Temple is not only the oldest among the seven Goswami temples but also one of the oldest and one of the most magnificent temples in the entire town of Vrindavan. However, like many other temples in Vrindavan, this one too had to bear the brunt of the Moghul king Aurangzeb's onslaught. The original idols were moved to Rajasthan for safekeeping and to protect them from the tyranny of Aurangzeb. Today, a replica of this idol is worshipped in the temple.

Since the original temple was partially destroyed, a new temple was built next to it. The new temple is at the bottom of the hill. This was built by Sri Nanda Kumar Bose of Bengal in the early 19th century. The new temple has replicated deities that were in the original one.

The main temple building is flanked by two other buildings. One noticeable feature is that both these buildings are reminiscent of the Moghul era. The left one had a huge gate that is now closed. The right one has a Bhajan Kutir and the *samadhi* of Sanatana Goswami. All the three buildings are made of red sandstone. The central building has the sanctum sanctorum. It houses the idols of Radha and Krishna at the centre of the altar. The idol of Chaitanya Mahaprabhu is on the left and that of Prabhu Nityananda on the right. The deity of Radha's friend, Lalitha, is in the front of these deities.

There are two versions regarding the discovery of the idol of Madan Mohan. Some believe that Saint Advaita Acharya discovered the original idol at the base of an old Banyan tree, when he visited Vrindavan. He entrusted the worship of this idol to his disciple, Purushottama who later gave the idol to his disciple, Sanatana Goswami. Sanatana Goswami spent many decades in Vrindavan worshipping this idol. There are many who believe that Sanatana Goswami himself discovered the original idol of Madan Mohan. It is also believed that Lord Chaitanya Mahaprabhu stayed at this temple during His visit to Vrindavan.

There are different versions about the past lives of Sanatana Goswami. Some believe him to be an incarnation of a gopi named Rati, who was Radha's close friend. Some considered him to be an extension of Lord Chaitanya Mahaprabhu. There are others who believe that he was an incarnation of Sanata Kumar, one of the four Kumara sons of Lord Brahma.

Sanatana Goswami had renounced all materialistic comforts. He could not afford to build a luxurious temple for his Madan Mohan. He used to constantly feel sad that he could not perform an elaborate *puja* of his deity with pomp and glory. However, all this despair was to end soon. The winds of change were not far away.

The gusty winds and the storms are making sailing very difficult for Ram Das Kapur. He is a rich merchant from Multan, who is sailing in the Yamuna River. The ship is fully loaded with merchandise. Suddenly, the ship begins to sink and he does not know what to do.

He starts to scream, "Help! Help! I am drowning and my ship is sinking."

Sanatana Goswami is sitting on the banks of the Yamuna. He hears Ram Das Kapoor's screams for help.

He makes a mental contact with Ram Das Kapoor and advises him, "Please pray to Lord Madan Mohan for help."

Ram Das obeys him and begins to pray to Lord Madan Mohan, "Oh Supreme Lord! Please save me. Please rescue Your humble devotee."

Immediately his ship recovers and he and his crew and the merchandise are saved. He reaches the banks of the Yamuna safely. He finds Sanatana Goswami meditating on the banks of the river.

Ram Das falls at Sanatana Goswami's feet and pays obeisance.

He says to Sanatana, "Oh Holy Saint! I know that it was you who came into my thoughts and suggested that I pray to Lord Madan Mohan. I was saved because of you."

Sanatana Goswami opens his eyes and smiles, "Oh Ram Das! Please get up. Please don't thank me. I have done nothing. Your saviour is Lord Madan Mohan."

Ram Das Kapur realises the greatness of Lord Madan Mohan.

He asks Sanatana, "Oh Holy One! Please tell me how to show my gratitude towards the Supreme Lord."

Sanatana shows him the Lord Madan Mohan idol and says, "I am a poor brahmin. I do not have any money to build a temple where I can worship this beautiful idol. If you have sufficient money then please build a temple which is worthy of this idol."

Ram Das replies, "Oh Saint! I will do as you wish. I will build a temple which will be the most beautiful temple in this town."

Saying this, he builds the Radha Madan Mohan Temple in 1580.

BANKE BIHARI TEMPLE

Banke Bihari Temple is one the most popular temples in Vrindavan and attracts many tourists. This temple is located near Loi Bazaar. This makes it the most crowded among all the temples in this temple town. I saw lots of hawkers selling flowers, reminiscent of the ambience near the temples in South India. Most of the devotees carried huge garlands of flowers to offer to Banke Bihari.

Banke Bihari is another name for Lord Krishna. *Banke* means 'bent at three places'. When Lord Krishna, stands while playing His flute, He is bent at three places — His right knee is bent to cross the left leg, His right hand is bent to hold the flute and His

Banke Bihari Temple

head is also bent while playing His flute. *Bihari* means 'Supreme Enjoyer'.

The idol of Banke Bihari was discovered by Haridas Swami at Nidhivan, in the 16th century. The idol was discovered in a Kadamba grove where it was originally worshiped. The musician Saint Swami Haridas was a great Krishna devotee, belonging to the Nimbarka sect. He was well known for his bhajans. He was also the Guru of the famous musician, Tansen, who adorned the court of Mughal Emperor Akbar. Haridas Swami worshipped Lord Krishna as Kunja Bihari since he found the idol in a Kadamba grove – *kunja* means 'grove'.

The Banke Bihari Temple was built in 1864 and the Banke Bihari idol was moved here when this temple was constructed. The temple was rebuilt in 1921.

As I entered the imposing structure, I saw a huge inner courtyard. Black and white marble tiles made up the courtyard flooring. Arches adorned two sides of the courtyard. At the far end was the altar. Initially the temple had only the idol of Banke Bihari. Later, an idol of Radha was added.

There are a few unusual features about this temple. One salient feature is that a curtain is pulled to cover the idol and it is removed every few seconds. It is believed that the bright and glowing eyes of Banke Bihari will make you unconscious if you watch it for a long time. Hence the curtain covers the deity every few seconds. Another feature is that the temple opens very late in the morning. This is because people believe that Krishna is awake during most of the night, performing Ras Lila with the gopis and Radha and so He needs rest. Mangala Arati, which is performed every day in all the temples, is performed here only once a year — on Janmashtami Day. The lotus feet of the Lord are covered every day and can be seen only on one day of the year — on Akshaya Trithiya day. Unlike other temples in Vrindavan, this temple has lots of flowers and flower garlands all over the place – practically everywhere.

The temple attracts a large number of devotees during the Shravana month (July/August). This is the month when Jhulan Yatra (Swing Festival) is celebrated. The idol is placed on a huge golden swing amidst many other smaller golden and silver swings.

RADHA VALLABHA TEMPLE

Radha Vallabha Temple is another very popular temple in Vrindavan. Harivamsa Goswami, who started the Radha Vallabha sect, built this temple. This sect lays considerable emphasis on worshipping Radha. This temple is located quite close to the Banke Bihari Temple. There are different versions about the origin of the name Harivamsa. There are many who

Radha Vallabha Temple

believe that his parents performed severe austerities and penance and prayed to Lord Hari Vishnu in order to have a child, so they named their son as Harivamsa (a descendant of Hari), when he was born. There are others who believe that he was the incarnation of the divine flute (*Vamsi*) of Lord Krishna, hence he is known as Harivamsa (Flute of Hari).

Harivamsa Goswami renounces his family life and proceeds towards Vrindavan in search of his Lord. On the way, he meets a brahmin, Atmadeva, who is worshipping Radha Vallabha. Atmadeva had a dream the previous night, in which the Supreme Lord instructed him, "Tomorrow morning, a holy saint named Harivamsa Goswami will pass by. You must gift the Radha Vallabha idol to him."

As soon as Atmadeva meets Harivamsa, he remembers the dream. He follows the instructions and hands over the idol to Harivamsa Goswami.

Harivamsa Goswami builds a hermitage and begins to worship the Radha Vallabha idol. A Bengali devotee named Sundara Das, who was the disciple of Braja Chand, son of Haridas Goswami, constructs a temple for Radha Vallabha in 1626.

However, Aurangzeb destroyed this temple in 1670. A new temple was later built adjacent to the old one in 1972. The deity is now worshiped in the new temple.

A salient feature of this temple is that there is no idol of Radha. A crown is kept instead, next to the black idol of Krishna. Another salient feature here is that, first the oblations are offered to the crown of Radha and then to the idol of Krishna. The other unusual feature of this temple is the blend of Hindu and Islamic influences on the architecture of the place. Though the temple construction was started by Sundara Das, he ran into financial problems. He approached the Moghul emperor, Akbar for monetary help. Emperor Akbar, known for his liberal views on religion, was more than willing to help Hindus. He played an active role in the construction of this temple. This could probably be the reason for the mix of Hindu and Moghul influences.

I reached the temple in the evening. The temple has a very huge inner courtyard. Arches are built on all four sides of the inner courtyard. The courtyard also has the *samadhi* of Harivamsa Goswami. Hundreds of devotees had assembled in the courtyard. There was hardly any place to sit. Suddenly the doors of the altar opened and the devotees rushed towards the altar. The black idol of Krishna was placed on a silver throne. To the right, was the crown of Radha. There were about four or five steps that led me to the altar. At the top of the flight of steps, I saw a huge thick rope. This rope was connected to a fan inside the altar. Devotees pulled the rope to fan the idol of Lord Krishna.

SEVA KUNJ

Seva Kunj, like Nidhivan, is the place where Lord Krishna engaged in Ras Lila with Radha and the gopis of Vrindavan. The terrain of Seva Kunj is completely different from the nearby areas. This place is covered with trees and thick shrubs. All the walls have inscriptions in Sanskrit and Bengali. The *samadhi* of Haridas Swami is located here. The place is swarming with monkeys, most

of them quite mis-
chievous and ferocious.
They snatch any item
that you hold loosely in
your hands, like hand-
bags or purses. Some of
them even snatch away
the devotees' spectacles!

It is believed that
every night, Radha and
Krishna come to Seva
Kunj and perform Ras
Lila. After the Ras Lila,
they rest in the Rang

Seva Kunj

Mahal. No one is allowed to watch this divine spectacle, hence the
gates of Seva Kunj are locked in the evenings. Even the monkeys,
that are present here in large numbers throughout the day,
voluntarily leave the place after dark. It is also believed that if
anyone stays back and watches the Ras Lila being performed, he
will invariably die.

There are small pathways, a few close to the walls bordering
Seva Kunj and a few in the middle of the shrubs. I walked along
the pathway near the wall of Seva Kunj to reach the far end. Rang
Mahal, the famous temple of Seva Kunj is located here. The
sanctum sanctorum of this temple has a multi-step podium that is
normally seen at homes during the Navaratri season. It also
resembles a bed to indicate that Seva Kunj is the 'resting place' for
Radha and Krishna. There is a picture of Radha and Krishna at
the top of the altar.

All the walls have beautiful paintings of Radha, Krishna, and
the gopis. Each painting depicts a different aspect of Radha and
Krishna. One painting depicts Krishna decorating Radha's hair
with flowers. There is another beautiful painting that has Krishna
playing His flute and enthralling Radha. There is one more that
depicts Them playing Holi and sprinkling coloured water on each
other. Another depicts Lord Krishna massaging Radha's tired legs.
This shows that the Merciful Lord can perform any act to
reciprocate the love of His devotee. Just watching these paintings

took me back in time. All of a sudden, I heard the sound of the anklets of the gopis and the dancing feet of Krishna and Radha.

The beats of the Ras Lila sticks is getting louder. Krishna is engaged in the Ras Lila with Radha and the gopis. The gopis are dancing in a circle. Krishna and Radha are dancing in the middle. Krishna multiplies Himself into innumerable forms and each form dances with one gopi. This makes each gopi believe that her beloved Kanha is dancing only with her.

Suddenly Krishna lifts Radha and breaking the circle of gopis carries Her away. They are no longer amidst the gopis but in a secluded spot. Krishna goes around plucking the most colourful and sweet smelling flowers.

He asks Radha, "Shall I decorate Your hair with these flowers?"

Radha smiles, "Yes Kanha! You have plucked such lovely flowers for Me!"

Krishna adorns Radha's hair with the beautiful flowers.

Krishna tells her, "Oh Radha! You look lovelier than the full moon. You are the most beautiful among all the gopis of Vrindavan. Your have a childlike innocence that has made You dear to Me."

He asks Her, "Are You feeling tired after the dancing? Are You exhausted?"

Radha smiles and says, "My Kanha knows everything but He still asks Me! Oh Kanha! You have not only stolen My heart but also captured My mind. You know everything. Why do You ask?"

Krishna asks Radha to stretch Her tired legs. She obeys Him. Krishna sits beside Her. He massages and decorates Her tired lotus feet with flowers.

Outside this temple is a pair of footprints. The white footprints are believed to be those of Radha's and the black ones are Krishna's.

A walk further away from Rang Mahal towards the entrance of Seva Kunj brought me to Lalitha Kund. Krishna created this *kund* using His flute, to quench the thirst of Radha's friend, Lalitha. This is about 50 metres from the entrance of Seva Kunj. It is quite deep and there are steps going down to reach the water. I was surprised to see a water source in the middle of a small forest. The Lalitha Kund is much bigger and spacious than the Vishaka Kund at Nidhivan. A walk further along the pathway took me to the main gate of Seva Kunj.

IMLI TALA

On the Vrindavan Parikrama road, Imli Tala comes on the right side, past the Madan Mohan Temple. On the left side of the road I saw the River Yamuna flow by. On the right side, there was a white marble building which had the sacred Imli Tala in front of it. This sacred tree had been 'caged' to protect it from vandalism.

Entrance of Imli Tala Temple

Imli Tala means 'tamarind tree'. Under this sacred tamarind tree, Chaitanya Mahaprabhu spent many days, chanting the holy names of Lord Krishna. It is believed that He visited this sacred tree everyday. Sri Sanatana Goswami later established the worship of Nitai Gauranga here. Many centuries ago, the Yamuna used to flow right across Imli Tala. However, now the river has moved away a bit. The Parikrama Path separates the Imli Tala from the holy river.

Behind the Imli Tala tree was the Gaudiya Matha temple. The altar had beautiful idols of Radha, Krishna, Nitai, and Gauranga. All the walls of the temple were adorned with colourful paintings depicting the pastimes from the life of Chaitanya Mahaprabhu. The biggest painting was the one above the altar. It depicted Lord Krishna performing Ras Lila with the gopis.

There must be thousands of tamarind trees in Vrindavan alone. What makes this tree so special and prayer worthy? Ironically, the tree had to bear the brunt of Radha's curse 5000 years ago!

Radha is walking briskly to meet Krishna. There are many ripened imli (tamarind) fruits lying on the ground near this tree and Radha accidentally steps on one of them. Her foot is bruised and because of this, she has to stop

99

and wash her foot. Her foot begins to hurt and she is unable to walk swiftly towards Krishna, who is waiting for Her. This slowing down upsets Her a lot and she curses the imli tree.

She says, "Your ripened fruits lying on the ground have hardened and these hardened fruits have bruised My feet. Because of this injury, I am no longer able to walk swiftly towards my beloved Lord. I curse you, may you never be able to ripen your fruits! May you bear only half ripe fruits that are soft and do not bruise the passersby."

Till this date, this tree no longer bears ripened hard fruit. When the fruits are half ripe and soft, they fall to the ground.

Some people believe that this particular tamarind tree here dates back to the era of Radha and Krishna. Others believe that this tree is a descendant of the original tree.

RADHA DAMODHAR TEMPLE

Radha Damodhar Temple is also one of the most important temples in Vrindavan. The idol here was carved by the famous saint Rupa Goswami. Later, he handed it over to his disciple Jiva Goswami who built a temple here in 1542. It is believed that all the Goswamis used to meet here and discuss the stories of Radha and Krishna. This temple is very close to Seva Kunj. In fact, many centuries ago, it was a part of Seva Kunj. The temple is also close to the ever busy Loi Bazaar.

The temple has a huge courtyard in front of the sanctum sanctorum. I saw lots of devotees chanting in the courtyard. The style and the accent of the chants and the attire of the devotees reminded me of ISKCON. The reason is not difficult to comprehend. I learnt later that Srila Prabhupada, the founder of ISKCON

Samadhis of various saints behind the temple

had spent many years in Vrindavan, frequenting this temple. His influence is very evident among the present day devotees. Srila Prabhupada had prepared well before he launched the ISKCON movement worldwide.

On the right side of the temple premises was a small room which was used by Srila Prabhupada. Sitting in this small room, under the sweltering heat of Vrindavan, he translated the entire *Srimad Bhagvatam*. From his room, he could see the *samadhi* and Bhajan Kutir of Rupa Goswami which served as a continuous inspiration to him.

The cream-coloured temple building had three arches in front. Beautiful paintings adorned these arches. A huge bell hung on the right. As in many other temples of Brij Bhoomi, here also, the altar had a huge multi-stepped podium. This podium was covered with a colourful cloth. Many pairs of Radha–Krishna idols, known by different names, were kept on the podium. Sri Radha Vrindavan Chandraji's idols were worshipped by Krishnadas Kaviraj Goswami. Lalitha Sakhi Sri Radha Damodarji's idols were worshipped by Jiva Goswami. Sri Radha Madhavaji's idols were worshipped by Jaidev Goswami. Sri Radha Chail Chikanji's idols were worshipped by Bhugarbha Goswami. As in the case of Banke Bihari Temple, here too, huge curtains cover the deity every few seconds.

In front of the deities was a black stone. This was no ordinary stone, it was Goverdhan Shila. This is also known as *Girirajcharan Shila*. It was worshipped by Sanatana Goswami because it has the divine footprints of Lord Krishna on it. It also has imprints of a calf, flute and a *lathi* (stick used to control the cows while grazing).

Sanatana Goswami regularly performs the Parikrama of the sacred Goverdhan Hill. As he is growing old, he is finding it very difficult to do this.

He prays to Lord Krishna and says, "Lord, I am finding it increasingly difficult to walk all the way to Goverdhan and then perform the Parikrama. My body has grown old and weak. My bones are tired. Please help me."

The Supreme Lord is touched by his devotion. He picks up a black stone lying below His feet and gives it to Sanatana Goswami and tells him, "This is a stone from Goverdhan Hill. It is a Goverdhan Shila. Treat this as the Hill itself and pray and perform Parikrama around this sacred stone."

Sanatana Goswami begins to perform the puja of this sacred stone everyday. He also performs the Parikrama around this 'Shila', just as devotees perform Parikrama around the divine Hill. Since the Lord had stood on this stone, it has His footprints. Hence it is known as Girirajcharan Shila, which means the stone with the footprints of the Lord of Goverdhan.

While performing Parikrama of the altar, I was surprised to see numerous small temple-like structures on three sides. These were *samadhis* of holy saints. One more notable feature is that although these structures were small, there were many of them on the left side of the altar. And they were bigger in size and less in number on the right side of the altar. Among them were many bhajan kutirs. The bhajan kutirs and samadhis of Rupa Goswami and Jiva Goswami can be seen here. There was also a bhajan kutir of Srila Prabhupada.

RADHA SHYAMSUNDAR TEMPLE

'The only deity manifested from Srimati Radha Rani's heart' — says a board in front of the temple. Many believe that the most important temples in Vrindavan are the seven temples built by the Goswamis of Vrindavan. Though the Radha Madan Mohan Temple looks more magnificent, the Radha Shyamsundar Temple is considered to be the most sacred of them, since the deity is believed to have 'manifested' itself from none other than Radha, the divine consort of Lord Krishna.

Radha Shyamsundar Temple

Radha and Krishna are performing the Ras Lila. Suddenly, the anklet slips from Radha's left foot and falls down. It is nearing dawn, and Radha is in a hurry to get back home. In her hurry, She does not notice that her anklet has fallen down.

It is early morning. Radha notices that she has lost Her anklet. She is worried that Her mother-in-law will scold Her so She asks Lalitha to help her find it. Lalitha says, "Radha, I think You must have dropped it in the grove while performing Ras Lila with Kanha last night. I will go and search."

Lalitha goes to the grove where Radha and Krishna had danced the previous night.

Shyamananda Pandita (earlier known as Dukhi Krishna Das) is cleaning the grove. He finds the anklet lying on the ground. As soon as he holds the anklet in his hand, he discovers that it is no ordinary anklet and that it belongs to a Divine Soul.

Lalitha notices that Shyamananda Pandita has found the anklet. She disguises herself as an old lady and approaches him.

Lalitha says, "The anklet that you found belongs to my Friend. Please give it to me so that I can return it to Her."

Shyamananda replies, "When I touched the anklet, I felt a strange sensation in my body. I could feel energy surging through me. I immediately guessed that this belongs to a very divine lady. Please tell me who your friend is."

Lalitha smiles, "She is none other than Radha!"

Shyamananda exclaims, "Radha! Radha! This belongs to Radha! How fortunate I am! Please take me to Radha, the Queen of Brij Bhoomi."

Lalitha says, "You are in a material world and you have a physical body that belongs to this world. You should have a bath in Radha Kund. This will help you to take the form of a gopi. You will be able to see Radha once you do this."

Shyamananda bathes in the sacred Radha Kund. When he steps out, he finds that he has been transformed into a gopi. He is able to see Radha. He prostrates himself on the ground at Her feet and asks Her to bless him. Radha blesses him and asks him to return to the material world. Shyamananda weeps with joy, "Oh Radha! I do not want to return to the material world. I want to stay here and serve You for the rest of my life."

Radha says, "Each person is destined to stay for a certain period in the material world. You need to go back and serve the people of Vrindavan. I promise you that once your time is over, you will come back to Me."

Shyamananda Pandita is overjoyed. He falls at Radha's feet once again.

Radha closes Her eyes. A beautiful idol of Shyamsundar manifests from Her heart. She hands it over to Shyamananda and says, "Take this idol with you and worship it daily. You will be blessed."

Shyamananda returns to the material world. He begins to worship this idol daily at Vrindavan.

Radha created this idol and gave it to Shyamananda Pandita in 1578. This temple is located quite close to Radha Damodhar Temple and Loi Bazaar. As I approached this temple I experienced a pleasant change in the ambience. Unlike the hustle and bustle of the noisy and crowded Loi Bazaar, a serene atmosphere pervaded here. Once I stepped inside, I saw a huge open courtyard, probably bigger than what I had seen at the other temples. The courtyard is completely open at the top, with no enclosures or mesh. The sanctum sanctorum has a set of huge sandstone coloured arches in the front. The wall on the right has a white marble arch. The altar has a white idol of Radha and a black idol of Krishna. The original idol given by Radha Rani to Shyamananda Pandita is kept to the right of these idols.

At the centre of the courtyard is the deity of Vrinda Devi. Vrinda Devi is the Holy Tulsi, which is very sacred and dear to Lord Vishnu. It is believed that many centuries ago, the entire area around this place was covered with Tulsi plants, hence the name Vrindavan.

SHAHJI TEMPLE

Shahji Temple

Shahji Temple is popularly known as *Tede Khambe Wala Mandir* which is translated as 'Temple with Spiral Pillars'. This magnificent temple was built in 1876 by two wealthy brothers, Shah Kundan Lal and Shah Fundan Lal, hence it is known as Shahji Temple. They were wealthy jewellers from

Lucknow. Both of them were ardent followers of Chaitanya Mahaprabhu and great devotees of Lord Krishna.

This temple is located at one end of Loi Bazaar, close to Nidhivan. There are many small shops that obstruct one's view of this beautiful temple. When I was standing in Loi Bazaar, I didn't even realise that such a beautiful temple with exquisite carvings was just a few metres ahead. However, once I walked past the huge Loi Bazaar gate, I chanced upon a huge field and on the other side of the field was this stunning temple in its full splendour. The entire temple is made of Italian marble.

I asked my guide to tell me the history of this temple. He narrated, "I was told by my friends that at the entrance of the temple, you will see the faces of the two brothers engraved on the floor. At first sight, this may appear strange because, we are normally accustomed to seeing huge decorative portraits of the builders hanging from the walls in a majestic manner. You don't expect the portraits to be on the floor, hundreds of devotees are sure to step on them every day. But then, if you want to understand the reason, you should appreciate the meaning of the true divine love that the brothers had for Radha, Krishna, and Brij Bhoomi. Shah Kundan Lal and Shah Fundan Lal were fascinated by the sacredness of Brij Bhoomi. They knew that the Lord of the Universe had spent His childhood here and there could not be a more sacred place on earth than Brij Bhoomi. They consider the entire Brij Bhoomi to be one big temple. Since people don't wear shoes at places of worship, they decided not to ever wear any footwear, during their stay in Brij Bhoomi. It was their desire that, after their death, their bodies should not be burnt because they believed that their body, in the form of smoke, will go into the atmosphere, outside Brij Bhoomi. They also did not want their ashes to be thrown into the River Yamuna because the river will carry the ashes away from Brij Bhoomi. They wanted their dead bodies to be dragged through the streets of Vrindavan. They felt that if this was done, they would be covered by holy dust. They also wanted their faces to be engraved on the floor of the temple so that when devotees come to this temple, they will invariably step on them and cover their engraved faces with the holy sand of Vrindavan."

I was fascinated with this story of devotion!

The temple is well-known for its exquisite and beautiful architecture. It has 12 pillars, made of beautiful white marble. Each pillar is 13 feet high and 35 inches in diameter. The main deities of this temple are Radha and Krishna. Since the idols are quite small, they are known as Chote Radha Raman (*chote* means 'small'). To the right is the idol of Goddess Ganga.

The temple has a room known as *Basanti Kamra* which houses Belgian glass chandeliers and paintings. This room is situated in the eastern wing. The ceilings and walls have many paintings. This magnificent room has 15 Belgian chandeliers. In the olden days, candles were fitted into the chandeliers to illuminate the room. Since the advent of electricity, electric bulbs are used. There are three fountains in the centre of the room. This room is opened only twice a year. Unfortunately, the room was closed on the day I visited the temple.

NIDHIVAN

Entrance to Nidhivan

Nidhivan is located between Shahji Temple and Loi Bazaar. Nidhivan is also a grove, similar to Seva Kunj. It is believed that many centuries ago both, Seva Kunj and Nidhivan, were part of one big grove. That explains the similarity between the two places. *Nidhivan* means the 'forest where invaluable gems are found'. During the era of Lord Krishna, this part of Brij Bhoomi was probably a dense forest, hence the name Nidhivan. However, due to deforestation, Nidhivan is today only a small patch of land with a few trees and thorny shrubs. I could see many modern buildings surrounding this beautiful place. This is the venue for the famous Ras Lila, where Krishna and His consort Radha, along with the gopis, danced. Radha and Krishna also rested here on numerous occasions. Like Seva Kunj, Nidhivan is also locked up at night. Here too, the monkeys leave, as dusk approaches.

As in the case of Seva Kunj, this place was also swarming with monkeys. Most of them were quite fearless and aggressive. They are ready to snatch any article that we carried — handbags, cameras, flower garlands. During my first visit, a tourist who was standing beside me, offered chickpeas to a monkey. Seeing this, a herd of monkeys arrived from nowhere. They attacked the tourist who was carrying the bag of chickpeas. In no time, his bag was snatched by these monkeys. They also looked at my hands. Since I was not carrying any food for them, they got upset and chased me away! A few days later, after gathering sufficient courage, I made my second visit.

There were a few muddy pathways between the shrubs and also near the walls surrounding Nidhivan. A walk on the pathway along the wall in an anti-clockwise manner led me to the *samadhi* of the poet saint, Swami Haridas. The inscription on the *samadhi* reads 'Swami Sri Haridasji Ki Jai'. Swami Haridas, born in 1535, was a great Krishna devotee, belonging to the Nimbarka sect. He was well known for his *bhajans*. He was also the Guru (teacher) of the famous musician Tansen, who sang in the court of the Moghul emperor Akbar.

Haridas is chanting and singing divine songs praising the Supreme Lord. Emperor Akbar, who is passing by, is fascinated. He asks his men to stop and listens to the sweet melody coming from the grove. He asks his commander to find out who is singing such a melodious tune. The commander goes into the grove and sees a saint sitting below a tree, singing the holy names of the Lord. He goes back and reports this to his master. Akbar, known for his liberal views and artistic tastes, immediately feels that he must make him his court singer. He goes to the saint and bows down.

Swami Haridas opens his eyes and asks, "Who are you? What brings you here?"

Emperor Akbar introduces himself, "I am Emperor Akbar. I am fascinated by your song and your melodious voice. Oh Holy Saint! Please come and bless my court with your sweet melodies."

Swami Haridas replies, "For me, this grove is my court and Lord

Krishna is my King. I will neither leave this place, nor will I serve anyone else."

Emperor Akbar begs him to come. Swami Haridas is silent and thoughtful for a few minutes.

Finally, he replies, "I will not come. However, I do not want to disappoint you. I will send my favourite disciple to accompany you to your court."

The Emperor agrees and takes Swami Haridas' favourite disciple with him. This disciple later, becomes one of the most famous singers in the history of India and is well known as Tansen.

Behind the *samadhi* is an idol of a lady playing the musical instrument Veena. This lady is Lalitha, one among the *ashta sakhis* (eight friends) of Radha. It is believed that Lalitha was later reborn as Swami Haridas.

As I walked along the wall of Nidhivan and went past the *samadhi* of Swami Haridas, I came across a temple which had three deities. At the centre was the idol of Radha, flanked by Her friends, Lalitha and Vishaka. One unusual feature is that it is not Krishna but Radha who is playing the flute.

As I walked along the muddy path, I came across a small temple, known as Rang Mahal. Next to it was an open courtyard, known as Ras Sthal (location of Ras dance). It is believed that Krishna had performed Ras Lila at this very place with Radha and the gopis of Vrindavan. I could still hear the musical sounds of their dancing feet.

It is full moon night in the Sharad season, also known as Sharad Poornima. Lord Krishna remembers the previous birth of the gopis. They had been great sages and had performed severe penances and austerities to please Lord Vishnu. When Lord Vishnu asked them to seek a boon, they desired to experience conjugal love with the Supreme Lord. Lord Vishnu told them that this was not possible in His current incarnation of Lord Rama. The sages were disappointed. Lord Vishnu, the ever merciful Lord, took pity on His devotees. He promised them that they would be able to experience this in their next birth as gopis, the milkmaids of Vrindavan when He would descend once again to Earth as Lord Krishna.

Krishna remembers His promise to them. He feels that it is time to fulfil his promise. He picks up His divine flute and begins to play melodious tunes. The entire Vrindavan is filled with the entertaining tunes from His flute. The enchanting tune reaches the homes of each and every gopi. When they hear the music, they realise that He is calling them. Their desire to be with Him increases. They stop their household chores and rush to Him. Krishna was only eight years old then and the gopis are much older than Him. Most of them are married. They are busy with their chores, when the sound of the flute fills the air. Some gopis are cooking. Some are feeding their children and husbands. Some are eating. However, they drop all their work and run towards the forest of Vrindavan. The husbands of some of them try to stop them from leaving the house at night, but they don't care. They are so anxious to see the lotus-eyed Krishna and dance with Him on this full moon night that nothing in this world will stop them from doing so.

The gopis are living in different parts of Vrindavan. They come out of their homes and run swiftly in the direction of the melodious sound of the flute. It looks as if the entire Vrindavan is headed towards the forests at Nidhivan.

The gopis reach Nidhivan. They surround Krishna, who is playing His flute and unmindful of what chaos He has caused in the middle of the night! As He opens his lotus eyes, He notices that He is surrounded by hundreds of gopis.

He smiles, "Oh Beautiful Maidens of Vrindavan! Please tell me what brings you here in the middle of the night? Why have you left your husbands, brothers, sisters, sons, and daughters and come here like this?"

The gopis reply in a chorus, "Oh Kanha! We heard the melodious tunes of your Divine Flute. It is also Sharad Poornima. The beautiful moon has filled the entire town with a glow that can be only matched by Your divine looks. We desire to dance with You through the night."

Krishna once again smiles and rebukes them, "Each of you has come here alone in the middle of the night. You have passed through the thick forest that is infested with wild animals. I admire your courage. However, are you doing the right thing in leaving your family and coming here? Won't they be worried about your whereabouts, especially since they have seen you disappear in the middle of the night?"

The gopis are stunned to hear this. They have come here to fulfil their desire to dance and spend the night with Krishna. They do not expect such a welcome. They have tears in their eyes. Some of them sob inconsolably.

The gopis say, "Oh Kanha! Please do not reject us this way. We have left our homes to spend the night dancing with You. We are unable to control ourselves on this enchanting night. Though we are married, You are our eternal Husband. We know that we can have a good family life only with Your blessings. We want to enjoy Your presence. We want to spend this night dancing with You. We want to embrace You. We want to taste the nectar of Your divine love. We want to worship Your lotus feet. You have stolen our hearts. We constantly remember You. Our lips are constantly chanting Your name."

The gopis continue, "Oh Kanha! Please do not turn us away like this. We do not have the power to go back. We do not have the wish to return to our homes without experiencing divine bliss with You. We are slaves of Your sublime beauty. Your face is shining brighter than the full moon. We have totally surrendered ourselves and wish to take refuge in Your Lotus Feet."

Hearing this, Krishna begins to smile. He multiplies Himself into hundreds of Krishnas! Each form holds one gopi and dances with her. The gopis do not realise that the Supreme Lord has multiplied Himself. Each gopi thinks that her Kanha is dancing only with her. As they dance, hand in hand, with Krishna, they experience the eternal bliss that even many of the Gods and the Gandharvas in Heaven do not know. All the Gods and Goddesses appear from Heaven to watch this wonderful spectacle. They begin to chant the holy names of Lord Krishna. They drop the most beautiful celestial flowers from Heaven. As the flowers begin their descent they get woven into beautiful garlands. These garlands fall around the neck of each form of Krishna. The fragrance of the beautiful celestial flowers fills the enchanting air of Vrindavan. The moon is shining in all its glory. There are hundreds of beautiful milkmaids from Vrindavan singing, chanting, and dancing in the forests. The beautiful tunes from Krishna's flute fill the celestial atmosphere. Each gopi is dancing with her Lord, hand in hand. Krishna embraces the gopis. As His hands touch them, they experience the kind of eternal bliss that they had desired in their previous birth as sages. They look at the handsome, shining face of Krishna and feel their desires have been fulfilled.

Radha is the supreme Lady, among the gopis. All the gopis are dear to Krishna, but Radha is the dearest to Him. He puts His arm around Her shoulder and gently leads Her to the centre of the circle formed by the dancing gopis and Krishnas. Krishna and Radha are surrounded by everyone else. Krishna starts playing His flute once again and Radha is dancing next to Him. The Gods and Goddesses shower Krishna and Radha with celestial flowers. They bow to Them from Heaven and seek Their Blessings.

Rang Mahal is also known as the Sleeping Temple because Radha and Krishna used to rest here after the Ras Lila. This temple has a bed and the people of Vrindavan believe that Radha and Krishna come here every night and rest. The Rang Mahal has numerous pictures of Radha and Krishna. The walls are decorated with colourful pieces of glass.

The devotees keep flowers and *kumkum* here every day. It is believed that Radha and Krishna perform Ras Lila in the groves every night and then they come and relax on this bed. They also believe that Krishna decorates Radha with the flowers and *kumkum* that are kept here by the devotees. When the caretakers open the door of the *Rang Mahal* each morning, they find that the flowers and the *kumkum*, kept on the bed by the devotees during the day, would have been used.

As I walked further down the path, I came to the spot where Swami Haridas found the famous Banke Bihari idol. It was originally worshipped here and later moved to Banke Bihari Temple, when the temple was built in 1864.

As I walked further along the walls of Nidhivan, I reached Vishaka Kund. Krishna had created this *kund* using His flute, to quench the thirst of Radha's friend, Vishaka. This *kund* is quite deep and there are steps leading down to the water source. The *kund* cannot be seen even while one is standing close to it since a major part of it is below ground level.

CHIR GHAT

On the Vrindavan Parikrama path, Chir Ghat comes soon after Imli Tala. It has the Yamuna on the left and an ancient tree on the right side of the road. This place is known as

Tree on which Krishna hid Himself

Chir Ghat because this is place where Lord Krishna hid the gopis' clothes (*chir*), while they were bathing in the Yamuna.

All the gopis come to River Yamuna to bathe. Krishna sees that the gopis undress themselves before stepping into the waters of the Yamuna. Krishna finds this revolting. He tells his friends, "The gopis should not remove all their clothes while taking a bath."

His friends ask Him, "Why Krishna? Please tell us what is wrong."

Krishna replies, "They are insulting the River God by bathing without clothes. They should wear atleast one piece of cloth when they step into the Yamuna."

His friends ask, "Please tell us what we should do."

Krishna tells them His plan, "Let us take away all their clothes and hide them. We will teach them a lesson."

Krishna and His friends gather the clothes that are lying on the banks of the river. He keeps all the clothes on a tree and finally He climbs the tree and hides Himself. His friends also hide themselves on adjacent trees.

The gopis are bathing. They are singing and dancing in the Yamuna. Soon, they finish their bath. They step out of the river and walk to where they have left their clothes. The clothes seem to have mysteriously vanished. They ask one other, "Who could have stolen our clothes?" The gopis look in different directions and search everywhere, but don't find a trace of who could have taken them.

Suddenly, a sweet melody fills the air. The tune is as gentle as the breeze that is blowing. The gopis stand still. They stop their search and begin to look towards the source of this beautiful tune. One of them notices Krishna sitting on a tree playing His flute. A gopi screams, "There He is! I have spotted Kanha sitting on that tree. He is hiding Himself and playing His flute. He is the culprit who has stolen our clothes. Look! Our clothes are also hanging from different branches of the same tree."

All the gopis feel embarrassed since they are not wearing a single piece of cloth. They rush and jump into the river once again. One of the gopis shouts at Him, "Kanha! How dare You steal and hide our clothes."

Krishna says, "It is your fault. You should not have a bath without any clothes since it is an insult to the River God."

The gopis feel ashamed and realise their transgression.

They shout in unison, "We agree what we have done is wrong. We have inadvertently insulted River Yamuna. We promise never to do this in future. Please return our clothes."

Krishna replies, "Please come out of the river, one by one. Please walk up to the place where I am sitting. I will return your clothes."

The gopis plead, "We can't come out of the river without any clothes. We feel ashamed to come out and stand before you."

Krishna replies, "You were not ashamed to take bath without your clothes, so why do you feel ashamed to come out without your clothes?"

The gopis are upset and tell Him, "If You do not return our clothes, we will complain to Yashoda about your pranks."

On hearing this, one of Krishna's friends replies, "If you complain to Yashoda about Krishna, then we will tell the whole village how you all look without clothes!"

The gopis are now helpless. They realise that they have no choice but to obey Kanha. Each gopi comes out of the water and goes to the tree where Krishna is sitting. Krishna hands over the clothes he has taken. The gopis wear their clothes and promise Krishna never to repeat this again.

People believe that the ancient tree at Chir Ghat is the one on which Lord Krishna sat after hiding the clothes of the gopis. A black idol of Lord Krishna is kept near the tree. A picture depicting this event is kept next to the idol. Lots of *duppattas* (colourful cloth pieces), which are generally worn by the local women are tied to the branches of this tree, symbolising this event. Next to the tree is a temple which houses the white marble idol of Goddess Yamuna.

RADHA RAMAN TEMPLE

Radha Raman Temple was built in 1826 by Shah Behari Lall, the grandfather of Shah Kundan Lall and Shah Fundan Lall, who built the Shahji Temple. This temple is located quite close to Nidhivan and Loi Bazaar. *Radha Raman* means 'one who gives pleasure to Radha'.

At the entrance are two huge gates reminiscent of the Moghul style of architecture. Even the main brown-coloured building is similarly designed. When I walked through the gates, to my left, I saw a small building that had two small rooms. The inner of the two rooms contains the *samadhi* of Gopal Bhatta. Gopala Bhatta Goswami found the idol in this temple in 1542. He was the son of Venkata Bhatta, from Srirangam in south India. He was an ardent devotee of Chaitanya Mahaprabhu who had sent him to Vrindavan to pursue spiritual studies. As I proceeded further, I saw a huge courtyard. To the left was the altar with a black idol of Lord Krishna (Radha Raman).There was no idol of Radha. Instead, there was a silver crown, to the left of Lord Krishna's idol, symbolising Radha Rani.

Radha Raman idol is one of the few original idols left in Vrindavan. In most of the other Goswami Temples, the original idols had been moved, during the days of Aurangzeb, to other places for safekeeping. What remains are replicas of the original deity. The idol in Radha Raman is considered to be very sacred because it is believed to have manifested itself from a Saligrama to satisfy the wishes of Gopala Bhatta Goswami.

It is early morning. Gopala Bhatta is bathing in the Gandaki river. Suddenly, he notices 12 stones inside his copper vessel that he uses while bathing. He puts the stones back into the river. As he dips the copper vessel once again in the water, he notices the same set of 12 stones entering his vessel. He finds this strange. He removes them and puts them back in the river. As he dips the copper vessel the third time into the holy river, the same set of stones enter his vessel.

He thinks, "These 12 stones must have some special qualities. They are no ordinary stones. Let me take them home."

He puts the stones in his sacred cloth and takes them home. That night, Chaitanya Mahaprabhu appears in his dream.

Chaitanya Mahaprabhu tells him, "The stones that you found in the holy river today are no ordinary stones. They are sacred Saligramas. I am glad that you brought them home. Please worship them daily, the way you would worship any idol."

Gopala Bhatta is thrilled and He begins to worship them daily.

It is the full moon night in the month of Vishaka.

Gopala Bhatta prays to the Lord, "I wish I had found You in the form of an idol and not Saligrama. I would have been able to decorate You daily with different clothes which I can't do now since You are in the form of a stone. My friends, who are priests in other temples, are so lucky. They have idols which they are able to decorate with fine clothes everyday."

The next morning, when Gopala Bhatta Goswami wakes up, he has a pleasant surprise. He finds that one of the Saligramas has turned into a Krishna idol. He is able to perform pujas, abhisheka, and decorate the Lord with different clothes like his fellow priests in the other Vrindavan Temples do.

This self-manifested idol is worshipped to this date at this temple. Every year, during full moon night in the month of Vaishaka, this event is celebrated in a grand manner. The Panchamritha Abhisheka is performed for the Radha Raman idol.

Since Gopal Bhatta was not a rich man, he could not afford to build a temple. He kept the Radha Raman idol on a tree and worshiped the deity daily. Since he was worried about the safety of the idol at night, he would remove the idol from the tree and keep it in a boat that was anchored in the middle of a lake. Gopal Bhatta and his friends would guard the idol with bows and arrows. It is believed that the bows and arrows are still kept in the temple premises. Gopal Bhatta had brought Lord Chaitanya Mahaprabhu's clothes and seat from Jagannath Puri. These are also kept in the temple premises and displayed to the public a few times a year.

One needs to be extremely careful about the ferocious monkeys that surround this place. The temple priest gave us *prasada* (holy offerings) in earthern pots. The *prasada* was *khova* (a sweet made of milk and sugar). It tasted delicious, just out of this world. As luck would have it, one of the monkeys came swiftly and snatched the earthern pot containing the delicious *prasada* from my son's hands. My son began to cry. I consoled him saying that monkey is an *avatara* of Lord Hanuman, the greatest devotee of Lord Rama and since Lord Krishna is none other than the re-incarnation of Lord Rama, fate had willed that the *prasada* of Lord Rama (Krishna) should go to His prime devotee — Lord Hanuman. We must remember that Lord Hanuman always has the first right to the *prasada* of the Supreme Lord.

RADHA GOKULANANDA TEMPLE

Radha Gokulananda Temple

This temple is located between the Radha Raman Temple and Kesi Ghat. At the entrance, there is an enclosed courtyard that has numerous small Tulsi plants with a huge Tulsi plant at the centre. I took the path to my right, which brought me to the second courtyard. A path from here led me to the third and the innermost courtyard. This court-yard contains the *samadhis* of the people who were associated with this temple like Vishwanath Chakravarthi, Loknatha Goswami, and Narottama Dasa. The sanctum sanctorum is to the right.

The Bengali influence is quite evident here also, as in other Goswami temples. I saw many women devotees sitting on floormats near the deities. They were playing different musical instruments and singing melodious Bengali songs. Though I could not follow the language, it sounded very soothing and melodious. No wonder Bengali is considered to be one of the sweetest languages in India! The priest had closed the altar door since he was decorating the idols. After a long wait, the door opened. The women stopped singing and stood up. The priest performed the Mangala Arati for the deities.

The sanctum sanctorum has two pairs of black Radha Krishna idols. It is believed that there were two Goswamis and each of them worshipped one pair of Radha Krishna idols at different locations. Loknatha Goswami worshipped the small pair of Radha Vinoda idols at Vrindavan and Vishwanath Chakravarthi worshipped the bigger pair of Radha Gokulananda idols at Radha Kund. One day, Vishwanath Chakravarthi came to Vrindavan with his set of Radha Gokulananda idols. He stayed with Loknatha Goswami. He placed them in the same altar where Loknatha

Goswami had kept his Radha Vinoda idols. That temple was later broken down, so the current Radha Gokulananda Temple was built where both the pairs of Radha Krishna idols were kept. This is why there are two pairs of Radha Krishna idols. The bigger pair of Radha Krishna idols is on the right and the smaller pair of idols on the left. As in the case of other Vrindavan temples, here too, the idol of Lord Krishna is black in colour and holding a flute. There is a golden-coloured idol of Chaitanya Mahaprabhu on the left side of the altar. This was the idol that was installed and worshipped by Narottama Dasa. Lord Chaitanya Mahaprabhu was golden complexioned, so he was also known as *Gauranga* (one whose body is of golden hue) and so it is appropriate that His idol is also of the same colour.

A Goverdhan Shila is also kept near the idols. It is believed that Lord Chaitanya Mahaprabhu used to chant the holy name of the Lord while holding this Goverdhan Shila in His hand, so it has the thumb impression of Chaitanya Mahaprabhu. Lord Chaitanya Mahaprabhu handed over this stone to His devotees.

KESI GHAT

Kesi Ghat is at the farthest tip of Vrindavan town and located quite close to the Radha Gokulananda Temple. This is the spot where Lord Krishna killed the Kesi demon. This is the reason why Lord Krishna is also known as Keshava though there are others who believe that He is known as Keshava because of His thick hair (*Kesh*).

Kesi Ghat

Kesi Ghat is on the banks of the Yamuna. This is probably the biggest and the most picturesque of all the ghats in Vrindavan. Thousands of years ago,

117

all the ghats of Vrindavan were built on the banks of River Yamuna. However, today, in most cases, the river's course has shifted. Kesi Ghat is among the few ghats where the Yamuna still flows beside it. This could be one of the reasons for its popularity as a bathing place. Every evening, an aarti is performed similar to the one performed at Vishram Ghat in Mathura. It is very picturesque. Hundreds of small *diyas* (earthern lamps) float in the river, resembling the sky on a clear starry night.

Many people had cautioned me that Kesi Ghat was notorious for robbery and theft. I was also warned not to go there alone and unarmed. Luckily, Lord Krishna protected me and I had no untoward experience. As I approached the steps of the ghat, I found many ferrymen waiting to ferry me across the Yamuna. From the other side of the riverbank, I got a good view of the ghat with its magnificent sandstone coloured structure. The architecture style, structure, and the colour of the building reminded me a lot of the one at Kusum Sarovar, near Goverdhan.

At the entrance of the ghat is a Shiva Temple. Next to it is the Goddess Yamuna Temple. There is a picture depicting the famous fight between Lord Krishna and the demon Kesi.

Kansa is frustrated. All his efforts to kill Krishna have failed. He had sent the most powerful Asuras to kill Krishna, but they all were killed instead. Putana, Kakasura, Shakatasura, Trinavarta, the list was growing and endless. He is sitting on his throne, helpless.

His chief minister says to Him, "Oh King, why you are so worried?"

Kansa lists the number of Asuras who have been killed by Krishna.

He says, "I am totally shattered. It looks like the prediction will come true. Krishna will indeed kill me."

His minister says, "Please summon Kesi. He may be able to help you."

Kansa thinks for a while and replies, "Yes. That's a very good idea. Kesi is one of the most powerful demons in Brij. He can also take any form, using his knowledge of Maya. Call him immediately."

Kesi is soon summoned to Kansa's court.

Kesi bows before Kansa and says, "Oh King, what has made a powerful king like you remember an ordinary asura like me?"

Kansa explains why Kesi has been summoned.

Kesi laughs arrogantly, "I am surprised that a small Boy has been giving you sleepless nights. Just tell me where He stays and I will take care of Him."

Kansa orders his men to take Kesi to places Krishna visits frequently.

Krishna is playing on the banks of River Yamuna with His friends. Kesi has reached the same place. He asks Kansa's guards to show him who Krishna is. The guards point towards the handsome Boy dressed in golden clothes. Using his power of Maya, Kesi changes his form and becomes a powerful horse. He is strongly built and majestic looking. He rubs his front hooves on the ground and neighs loudly. Krishna and His friends hear the loud neighing. They look around and see a ferocious looking horse running towards them. Its thick black mane is fluttering in the strong breeze.

The cowherd boys scream, "Krishna! Watch out! Look! A mad horse is running towards us. Run quickly and escape before we get trampled by this creature."

Lord Krishna, through His divine vision, has seen through the disguise of Kesi. He knows this is a demon in the form of a horse. He stands rooted to His spot even as His friends begin to run away. Some of them climb trees. Some run into the open fields. They shout, "Krishna! Don't just stand there, watching! The horse will trample You."

Krishna ignores them. He stands still, waiting for the horse to come closer. The horse is now within touching distance. Kesi is surprised at Krishna's bravery. He thinks, all the boys of Vrindavan have fled at my ferocious roar and my menacing form. This Boy seems to be fearless. He is standing alone, ready to take me on.

Kesi bends his head. With one mighty heave of his head, he tries to lift Krishna and throw Him to the ground. Who could ever dare to lift the Lord who is Himself capable of lifting the world on His shoulders? Kesi's mighty blow is just a gentle nudge to the Supreme Lord. Krishna brushes aside Kesi's massive body just as an elephant would brush aside an ant on its path. Kesi is wonderstruck. He can't believe his own eyes. He once again neighs loudly and charges at Krishna. Krishna is prepared. He holds Kesi by his head and with one mighty twist throws him to the ground. Kesi has never experienced such a blow before. He falls to the ground with a huge thud. However, within a few seconds, he is once again up on his feet. He charges once more. Krishna holds the horse by his head and twists him till the bones of his neck break.

The sound of the breaking bones reverberates in the air of Vrindavan. Large dark clouds fill the sky, the sounds of thunder fill the air and blinding strokes of lightning flash across the sky. People come out of their homes and wonder what is happening in their sleepy town. Krishna is now holding the huge horse in His left hand. He whirls the horse three times and throws him. Kesi lands a hundred feet from where Krishna is standing. He gives one mighty groan and dies. Krishna's friends hiding in the trees watch this fascinating duel between their Friend and the mad horse. They climb down and rush towards Him, exclaiming in joy, "Krishna! Krishna! You have once again come to our rescue."

Krishna smiles. He looks towards the heavens and sees all the Gods witnessing this spectacle. They bow to Him and drop garlands of flowers on His divine body. Krishna smiles at them and lifts His right hand to bless them.

Jugal Kishore Temple is located near Kesi Ghat. Since it is very close to Kesi Ghat, it is popularly known as Kesi Ghat Temple. This temple has now been closed to the public.

RADHA GOPINATH TEMPLE

This temple is located quite close to the Radha Raman Temple. It is a red-coloured sandstone building. As I passed through the main door and walked towards the courtyard, I saw the old temple to my right. The new temple is on the left, beyond the courtyard. The old temple was partly destroyed by Aurangzeb, hence a new temple has been built adjacent to it.

Lord Krishna's great-grandson, Vajranabha installed the original idol of Gopinathji. The idol was lost for many years and later found by Paramananda Goswami in the Vamsi Vata area. He handed it to Paramananda Bhattacharya, who later passed them on to Madhu Pandita Goswami. Madhu Pandita Goswami began to worship Lord Gopinath. Later, these idols were moved out because of frequent attacks by Aurangzeb.

The temple has an outer and an inner courtyard. The outer courtyard has a black and white marble tiled floor. It is surrounded by huge white arches that are reminiscent of Moghul architecture. On one of the walls, there is a huge painting depicting the famous Ras Lila of Krishna with Radha and the gopis.

The sanctum sanctorum has five deities, all of them dressed in green coloured silk robes. At the centre is the idol of Lord Krishna, Gopinathji. This is a black idol, holding a flute. In front of this idol, there are idols of two of Radha's friends, Lalitha on the left, and Vishaka on the right. Behind the idol of Lord Krishna are two more idols. The one in the left corner of the altar is Radha and the one in the right corner is Her younger sister, Ananga Manjari. The placement of the deities is quite unusual because, in all the Radha Krishna Temples in Vrindavan, Radha stands to Krishna's left, this is the only temple where Radha stands to the right of Krishna.

It is believed that Ananga Manjari, the younger sister of Radha, was later reborn as Jahnava Devi and she became the wife of Nityananda. It is believed that Jahnava Devi used to visit the temple frequently and pray to Lord Gopinath. One day, Lord Gopinath, touched by His devotee's prayers, came down from the altar and took her away into the altar. In order to symbolise this event, an idol of Ananga Manjari (Jahnava Devi) is kept on the altar.

BRAHMA KUND

Brahma Kund is located next to Rangaji Temple. Earlier, this *kund* was very badly maintained and was used as a dumping ground for garbage. Thankfully, this place has now been renovated by Brahma Kund Restoration and Maintenance, The Brij Foundation.

As I reached this sacred place, I noticed there were several steps leading me down to the holy *kund*. This circular *kund* had a huge white idol of Lord Brahma, sitting on a lotus. When Mirabai had come to

Idol of Lord Brahma

Mirabai and the six Goswamis

Vrindavan, she had spent her first night at Brahma Kund. At the far end of this *kund*, there are statues of Mirabai and the six Goswamis of Vrindavan. On the right side of this *kund* is a Shiva Temple (Sri Brahmakundeshwar Mahadev). There is a huge board that depicts the two versions of the legend associated with this place.

Lord Shiva wants to witness the life led by Lord Krishna. He prepares to come down to Earth from His Heavenly Abode.

As he is approaching Earth, He hears a heavenly voice, "Oh Lord! Only the gopis have been blessed by the Supreme Lord Himself to be able to watch His pastimes. You cannot watch it, since You are not a gopi."

Lord Shiva feels sad. He asks, "How can I watch Lord Krishna at Vrindavan? Please tell me. There must be some way."

The voice replies, "Bathe in Brahma Kund at Vrindavan. This is a holy tank dedicated to Lord Brahma. If you bathe here then You will assume the form of a gopi. In this form, You can watch Lord Krishna."

Lord Shiva is ecstatic on hearing this. He rushes to Brahma Kund and takes a dip. His body is transformed immediately into that of a lovely Gopi. He moves towards Nidhivan to witness and participate in the Ras Lila that Lord Krishna performs with Radha and the gopis.

One day, Sage Narada wants to have a glimpse of Lord Krishna and His pastimes in Brij Bhoomi. He prays to Goddess Yogamaya, "Oh Goddess! I want to witness the pastimes of Krishna at Vrindavan. I am told that only gopis can witness and participate in the Ras Lila of Krishna. Please tell me what I should do."

Goddess Yogamaya tells him, "Bathe in the Brahma Kund at Vrindavan. You will be transformed into a beautiful gopi. You can then enter the Ras Lila area and witness the pastimes of the Supreme Lord."

Sage Narada follows the instructions of Goddess Yogamaya. When he steps out of Brahma Kund, he has been transformed into a lovely gopi. He heads towards Ras Sthal to witness the pastimes of Lord Krishna.

RANGAJI TEMPLE

Rangaji Temple is located at one end of the town, close to Brahma Kund and Govind Dev Temple. This temple is dedicated to Lord Vishnu, in His form of Ranganatha, reclining on Sheshanag. It is quite similar to the Ranganatha Temples seen in the south Indian towns of Srirangapatna and Srirangam. The locals probably found it difficult to pronounce *Ranganathaswamy*, so they shortened it to Ranga and added the respectful suffix *'ji'* and called Him *Rangaji*. This temple was built in 1851 AD.

South Indian style Gopura

A striking feature of this temple is that even from a distance, once can see the 100 ft high South Indian style *gopura* that adorns the temple. The tall *gopura* is six storeys high. It is believed that the businessman who built this temple had hired a south Indian priest. This priest was a follower of Ramanujacharya, hence the Dravidian architecture and a striking resemblance to the temples of south India. In front of this tall south Indian style *gopura*, is a huge gate, which is built according to the Rajasthani style. As I went past this gate, I noticed a huge water tank and a well-maintained garden nearby.

Rajasthani style gate

123

To my left, I saw the main temple. This temple has an idol of Lord Vishnu in His famous reclining posture. He is lying on the Serpent King, Sheshanag. Next to this temple is another *gopuram* which leads to a huge open courtyard. At the centre of this courtyard, is a huge gold pillar, weighing 500 kg. This pillar is known as Dwaja Stamba. It is approximately 50 ft high. The businessman who built this temple, constructed it in the memory of his late parents. Similar to Tirupathi, here also Brahmotsava is celebrated every year, when devotees pull the chariots carrying the deities. This 10-day long festival is annually held in the month of March/April.

There are many other temples in the same premises. There is one temple that has deities of Vishnu, Lakshmi, and Garuda, all made of black stone. There is another one of Tirupathi Balaji. On the right is a temple dedicated to Rama, Sita, and Lakshmana. Interestingly, this has two sets of idols. The ones in the front are made of black stone and the ones at the back are made of gold.

RADHA GOVIND DEV TEMPLE

Radha Govind Dev Temple

This breathtaking temple, one of the biggest in Vrindavan, is very close to the Rangaji Temple. It is situated in an area known as Yoga Peetha. When this temple was built in 1590 AD by Maharaja Mansingh, it was a magnificent seven-storied building.

It is a hot afternoon in Vrindavan. Rupa Goswami is resting. He is approached by a small boy who narrates a very strange phenomenon.

The boy says, "Oh Holy Saint! Every day I see a cow come and give its entire milk into a hole."

Rupa Goswami is astonished.

He asks the boy "Can you show me this place? Do you remember where it is?"

The boy replies, "Yes! Please follow me."

Rupa Goswami follows the boy to see the hole. There, he sees a beautiful idol of Govinda. He carries this idol and begins to worship it everyday. Rupa is a poor brahmin and he does not have enough money to build a temple. He requests Maharaja Mansingh to build a beautiful temple.

It is believed that Maharaja Mansingh ran out of red sandstone needed for the construction of this beautiful temple. When Emperor Akbar, known for his liberal views and respect for different religions found out about this, he donated him enough red sandstone to complete the construction of this temple. It was ironic that in 1670 AD, his descendant, Aurangzeb chose to destroy the top four floors of this same temple.

This temple has three huge pillars. One was made of gold, the second of silver and the third was made of copper. Each of them is 240 ft tall. During the Deepotsava festival in the month of Karthik, it was a common practice to place lamps on top of these three pillars. The light was so dazzling that Aurangzeb noticed the flames from his capital, Delhi. He felt jealous seeing a Hindu temple with so much opulence. Immediately, he marched to Vrindavan along with his soldiers and tried to destroy the entire temple. However, after he had demolished four floors, the ground began to shake violently. He and his men panicked and fled. People believe that this divine intervention prevented the total destruction of this magnificent temple.

The inner courtyard has several carvings that blend Hindu, Moghul, and Western architectural influences. In the centre of the inner courtyard, on the ceiling, there is a beautifully sculpted lotus. It is said that when this temple was built, the lotus was studded with diamonds. However, Aurangzeb and his men looted the diamonds.

The sanctum sanctorum has a big black idol of Krishna, flanked by Chaitanya Mahaprabhu and Nityananda. In front of these idols, there are idols of Radha, Krishna, and Jagannath. A Goverdhan Shila is also kept nearby. The idols at this temple are replicas, since the original ones were moved to Jaipur for safekeeping.

JAIPUR TEMPLE

Jaipur Temple

Is this a palace? Or is it a fort? No. This is the Jaipur Temple! This is known as Jaipur Temple because it was built by Sawai Madhav Singh, Maharaja of Jaipur in 1917 AD. It is also known as Radha Madhawa Temple. This temple, with its rich architecture, is one of the most beautiful and aesthetically built temples in the temple town of Vrindavan. Its opulence makes it look more like the palace of a Rajput king, than a temple.

The entire temple is built of sandstone. As I passed through the gigantic gate, I came across a huge courtyard, flanked by well-maintained gardens on either side. The outer courtyard has magnificent arches on all sides, reminiscent of the Moghul style of architecture. An exquisitely carved pot-like structure containing a Tulsi plant is kept at one end of the outer courtyard. A walk towards the other end took me to another gate that led me to the inner courtyard. The inner courtyard too had beautiful pillars and arches with exquisite carvings. These pillars and arches were handcrafted by the artisans of that era.

The sanctum sanctorum had a wall of Italian marble. It was well decorated with beautiful paintings. The temple had three altars. The altar in the middle had a black idol of *Madhawa* (another name for Krishna) and a golden idol of Radha. Both were surrounded by Ashta-sakhis (eight of Radha's gopi-friends). On the right altar, there was an identical pair of idols of Radha and Krishna, but smaller in size. They were flanked by Lalitha and Vishaka, gopi-friends of Radha. On the left altar, there was an idol of Lord Krishna in his Hamsa Avatar (Swan Form). To the left of this idol were four small black idols representing the four

Kumara sons of Lord Brahma. It is believed that Lord Krishna assumed the Hamsa Avatar before He began teaching the four Kumara sons of Lord Brahma. This altar also has a Swami Nimbakacharya idol.

GITA MANDIR

Gita Mandir is on the Vrindavan-Mathura highway. While going from Vrindavan towards Mathura, this temple is on the right. Since it was built by the Birlas, it is also known as the Birla Temple. This is a red sandstone temple that looks quite modern, compared to the older temples in Vrindavan. The temple architecture and the colour combination of maroon and beige is very similar to the Birla Temple in New Delhi. Cleanliness is a hallmark of all Birla Temples and this one did not disappoint me. This temple and the ISKCON Temple are probably the cleanest temples in Vrindavan.

The temple has a huge courtyard that has the Gita Stamba (Gita Pillar), so called because all the verses of the *Bhagvad Gita* are inscribed on it. Lord Krishna had recited the *Bhagavad Gita* to Arjuna at the start of the famous Mahabharata war at Kurukshetra. This temple has a huge beautiful idol of Lord Krishna, made of white marble. Here, He is not

Outside Gita Mandir

seen playing the flute, as He is seen in other temples. Instead, He holds the Sudarshana Chakra, the Divine Discus, in His right hand. The Sudarshana Chakra has been motorised so it is continuously rotating around the index finger of His right hand. Beside the main altar, there is another altar that houses the idols of Goddess Lakshmi and Lord Narayana. These are also made of white marble.

The walls of the temple have colourful paintings, depicting the pastimes of Krishna and Narayana. Among them are the stories of Dhruva praying to Lord Vishnu in a forest, Lord Narasimha killing Hiranyakashyapu, Krishna helping Draupadi when Dushasana tries to strip her, Krishna killing His cousin Shishupal and Krishna killing His maternal uncle Kansa. The one that I liked the most was the painting that depicted the famous court scene where Duryodhana tries to arrest Krishna and the latter shows him His Viraat Swaroop (Universal Form) and stuns the entire court.

GLASS TEMPLE

Krishna lifting Goverdhan Hill

The Glass Temple is located opposite Gita Temple, on the outskirts of Vrindavan. While travelling from Vrindavan towards Mathura, this temple was to my left. It is known as Glass Temple because glass has been extensively used while making this temple. As I entered, on the right I saw a beautiful idol of Lord Krishna lifting Goverdhan Hill on the little finger of His left hand. Residents of Brij are taking shelter under the sacred Goverdhan to protect themselves from Lord Indra's fury. These clay figures resemble the clay dolls that are made during Navaratri, but are probably a hundred times larger in size.

Entering the temple, I saw five pillars on each side of the altar. Glass is used everywhere — on the pillars, walls, and ceiling. The temple has idols of Radha and Krishna.

PAGAL BABA TEMPLE

Pagal Baba Temple is on the same street as the Glass Temple and Gita Temple. While going towards Mathura, this imposing structure is on the right, after the Gita Temple. It was built by Srimad Lila Nanda Thakur who was popularly known as Pagal Baba Maharaj. It is a massive eight-storied white temple that can't be missed from the highway.

Pagal Baba Temple

Cars are not allowed inside hence we had to park on the main road and walk to the temple. The ambience was similar to that of a typical tourist place rather than a temple. Maybe, the presence of hundreds of school-children made me feel like that. There were lots of shops selling different things like idols, key chains, embroidered cloth, CDs, DVDs, film rolls, etc.

The temple has eight floors and each floor is quite distinct from the rest. There are no elevators so it was a long climb for all devotees. It can be quite tough for aged people.

The ground floor has lots of puppets, most of them mechanised. The left wing has puppets depicting the story of Krishna and the right wing depicts the story of the Ramayana. At the centre is a mechanised idol of Pagal Baba. He blesses all devotees by moving his right hand.

The first floor has a white marble idol of Radha and a black idol of Krishna. In front of these huge idols, there are lots of small idols of Radha and Krishna. Surprisingly, the second floor has no idols. The third floor has huge idols of Krishna and Balarama, made of white marble. The fourth floor has idols of Nanda Rai and Yashoda. Yashoda holds Infant Krishna. The fifth floor has white marble idols of Rama, Sita, Lakshmana, Hanuman, and Tulsidas. The sixth floor altar has an unusual scene not found in most Temples. This altar is dedicated to the Vamana Avatara of Lord Vishnu. It depicts Bali and his wife bowing before Lord Vishnu in His four-armed Form. Vamana, emanating from the body of Lord Vishnu, is pressing down Bali's head with His divine foot. The seventh floor has idols of Lakshmi and Narayana. The eighth floor does not have any idols. A light-grey marble idol of the holy mantra 'Om' adorns this room..

Pagal Baba was a staunch devotee of Lord Chaitanya Mahaprabhu. This is probably why I found the ambience and manner of chanting similar to that in the ISKCON temples. I could hear the continuous chanting of the Hare Krishna Mahamantra.

MANSAROVAR

Mansarovar is a 30-minute drive from Vrindavan, on the outskirts of the town. This place is serene, unlike the other temples of Vrindavan that are in the middle of busy streets. It was quite tough to locate this place. I asked the locals for directions and everyone would say 'Please go another couple of kilometres from here'. I was amazed at how everyone told us it was only a 'couple of kilometres' away, even though we eventually travelled more than 10 km! We had to drive on muddy roads and cut across green fields to reach this place. It was a miracle that none of the farmers came chasing after us. Just when I was getting a bit pessimistic about locating this place, we found it. Mathuresh, my guide, did an excellent job of a navigator and managed to cut across several sunflower fields and canals to find this place out of nowhere.

Mansarovar Lake

To me, Mansarovar is the most serene and tranquil place in the whole of Vrindavan. No commercialisation, no gift shops, no tea stalls, no unruly crowds. I could have stayed here forever. Since this place does not find a mention in most of the tourist books and is quite far away from town, I saw very few people here. Most of the people who come here are serious visitors who have heard the legend of this place and want to see it. There are no tourist buses stopping here with hordes of tourists pouring out all over the place.

As I got off the car, I saw a lake to my right and the temple was on the left. The lake was clean and well-maintained. It is home to many birds and can be a serious contender to the famous Bharatpur Bird Sanctuary which is just a couple of hours from here. Thankfully, there are no residences nearby, so this is an ideal place for meditation.

The temple near the lake is made of white marble. The inner courtyard is circular with black marble pillars. When I stood in the inner courtyard, I saw a strange sight. The altar has only Radha's idol. This is to depict the incident when Krishna left Radha alone for a few minutes during Ras Lila in order to rid Her of Her arrogance. It is also believed that when Radha cried, unable to bear the pangs of separation from Her beloved Krishna, her tears formed the lake, Mansarovar.

It is Ras Lila time. Radha and Krishna are dancing in the middle of a huge playground. They are surrounded by gopis. The Supreme Lord has replicated Himself so that each gopi, including Radha, thinks that Krishna is dancing only with her. This makes some of them arrogant. Krishna wants to teach them a lesson. He suddenly disappears.

The gopis continue dancing. They suddenly realise that the divine music of Kanha's flute has stopped. They stop dancing and look around. They cannot find Krishna, so they begin to frantically search for Him. He is nowhere to be seen.

One of the gopis cries out, "Our Kanha is missing and so is Radha. They must have gone off together somewhere. Let us search for them."

The gopis leave the Ras Sthal and begin to search throughout Vrindavan. They search from lane to lane. They become crazy due to their separation from Krishna. They begin to ask every tree, animal, and insect if they have seen their Lord. They get no answer from any of them.

The gopis are completely absorbed in the thoughts of Krishna. They begin to re-enact some of His famous stories. One gopi acts like Putana and the other acts like Shakatasura. The third one, acting like Krishna, 'kills' them both. One gopi imitates Krishna playing the flute while another one imitates the way He walks. As the gopis enact Krishna's pastimes, they wander deep into the forest.

They have walked many miles now, in search of their Kanha. They have reached an isolated spot. There is no sign of any civilisation here.

One of the gopis says, "I am feeling very tired. I know I will not find my Kanha. He is displeased with me, so He has disappeared. I had become arrogant, thinking that He is only mine. I thought I am the greatest gopi to possess Him completely. He has taught me a lesson. How conceited of me, to have such thoughts!"

Hearing this, another gopi too shares similar feelings. Within no time, all gopis recount similar experiences. They now realise the reason for Krishna's disappearance.

One of the gopis says, "We will not find Radha and Krishna here. This place is very isolated. Let us return to Vrindavan. There are so many wild animals here. It is not safe for us to roam around here in the middle of the night."

Even as they are thinking of turning back, they hear the sobs of a young Girl. They look around and find Radha sitting under a tree sobbing inconsolably.

One of the gopis cries out, "Oh Radha! What are you doing here? Where is Krishna? We thought You came here with Him. Where is He?"

Hearing the name of Krishna, Radha begins to sob louder.

She says, "As the Ras was reaching its climax, Krishna suddenly took Me off to a secluded spot, away from all of you. I was filled with arrogance. I thought I am the dearest Gopi to Him. I thought that He belongs only to Me. I decided to test His love for Me."

She continues, "I told Kanha that I was feeling very tired and asked if He could lift Me. Kanha agreed and asked Me to sit on His shoulder. As soon as I sat on His shoulder, He vanished from My sight. I immediately realised My mistake. I lost Him because of My arrogance."

Saying this She cries, "Oh Kanha! How arrogant of Me, that I made you serve me this way. How cruel of Me that I tested your divine love."

As Radha begins to cry, the tears accumulate and form a lake, today known as Mansarovar. Since this is formed by the tears of Radha, it is also known as the Lake of Tears.

Krishna sees that Radha and the gopis have been humbled and have repented. So He comes back once again. They return to Ras Sthal and the Ras Lila continues...

Since Krishna had left Radha and She was alone here, there is no idol of Krishna, unlike the other temples in Vrindavan that always have Radha and Krishna together. In the serene ambience, I could hear the melodious chants of *Radhe Radhe Jai Radhe Radhe* fill the air. This lent a musical note to the air in an otherwise quiet place.

9

Madhuvan and Talvan

...

"*ayyeva mana adhatsva mayi budhim niveshaya,*
Nivasishyasi mayyeva atha urdhvam na sanshayah"

("Fix your mind on Me and let your intellect dwell on Me. You will live solely in Me without any doubt.")

(*Bhagavad Gita* 12.8)

Madhuvan is one of the 12 famous forests in Brij Bhoomi. A demon named Madhu lived here hence the name Madhuvan (*van* meaning 'forest'). To reach Madhuvan, I took the highway from Mathura and travelled eastwards, towards Gokul. Within a few kilometres, I saw a huge palatial temple made of white marble on the right side — this was the Sri Gurudev Temple. Adjacent to this temple is a dusty road on the right, with a signboard 'Maholi'. In Lord Krishna's time, Maholi village was Madhuvan.

At first sight, Madhuvan village appeared to be another nondescript village in the Brij Bhoomi belt — it had dusty and narrow roads and small kids running around trying to keep pace with the stray dogs and fowls. However, as I got away from the village and moved towards the Dhruva Narayan Temple, the environment changed completely. Suddenly, I was in the middle of thick vegetation and greenery. There were no vehicles and no noisy village kids. It was as if I had been suddenly transferred to Lord Krishna's era. In the middle of the trees and shrubs, I saw beautiful peacocks dancing and showing off their dazzling feathers. It was a *vana* (forest) in every sense. No wonder Lord Krishna decided to make Brij Bhoomi His Abode.

DHRUVA NARAYAN TEMPLE

There are two routes to the Dhruva Narayan Temple. One route goes right through the village. The problem with this route is that as the road nears its destination, its quality deteriorates. So, tourists have to park their cars and walk the remaining distance, which is quite tedious. The better option would be to take the road on the left side, just before entering the village. This takes us to the foothills of Dhruva Tilla.

Dhruva Narayan Temple

The temple is on a small hillock hence this place is known as Dhruva Tilla meaning Dhruva Hillock. Twenty-five red steps up the hillock led us to the temple made of red stone.

As I entered the temple, I saw the statue of the famous Vaishnava saint Haridasji. I took a turn to the right, which led me to the main altar. This has three separate rooms. The room on the left has idols of Lakshmi and Sathya Narayana and a picture of Lord Vishnu blessing young Dhruva. The room on the right has Santoshi Maa's idol. Next to this room is an idol of Lord Hanuman. The room in the centre is the biggest room. It houses idols of Vishnu and Lakshmi at the centre and Sage Narada on the left and Dhruva on the right. On the main door, there is an inscription in Hindi — 'Om Namo Bhagawate Vasudevaya'. This is what Dhruva, as a young child, had chanted to receive the Blessings of Lord Narayana.

King Uthanapaad is the elder son of Manu. His first wife is Suniti and his second wife is Suruchi. Dhruva is the son of Suniti, and Uthama is the son of Suruchi. Both Dhruva and Uthama are playing in the garden. Their father, King Uthanapaad, comes to watch them play. He sits nearby and watches them lovingly. Seeing the King, Prince Uthama rushes towards him. He jumps and sits on his father's lap. Not to be left behind, Prince Dhruva too rushes towards his father to sit on the other side.

Queen Suruchi shouts, "Dhruva! How dare you sit on your father's lap? The lap is reserved only for my son, Uthama."

Prince Dhruva looks up and sees Queen Suruchi angrily glaring at him. He asks innocently, "Oh Mother! My father has two laps. Why can't I sit on one lap and my brother on the other?"

The Queen replies angrily, "The lap is reserved for my son and not Suniti's son. Don't you dare address me as your mother. I am not your mother."

Young Dhruva is too stunned to speak. He begins to cry. The King is scared of Suruchi and he remains quiet. He does not have the courage to support his son Dhruva.

Dhruva, feeling insulted, runs to his mother's chambers. He begins to wail loudly.

Queen Suniti runs out of her chambers. She has heard the wails of her son and is wondering what has happened to him. Maybe he has fallen down. Maybe he has hurt himself.

Dhruva flings his arms around his mother. She hugs him lovingly and asks, "Oh My son! Why are you crying? Have you hurt yourself? What happened?"

Dhruva narrates everything to his mother.

His mother says, "Please don't worry over such trivial incidents. Lord Narayana is there to protect all of us."

Dhruva is still weeping. He asks his mother innocently, "Oh Mother! Where can I find Lord Narayana? I want to meet Him and ask Him for justice."

Suniti laughs and says, "My son! I was just joking. It is not so easy to see Lord Narayana. Even the great sages have failed to see Him though they have been performing severe austerities and penances."

Dhruva says with a determined look on his face, "I too will perform severe penances like the sages. I will go to the forest right now."

Queen Suniti is shocked, "Oh no! You are too young to perform penances.

Moreover, you have always had a sheltered and comfortable life as a prince. You will not be able to withstand the harsh life in the forest. How will you protect yourself from the heat, cold and rains? The forest also has many wild animals prowling around. You are a tiny five-year-old boy. How can you protect yourself from the wild beasts?"

Dhruva is adamant. He says, "Mother! The same Lord Narayana will protect me against the heat, cold, and rains. He will also protect me from the wild beasts."

Saying this, he falls at his mother's feet and seeks her blessings.

His mother realises that it is futile to argue with him. She blesses him and wishes him success.

Dhruva walks barefoot towards the forest. He crosses the city limits and enters the forest. He does not see any people around. The humming of the birds and bees is all that he can hear. Occasionally, he hears the roar of a lion prowling nearby. He sits under a tree. Narada has been watching all these incidents with his usual sense of curiousity. He descends to Earth. He stands before Dhruva and chants loudly, "Narayana! Narayana!"

Dhruva looks up and sees Narada standing in front of him.

He bows to Narada and says, "Oh Holy One! Please tell me who you are and why you have come here."

Sage Narada says, "I am Narada, a devotee of Lord Narayana. I came to see what a small boy like you is doing in a big forest like this."

Dhruva exclaims, "A devotee of Lord Narayana! Then you can help me achieve my goal."

Narada smiles when he hears such words from the mouth of a five-year-old.

He asks Dhruva, "Please tell me what help you need from me."

Dhruva narrates the incident that drove him to the forest.

He concludes by saying, "I have come here to perform austerities. I want to meet Lord Narayana and ask Him for justice. I want Him to make me the future king of the kingdom."

Narada once again laughs, "Oh Prince! Please return to your palace. Many great sages who have been performing penance for hundreds of years have not been able to get a glimpse of the Supreme Lord. What is the guarantee that you will get to see Him? The rigorous forest life is not for you.

This forest is full of wild beasts. They may attack you. It is not a safe place to be in, unarmed."

Dhruva replies, "Oh Sage! I know you are trying to test me and my courage. I have full faith in my Lord Narayana. He will protect me."

Narada realises that this five-year-old is no ordinary boy. He will not leave the forest till he meets Lord Narayana.

He advises Dhruva, "Please continuously chant 'Om Namo Bhagawate Vasudevaya'. Lord Narayana will be pleased. He will come and bless you. I will leave now."

Dhruva once again bows and says, "Thank you. Please bless me that I may be successful."

Narada blesses him and departs.

Dhruva sits under the tree and begins to chant 'Om Namo Bhagawate Vasudevaya'. He is totally engrossed in chanting the Lord's name. Many days and months pass. He has given up eating food and drinking water. He does not think of, or see, anything other than Lord Narayana. Many wild animals come near the tree where he is sitting. They get scared seeing the brilliant aura of light emanating from his body. They depart hastily.

Dhruva reflects, Oh Lord Narayana! I think You are still not pleased with me. I have given up food and water. Now I will give up air too.

Saying this, Dhruva keeps out the air from entering his body. This blocks the flow of air in all the universe. There is no breeze on Earth. Heaven too experiences a similar fate. All the Gods and Goddesses panic. They go to Vaikunta and inform Lord Vishnu, "Oh Supreme Lord! Oh Narayana! Your devotee Dhruva has stopped the flow of air in the three worlds. At this rate, everyone will be killed. Please appear before him and ask him to stop such austerities."

Lord Vishnu says, "So be it."

Saying this, He descends from Vaikunta. He stands in front of Dhruva and says, "Oh Dhruva! Open your eyes. Tell me your wish."

Dhruva opens his eyes. Seeing the Lord surrounded by a divine halo, he realises He must be none other than his Lord Narayana. He touches the Lotus Feet of Lord Vishnu. Lord Vishnu places the child on His lap and asks him, "Oh Dhruva! Tell me what you desire."

The moment Dhruva sits on Lord Vishnu's lap, a strange sensation fills his body. His physical body, battered by the extreme heat and cold, once again becomes healthy. His body had become a set of bones, within a flash, it is filled with muscles and flesh. His mind is at rest and filled with a sense of joy. His soul transcends the materialistic desires of life.

Dhruva replies, "Oh Lord Narayana! I came to the forest to meet You and seek justice. I wanted to sit on my father's lap. However, after sitting on Your lap, all this now seems too mundane and materialistic. I have no desire to enjoy the riches of the kingdom. I have no desire to go back and lead a princely life. I seek refuge in Your Lotus Feet. Please take me with You to Your Heavenly Abode."

Lord Vishnu smiles and blesses him, "You are too young to come with Me. You should return to your city. Your parents are anxiously waiting for you. Queen Suruchi is also repentant. She realises that being the son of the first wife of King Uthanapaad, you are the rightful heir to the throne. I bless you with happiness, joy, and good health. I will now return to Vaikunta."

Dhruva touches the Lotus Feet of Lord Vishnu and says, "Oh Lord! I will do as You command."

Dhruva returns to his city. He gets a joyous welcome from the citizens and his family who are anxiously awaiting his return. His father hands over the kingdom to him and he himself retires to the forest. Dhruva rules the kingdom for many years. After his death, as promised by Lord Narayana, he turns into the brightest star of the entire Universe and is given a prominent place in the sky. He is known as Dhruva-Tara meaning Dhruva Star. The Dhruva-Tara is also known as the Pole Star (North Star) which is always seen in the northern sky and is the only star that is rooted to one place and this fixed state symbolises the focus and determination of Dhruva in his quest to meet his Lord Narayana.

KRISHNA KUND

Krishna Kund is a big pool in the Madhuvan forest located between the Balarama Temple and the Shatrughna Temple. This *kund* has a lot of water and is very well maintained. This is known as Krishna Kund because it was created by Krishna to quench the thirst of His friends and cattle.

Krishna comes to Madhuvan forest along with Balarama and all the cowherds. They bring the cattle and play on the grass. Krishna plays His Flute and the melody fills Madhuvan forest. All the birds and animals come to watch and listen to Krishna play His flute.

After some time, the cowherds tell Krishna, "We are very thirsty, and so are our cattle."

Krishna asks them to go to River Yamuna to quench their thirst.

The boys tell Him, "We are too tired and thirsty to walk all the way to River Yamuna."

Krishna Kund

Krishna takes pity on the cowherds and the cattle. He is after all Govinda, the protector of the cows. He immediately strikes the ground with His Flute. At once, the ground cracks. Water begins to gush out and within a few minutes, the entire area turns into a huge pool. Since this happens due to the blessings of Lord Krishna, this sacred pool is known as Krishna Kund.

BALARAMA TEMPLE

Balarama Temple is to the left of Krishna Kund. This temple is also known as Dauji Temple since Lord Balarama is lovingly known as Dauji. One striking feature about the Balarama deity is that the idol is black in colour. In most of the temples in Brij Bhoomi, the idol of Lord Krishna is black and that of Lord Balarama is white. However, this temple seems to be an exception.

Entrance of Balarama Temple

After Krishna and Balarama return to Mathura, the gopis and Radha

141

begin to feel the pangs of separation from their Lord. They begin to weep and pray to Krishna to return to the forests of Brij Bhoomi. Their minds are filled with the joyous times that they had enjoyed with Krishna. Krishna, the Supreme Lord, hears their wails though He is seated on the throne of Mathura.

Krishna calls His elder Brother Balarama and says, "All the gopis and Radha are missing Me and feeling the pangs of separation. I am not in a position to leave Mathura. Could you please visit Brij Bhoomi and pacify them?"

Balarama agrees at once. He leaves for Brij Bhoomi. When He reaches the groves of Brij Bhoomi, He sees all the gopis and Radha absorbed in thoughts of Krishna and they are crying out, "Krishna! Krishna!"

Seeing this sight, Lord Balarama too is lost in the thoughts of Lord Krishna and He too begins to cry out, "Krishna! Krishna!"

It is believed that since Balarama was totally engrossed in the thoughts of Krishna, His body also became black, like that of Krishna.

To depict this story, the idol of Balarama in this temple is made of black stone. As in the case of the other temples of Madhuvan, here too, there were not many visitors.

DAUJI TEMPLE, TALVAN

Idols of Krishna, Balarama and Revathi

Talvan is located around 10 km to the west of Mathura. A drive along the Mathura-Bharatpur road took us to Talvan village. Here, we came across a sign-board, indicating the right turn. Since the road appeared to be quite narrow, we decided to walk the rest of the way. It took us 20 minutes to reach Dauji Temple at Talvan.

As we entered the temple premises, we went past the outer courtyard and reached the main altar. There is an idol of Balarama (Dauji), flanked by idols of Krishna and Revathi. Since this place was associated with incidents pertaining to Balarama, His idol was bigger than the idols of Krishna and Revathi. To the right of this temple was the Balbhadra Kund. Unlike some of the other *kunds* in Brij Bhoomi, this one looked very clean. The priest told me that the Brij Foundation had cleaned up and renovated the entire *kund*.

Between the Balbhadra Kund and the Dauji Temple, I noticed a few trees that resembled date-palm trees. Many devotees were bowing their heads in front of them. Seeing the surprised look on my face, the priest laughed, "These are *tal* trees. During the era of Krishna and Balarama, this entire forest was filled with *tal* trees hence this place was known as *Talvan* (forest filled with *tal* trees). They bear fruits which are similar to dates and taste as sweet as honey. People consider these trees sacred due to the legend associated with them."

"There is a place known as Talvan which has many tal trees. These bear very sweet fruits. Some of these ripened fruits are lying on the ground, but no one has access to them. A powerful donkey-demon, Dhenukasura, guards all the tal trees. No one has ever come out alive from Talvan. Oh Balarama! You are the mightiest among men. Oh Krishna! You are the slayer of all demons. Only You two can help us taste these sweet tal fruits by slaying Dhenukasura," say the cowherd friends of Krishna and Balarama.

Hearing this, Krishna and Balarama decide to go to Talvan forest along with their cowherd friends. Balarama holds the tal trees and begins to shake them vigorously. All the fruits begin to fall on the ground. Hearing this sound, Dhenukasura wakes up. He is aroused and angry. He rushes towards the trees. The entire forest trembles with the power of the demon's hooves. As he comes near Balarama, he turns around and with his strong rear legs, he gives a mighty kick. Balarama, the strongest among men, catches the hind legs of the donkey demon and twirls him round and round. He throws the donkey away like a javelin. The demon lands atop a tal tree and dies. Because of its heavy weight, the tal tree comes crashing down. It falls on its neighbouring tree, which also falls down. This has a domino effect and within a short while, most of the tal trees fall down. Seeing Dhenukasura dead, hundreds of other donkey-demons charge towards Krishna and Balarama. The duo catch the hind legs of all the donkey-demons and twirl them and throw them on the remaining tal *trees. Soon, all the donkey-demons are dead.*

The cowherd friends shout, "Glory to Krishna! Glory to Balarama! Let us eat the sweet tal *fruits in peace."*

I looked around. The ambience was very serene. The devotees were sitting in the courtyard, singing *bhajans* (devotional songs). It was difficult to imagine that this tranquil place was once infested with hundreds of donkey demons and had also witnessed their gory end.

10

Radha Kund

• • •

"*achchitta madgataprana bodhayantah parasparam,
Kathayantascha mam nityam tushyanti cha ramanti cha.*"

("The minds of the devotees are fully fixed on Me and their
lives are devoted to Me. They are enlightening one another about
Me and perpetually remain in a state of bliss by taking delight in
Me.")

(*Bhagavad Gita* 10.9)

Radha Kund is the name of both, the town and the sacred tank.
This town is about 25 km to the west of Mathura and five
kilometres to the north of Goverdhan. While travelling from
Mathura, I arrived at a toll gate where they collected an entry fee.
There was a Y-junction here. The road to the left goes
southwards, towards Goverdhan. The road on the right goes
northwards, towards Radha Kund.

As I entered the narrow bylanes of Radha Kund town, I
noticed small temples on either side of the road. I longed to visit
the holiest of all *kunds* of Brij Bhoomi — Radha Kund and
Shyam Kund. I went twice on Bazaar Road by car but there was
no sign of these *kunds*. Finally, I decided to conduct my search on
foot. So I asked Ashwani to park the car at one end of the town.
As I was walking through Bazaar Road, I suddenly noticed an
inconspicuous signboard that said 'Sangam of Radha Kund and
Shyam Kund'. I took a right turn and reached my destination.

RADHA KUND AND SHYAM KUND

Radha Kund

Radha Kund and Shyam Kund are located next to each other. The one on the left is Radha Kund and the one on the right is Shyam Kund. The two *kunds* are separated by a pathway. At the beginning of the pathway, I could see Radha's and Krishna's footprints. Behind the footprints, on the other side, there are many rocks stacked together. These are the sacred Goverdhan Shilas (stones from the sacred Goverdhan Hill).

Shyam Kund

It is believed that both these *kunds* were covered with lots of shrubs and plants. For many centuries people did not know of the existence of these sacred tanks. In 1513 AD, Lord Chaitanya Mahaprabhu came to this region in search of these two *kunds*. He danced with joy when He saw Radha Kund and Shyam Kund. He called His disciples and narrated the fascinating story of this holy place.

A demon named Aristasura attacks Brij Bhoomi. He comes in the form of a bull and attacks the villagers with his strong horns and hooves. He kills many women and children. The villagers panic and turn to their Saviour, Lord Krishna.

They plead, *"Oh Lord! Please save us from Aristasura. He is killing innocent villagers. Please protect us."*

Krishna says, *"Return to your village in peace. I will free you from this demon."*

The villagers return.

Krishna finds Aristasura creating havoc in the village.

He shouts, *"Aristasura! If you are really strong and confident of your strength then come and attack me. Leave the women and children alone."*

Aristasura now notices Krishna's arrival. Hearing Krishna's taunts, he roars. He heads straight towards Krishna. His eyes are blood red. He charges at Krishna with his mighty horns. Krishna just smiles at him. He catches hold of his horns and twists them. The entire body of the bull twists and falls flat on the ground. Before the bull can get up and attack, Krishna pounces on him quick as lightning and kicks him. The bull begins to roar furiously but in vain. Krishna easily overpowers the bull demon and kills him with one heavy blow. Hearing the shouts and roars, the villagers run out of their homes. They see that Krishna has killed Aristasura and has once again saved them.

They gather around Krishna and say, *"We are indebted to You. Otherwise all of us would have died."*

They leave, Krishna is now standing alone.

Radha has come to meet Krishna. She asks Krishna what has happened. Krishna tells her about the end of Aristasura's reign of terror.

Radha says thoughtfully, *"Kanha! Though you have killed Aristasura and protected the villagers, you have committed a sin."*

Krishna acts surprised and asks Radha, *"Sin? What sin?"*

Radha replies, *"Arista was a demon no doubt. However, when You killed him, he had taken the form of a bull. It is a sin to kill a cow or a bull in Brij Bhoomi."*

Krishna asks Radha innocently, *"Oh is it? What should I do?"*

Radha, unmindful of the fact that She is speaking to the Supreme Lord, feels it is Her duty to educate Krishna about the sins of killing cows and bulls.

She advises Him, *"Please build a sacred kund. This will free you from your sins and serve as an act of repentance."*

Krishna agrees and with His divine powers, creates a sacred tank in a flash. Since it is created by Krishna it is known as Krishna Kund, or Shyam Kund.

After this, Krishna tells Radha innocently, "I agree that I have committed a sin but please understand that in a kingdom when a subject commits a sin, part of the sin will go to the king and the queen of that kingdom. I am just an ordinary subject in Brij Bhoomi. However, You are the Queen of Brij Bhoomi. So any crime committed by Me, will have repercussions on You also. So You have also committed a sin indirectly. You should also repent and wash away Your sins by building another sacred tank."

Radha picks up a small pebble and with Her divine powers creates another sacred tank. Since the creator of this tank is Radha it is known as Radha Kund. However, Radha notices that the kund is dry. Radha asks all the gopis to line up. This long chain extends a few kilometres. The gopi standing at the end of the line has reached Manasi Ganga, near Goverdhan. Radha asks this gopi to collect the sacred water from Manasi Ganga. It is passed on from gopi to gopi. Soon Radha Kund is filled with water from Manasi Ganga.

When I was standing near the sacred tank, a priest came to me and said, "Do you know that Radha Kund is the holiest among all *kunds?* Please sprinkle a few drops on your head and get blessed."

I hesitated, looking at the condition of the tank. The water did not appear to be clean and I stood wondering what to do. Just then I noticed a foreigner come out of a building and walk towards Radha Kund. She was clad in a saree and chanting the holy names of the Lord. Suddenly, she took a big leap and dived into Radha Kund. She began bathing, unmindful of the condition of the water. I felt ashamed that inspite of considering myself a devout Indian, I was hesitant to sprinkle a few drops of water on my head and here was a lady, from a far off country, who had jumped into the pool of water, unmindful of its cleanliness. Her state of bliss and true devotion made me feel ashamed of myself.

I continued my walk along the pathway and reached the other end. There was a building at the far end which appeared to be some kind of an *ashram.* I saw many people sitting and chanting the holy names of the Supreme Lord. I took a turn and walked back along the pathway, my mind still in a state of turmoil over the recent incident.

11

Goverdhan

...

" *ham sarvasya prabhavo mattah sarvam pravartate,*
Itti matva bhajante mam budha bhavasamanvitah. "

("I am the source of all creation and everything emanates
from Me. The learned people know this and worship Me with all
their attention and full of devotion.")

(*Bhagavad Gita* 10.8)

Goverdhan Hill is situated 25 km to the west of Mathura and five
kilometres to the south of Radha Kund. The town where the
sacred Goverdhan Hill is located is also known as Goverdhan.
The entire region looks like a peacock with its head tucked into its
stomach. Kusum Sarovar is the face, Radha Kund and Shyam
Kund form the two eyes, Manasi Ganga is the neck, Mukharavind
its mouth, and Punchari Kund (Naval Kund) its tail.

People consider Goverdhan Hill to be no different from Lord
Krishna Himself. He is worshipped as Girirajji (King of the hills).
Girirajji is a very common name in Goverdhan town. You will
find not just temples, but even roadside eateries and small shops
named after Girirajji. There are lots of 'Girirajji Restaurants',
'Girirajji Lassi Ghars' and 'Girirajji Gift Shops'! The stones of
Goverdhan are known as Goverdhan Shilas and they are
considered sacred and worshipped. Don't be surprised if you see
devotees bend down while walking on the roads of Goverdhan.
They are busy collecting pebbles that will soon find their way into

the *puja* rooms once the devotee returns home.

GOVERDHAN HILL

If you are a first-time visitor looking for a huge mountain, as you may have imagined based on the stories you have read, then prepare yourself for a shock! Today, this legendary hill is no more than a hillock because of Pulastya Muni's curse. This sacred hill, was 30,000 metres high thousands of years ago, but today peaks at just 25 metres. It has been shrinking by the size of a mustard seed, one-sixteenth of an inch, each day and some believe that by the end of Kali Yuga, it will vanish completely.

It is Satya Yuga. Sage Pulastya is depressed. He is staying in the holy city of Varanasi. However, he feels dejected since there is no sacred mountain there which can match the sacred River Ganga.

He approaches Dronachala, who is the King of Mountains.

Dronachala bows his head in reverence and asks Sage Pulastya, "Oh Holy Saint! What brings you here? Please tell me how I can serve you and receive your blessings."

Sage Pulastya blesses him and says, "I come from the holy city of Varanasi. I feel sad that there are no sacred mountains there. I would like to take Goverdhan with me."

Dronachala is unhappy because Goverdhan is his favourite son.

Sage Pulastya senses the reluctance. He angrily says, "Oh Dronachala! If you refuse to obey me then I will curse you!"

Goverdhan wants to save his father from getting cursed. He bows before Sage Pulastya and says, "Oh Holy One! I am ready to come with you. Please take me wherever you wish to. However, I have one condition. If you drop me anywhere, then I will no longer move. I will stay at that place."

Sage Pulastya happily agrees. He bids farewell to Dronachala and carries Goverdhan on his shoulders and leaves.

Sage Pulastya begins his journey towards Varanasi. They reach the beautiful forest of Brij Bhoomi. Goverdhan likes the beautiful flora and fauna of Brij Bhoomi. He thinks, "This is the most beautiful place on Earth. I should stay here. How do I continue to stay here?"

Suddenly, he has an idea. He uses his divine powers to make Sage

Pulastya feel the need to answer the call of nature. Sage Pulastya is not able to control himself. He keeps Goverdhan on the ground and goes to relieve himself.

Sage Pulastya relieves himself and returns to the spot where he has kept Goverdhan. He finds that he is unable to move Goverdhan.

Goverdhan says, "Oh Sage! I had warned you that if you kept me on the ground, I would get rooted to that spot. Since you kept me here to relieve yourself, I am now rooted to this spot. I will now remain here. Please go back to Varanasi."

Sage Pulastya, using his divine powers, is able to see through the devious plan of Goverdhan. He curses Goverdhan, "Oh Goverdhan! You used your divine powers to cheat me. I curse you for your devious trick. You will shrink every day by the size of a mustard seed."

Because of this curse, Goverdhan Hill has been shrinking every year. During my first visit to Goverdhan, I missed the hill completely. During my second visit, with great help from my guide, Mathuresh, I managed to locate the hill. The hill surrounds the entire Goverdhan town so I could see it in many places. However, due to its low altitude, I mistook the hill for flat land at most places. The highest point of Goverdhan Hill is where Srinathji Temple and Balarama Temple are located. There is a kund in front of it, known as Sankarshana Kund or Balbhadra Kund and as the name suggests, it is dedicated to Lord Balarama. To get a proper view of the hill, I decided to visit Sankarshana Kund since the highest point of Goverdhan hill is behind it.

GOVERDHAN PARIKRAMA

Just as people perform Brij Bhoomi Parikrama, they also perform Goverdhan Parikrama. There are two ways of performing this Parikrama. One is the short Parikrama, which is 25 km long. It encompasses the areas close to Goverdhan town. The longer Parikrama is 40 km long and encompasses many more areas.

Both versions of the Goverdhan Parikrama start and end at Manasi Ganga, which is in the middle of Goverdhan Hill. Pilgrims who intend to perform the Goverdhan Parikrama start by bathing in the holy waters of Manasi Ganga. As I walked further ahead, I saw Goverdhan Hill on my right. I passed by Hari Deva Temple, Mukharavind Temple, both located close by. I crossed Brahma Kund and after a couple of kilometres, I saw the ISKCON Temple on the left. I then saw Sankarshana Kund, Govinda Kund, Apsara Kund, and finally Punchari Kund. All along, I saw the Goverdhan Hill to my right. Punchari Kund is considered to be the tail of the peacock that represents Goverdhan. Here I made a curved 180 degree turn.

I then reached Kadamba Van. There are three more *kunds* here — Surabhi Kund, Indra Kund (Charana Kund), and Airavata Kund. Proceeding a few kilometres, I found myself at Kusum Sarovar. Another five kilometres and I was at Radha Kund. I turned back and reached Kusum Sarovar once again. As I proceeded further, I touched the holy waters of Manasi Ganga again.

There are different ways in which people perform the Goverdhan Parikrama. The most common way is to perform the Parikrama barefoot. There is a tougher method — the devotee pays obeisance to God by lying flat on the ground before taking each step. This kind of Parikrama is quite strenuous and can even take weeks to complete.

There are a few rules to be followed while performing the Parikrama. One should perform the Parikrama after bathing in the Manasi Ganga. The devotee should walk only barefoot irrespective of the condition of the road and the soaring mercury levels. People believe that Lord Krishna and Lord Goverdhan are one and the same, and so wearing footwear in Goverdhan is considered sacrilegious. It is for this reason that staunch devotees walk barefoot throughout their stay at Goverdhan and not just while performing the Parikrama. The other rule is that if night falls during the Parikrama, then one should stop and rest wherever they are. The next morning the journey should be resumed from the place where they had stopped.

If you do not have the time or energy to perform this kind of Parikrama, then there is an easier option — hire a taxi and go around Goverdhan!

MANASI GANGA

Pilgrims start and end the Goverdhan Parikrama at Manasi Ganga, which is at the centre of Goverdhan Hill. The Manasi Devi Temple is located at one end of Manasi Ganga. The deity here is Manasi Devi. Behind her idol is that of Lord Krishna. Both these idols are made of black stone. The idols look like huge black rocks with 'eyes'. A big lamp is lit in front of

Manasi Ganga

these idols. The priest tied a sacred red thread around my right wrist and asked me to light a small lamp in front of the big lamp.

Manasi means 'mind'. It is believed that Manasi Ganga was created by Krishna's meditating mind to fulfil His parents' wishes.

Nanda and Yashoda have heard of the glories of the holy Ganga. They are told that anyone who has a bath in its holy waters would be rid of all their sins and reach Heaven. They too are interested in bathing in this holy river. However, they do not know how they will travel such a long distance.

Nanda tells Krishna, "Yashoda and I would like to bathe in the waters of the holy Ganga."

Krishna says, "Why don't you visit the Ganga then? I will arrange for your visit."

However, Nanda is reluctant. He says, "The Ganga is too far away, it is difficult for Yashoda and me to travel long distances. Moreover, I cannot leave the people of Brij Bhoomi alone for so many days."

Krishna says, "Let me think of a solution."

Krishna closes His eyes and meditates. Goddess Ganga hears Him and comes and stands in front of Him.

Ganga says, "Oh Supreme Lord please tell Me what You wish."

155

Krishna says, "My parents want to take a dip in Your Holy Waters. However, they cannot travel that far. I wish that You could manifest Yourself here."

Immediately, a portion of Goverdhan Hill is flooded with the waters of the Ganga. Within a second, the dry land turns into a sacred lake. This place is known as Manasi Ganga.

Krishna tells Nanda, "Father, there is no need for you to travel to River Ganga since She has now come to Brij Bhoomi right here."

Nanda and Yashoda are thrilled to hear this. They, along with the other Brij Bhoomi residents, go to Manasi Ganga to touch its sacred waters.

MUKHARAVIND MUKUT TEMPLE

Mukharavind means 'lotus face' and *mukut* means 'crown'. This temple is adjacent to the Manasi Ganga Temple. At the entrance to this temple is a huge idol of Lord Krishna holding Goverdhan Hill on the little finger of His left hand. Nearby, I saw steps going down that took me to the main altar. I reached a huge circular area that housed many shops selling religious articles. At the centre was the main altar.

As in many Goverdhan Temples, here too, the Goverdhan Shila is worshipped as the Supreme Lord Himself. People believe that worshipping Goverdhan Hill is no different from worshipping Lord Krishna Himself. Since the *shilas* (stones) are considered equivalent to idols, it is a very common sight to see Goverdhan Shilas being worshipped.

There are two huge black *shilas* in this temple. The *shila* on the left represents the *crown* of Krishna, also known as Mukut Shila. The *shila* on the right represents the lotus face of Goverdhan, also known as Mukharavind Shila. Hence, this temple is known as Mukharavind Mukut Temple. At the entrance to the temple, I found vendors selling milk that is poured over these *shilas*. The priest noticed the bowl of milk I had purchased. He asked me to pour the milk on the *shilas* and place a coconut in front of them. He applied the holy *tilak* on my forehead. The main altar was octagonal and all the eight walls had paintings depicting the pastimes of Krishna.

BRAHMA KUND

Brahma Kund is located near the southern bank of Manasi Ganga. Unlike the Hari Deva Temple, this *kund* is a very famous landmark so it was quite easy to locate it. People who perform the Goverdhan Parikrama begin their journey with a bath at this *kund*, or at Manasi Ganga. This was probably the reason why there were hundreds of people bathing here. The *kund* was surrounded by many vendors who were selling flowers and other *puja* articles. Compared to Brahma Kund at Vrindavan, this one was much cleaner.

Brahma Kund derived its name because it was formed with the water that collected after Lord Brahma had bathed Lord Krishna. He did this to repent His sins for trying to test Lord Krishna's powers.

Let Me test Krishna's powers, thought Lord Brahma. He, like the denizens of Brij Bhoomi, had heard a good deal about the conquests of Infant Krishna. Some say He is the most powerful Being on this Earth. Others believe He is a Divine Soul. There are others who also say that He is none other than Lord Vishnu Himself in His eighth incarnation. The debate continues.

Lord Brahma is curious about the truth. Though He has heard that the Infant is the all powerful Supreme Lord of the Universe, He finds it hard to believe. He comes to Brij Bhoomi to test if Lord Krishna is really the Supreme Lord.

It is a bright and sunny morning at Goverdhan. Krishna has gone with His friends to the green meadows. They have taken the cattle along with them. The cattle are grazing in the meadows. Krishna is playing with the cowherds. He is also playing His flute. The cowherds are enjoying the mellifluous tunes. There is peace and harmony around them.

Krishna suggests to His cowherd friends, "It is time to eat lunch. Let us unpack what we have carried from home."

The cowherds obey Him. They sit in a circle and Krishna sits in the centre. They share their lunch with Krishna, who happily eats what they offer. They are laughing and talking loudly. In the meanwhile, the cows, have gradually walked deeper and deeper into the forest. When the cowherds realise this, they get scared.

Krishna, noticing the frightened look on their faces, assures them, "Please continue to eat your lunch. I will bring the cows back."

Even as the cowherds continue to eat, Krishna walks deep into the forest, in search of the cattle.

Lord Brahma arrives at the spot. He makes Himself invisible. He thinks of a devious plan. "Let me carry away and hide all the cowherds and the cattle. Krishna will be shocked. He will also panic. If Krishna returns alone then all the villagers will scold Him. They will attribute the loss of their children and cattle to Him. Let Me see how He will handle this situation," He says.

So thinking, Lord Brahma uses His mystical powers and carries away all the cowherds and the cattle. He transports them from Brij Bhoomi to Brahma Loka.

Krishna looks everywhere, but does not find the cattle. He decides to return to the place where He had left His friends. Silence greets him. He looks around. He does not see a soul. No cowherds. No cattle. He closes His eyes. With His Divine Vision, He realises what has happened. He is amused that Lord Brahma is testing Him. He decides to teach Him a lesson. Within a second, He replicates each and every cowherd boy and each and every cow. The entire meadow is back to its former state. The cattle are grazing. The boys are playing and screaming around. It appears as if nothing has changed!

Lord Brahma is pleased with Himself. He thinks He has successfully accomplished His task. He has hidden all the boys and cattle in Brahma Loka. He begins His journey back to the place where he had seen Krishna and the boys. He smiles to Himself, Krishna must be worried by now. He must be wondering what has happened to all His friends and cattle.

Lord Brahma reaches the same spot and is extremely shocked to see that everything is normal. Krishna is sitting under a tree playing His flute. The cows seem to be enjoying the melodious tunes that He is playing for them. The cowherds are playing near by.

Though Brahma had hidden them just a few moments earlier at Brahma Loka, on Earth the time it had taken was equivalent to one whole year. During that year, Krishna had spent His time with a duplicate set of cowherd boys and cattle. He had replicated them so well that on that fateful evening when He had returned home with the replicated boys and cattle, none of the

Brij Bhoomi villagers had realised what had happened. They did not guess that the kids were not their own, but replicated ones. Even the mothers did not notice any difference in their sons. Such is the creativity of the Supreme Lord of the Universe!

Lord Brahma is astonished at what he sees. Each kid and each cow seems to be back in Goverdhan. He thinks, This Boy is very smart. He has realised what has happened and had probably gone to Brahma Loka and rescued the kidnapped boys and cattle. Let Me go back and check. *He heads back to Brahma Loka. When He returns, He gets an even bigger shock. He sees that the boys and cattle He had kidnapped are still there!*

He begins to wonder, Those whom I had carried away are still in My abode. So who are these children playing with Krishna? How do they look so similar to the ones I kidnapped? I am the Creator of the Universe, so who has created them?

Lord Brahma returns to Brij Bhoomi. He once again looks at the cowherd boys playing with Krishna. Using His Divine Vision He realises that each cowherd has a bluish body and is wearing golden silk garments. All of them are four-armed, holding the Conch, Sudarshana Chakra, Mace, and Lotus! Their bodies are smeared with sandalwood paste and the neck is adorned with celestial flowers. He realises that all the cowherds and cattle had manifested from Lord Krishna! Realising the arrogant blunder He has committed in trying to test the Supreme Lord, He falls at the feet of the Supreme Lord, Krishna and begs for forgiveness.

He says, "Oh Supreme Lord! Please forgive Me for the grave sin that I have committed. I had heard a lot about you and decided to test You."

Krishna says, "When you and the other Gods came to me, pleading for help, I took pity on all of You. I decided to take birth on Earth to rid it of all the demons who were attacking the humans and the Gods. I am surprised that You forgot that incident and decided to come and test My powers. I forgive You this time, but do not test anyone this way. You should learn to appreciate and respect all beings that You have created."

Krishna tells Lord Brahma how He had replicated all the boys and the cattle as well. He also tells Lord Brahma that a full year had passed on Earth without the people in Brij Bhoomi noticing anything amiss.

Lord Brahma feels completely humbled and falls at the Lotus Feet of Lord Krishna. He cries, "Oh Supreme Lord! I failed to recognise You! I had heard so much about Your mystical powers. However, I still came and tested You!" Lord Brahma weeps. His tears wash the Lotus Feet of the Supreme Lord. Lord Brahma composes verses, known as Brahma Samhita, in praise of the Supreme Lord. He bathes Lord Krishna in water, milk, and honey. After performing the Abhisheka, He decorates Him with a garland of flowers. After offering His prayers, Lord Brahma performs the Parikrama of Lord Krishna thrice and bows at His Divine Feet. The water, milk, and honey that washed the body of the Supreme Lord form Brahma Kund.

ISKCON TEMPLE

The ISKCON Temple is about a kilometre from the central part of the town. While performing Goverdhan Parikrama, this temple is on the left. The temple is a two-storied sand-coloured structure. Behind it is a huge courtyard with a well-maintained lawn. The steps to the first storey rise from this courtyard. The main altar is on the first floor. The ambience in the temple is very serene. It is different from the noisy and crowded streets of Goverdhan town.

ISKCON Temple

The altar has two rooms. These are not really rooms, but more like huge cupboards. The main room has idols of Lord Krishna and Lord Balarama. Both idols are black in colour. The idols are kept on a Navaratri-type pedestal. One unique feature is that the idols are just faces. Colourful clothes are attached below the faces. There is no 'body' for these idols. It reminded me of similar idols I had seen at Jagannath Temple in Mahavan.

There is a painting of cows grazing on Goverdhan Hill behind these idols. The room on the right has idols of Nitai and Gauranga. Both these rooms have beautifully carved wooden doors. On the right side of the main room, there is a statue of Srila Prabhupada. A Tulsi plant is kept in the main hall in a small earthen pot on a carved wooden table.

Since we had reached the ISKCON Temple around noon, I thought it would be a good idea to have lunch here. Since ISKCON pays a great deal of attention to cleanliness and hygiene, the temptation to eat here was very strong. I asked one of the priests if I could eat here. He hesitated because they needed to inform the cook about a guest at least a day in advance. However, looking at the desperation in my eyes, he said he would check with the head priest and get back to me. After 15 minutes, he returned with the good news. I could have lunch there provided I was willing to wait for an hour. I readily agreed. I sat in the main hall in front of the main altar. A few minutes later a priest entered the main hall and proceeded towards the main altar. He was holding two plates that contained around 10 different dishes. He kept the food plate inside the main altar and told me, "It is time for Lord Krishna and Lord Balarama to have lunch." He closed the main altar doors. He disappeared into the kitchen and returned 10 minutes later with two more plates. Seeing my puzzled look, he smiled, "These are for Nitai and Gauranga." He kept the plates in the other room and closed that door too.

I noticed a few unusual things regarding the food offerings to the Gods. In most of the traditional temples, only one or two dishes are kept as *prasada*. However, here they had served the Gods with all the food items that had been cooked in the temple kitchen that morning. In a majority of the temples, the food is kept in front of the deities just for a couple of minutes as a token gesture. However, here they had kept it for more than 30 minutes. It was as if the Lord was really going to descend from Vaikunta to eat the food and go back.

Finally, it was the turn of the mortals to eat. The priests placed long cloth mats in the dining section on the ground floor. Steel plates were laid in front of the mats. I sat down on these mats and had a simple, but delicious lunch. The head priest sat at one end of the dining hall. They followed a very simple protocol. The devotees were allowed to start eating only after the head priest began to eat and they had to stop eating as soon as he finished eating!

SANKARSHANA KUND

I continued for a couple of kilometres on the Parikrama path and reached the neighbouring town of Aniyora. On my right, I came across Sankarshana Kund, named after Lord Balarama. This *kund* is also known as Balbhadra Kund.

The temple next to Sankarshana Kund is the Balarama Temple. This is on a hillock. Incidentally, this is the highest point of Goverdhan Hill. This temple has idols of Balarama and Krishna. The Balarama idol was installed by Krishna's greate grandson, Vajranabha.

Sankarshana Kund

GOVINDA KUND

After visiting Sankarshana Kund, I proceeded on the Goverdhan Parikrama. Within half a kilometre, I reached Govinda Kund. This was on the right side, a few metres off the main road. This was probably one of the cleanest and most well-maintained *kunds* in Brij Bhoomi. The water was refreshingly clear with absolutely no traces of weeds. This is the place where Lord Indra worshipped and bathed Lord Krishna to repent His folly of trying to challenge Lord Krishna.

The villagers are readying for a festival. People are cleaning their houses, farms, and cattle. They are

Govinda Kund

preparing sweets and other delicacies.

Krishna innocently asks Nanda Rai, "What are the villagers doing? Why are they decorating their houses? Why is there a festive atmosphere everywhere?"

Nanda Rai explains, "We are preparing for Indra Puja. This is an annual festival when we clean and decorate our homes. We prepare different varieties of sweets and offer them to Lord Indra."

Krishna laughs and asks, "Pray tell me. Why do you want to worship Lord Indra?"

His father replies, "Lord Indra is the King of Gods. He is the God who controls the rains, thunder, lightning, and clouds. Our cattle and crops need these rains to survive. Our livelihood depends on Him."

Krishna asks innocently, "What will happen if you do not worship Lord Indra?"

Nanda replies, "We are scared of Lord Indra and hence we worship Him to escape His wrath. We need to offer Him all this to please Him. We need to keep up this tradition."

Krishna advises him and the other villagers, "Your fate is controlled by your deeds and no one else. You need not worship Lord Indra. Instead, please worship our cattle and the Goverdhan Hill, since the cows and Goverdhan Hill are more important than Lord Indra. We are all cowherds by profession and live near the mountains, so it is fair that We worship them instead of Lord Indra."

The villagers ask Krishna, "Please tell us what we should do if Lord Indra gets upset and directs His wrath on us."

Krishna once again laughs and says, "Don't worry! I will take care of all of you."

The debate goes on. The villagers are convinced by His logic and decide that they should worship the cows and Goverdhan Hill. They take their cattle and head towards the Hill. The sages begin to perform 'Homa' and all the villagers begin to pray to Goverdhan Hill and the cows. Lord Goverdhan is pleased and comes and gives darshan to all the devotees who have come for the puja. The villagers notice that His face resembles that of Lord Krishna who is in their midst. Lord Goverdhan accepts all their offerings.

Lord Indra is very upset.

Every year, He has been worshipped by the villagers and this year, His ego is hurt. The villagers have not worshipped Him and have instead chosen to worship the cows and Goverdhan Hill. He is unable to control his wrath.

He thunders, "Who took this decision? Who is responsible for this?"

His courtiers tell Him, "The decision has been taken by a Boy named Krishna. He has convinced all the people of Brij not to worship You and instead worship Goverdhan Hill."

Indra is furious.

He declares, "I will take revenge on Krishna and the villagers for this."

He is advised not to take such a hasty decision. The courtiers also caution Him, "Oh Lord! Krishna is no ordinary Boy but the Supreme Lord Himself. Do not take any impulsive decision that will harm you"

Lord Indra is blinded by arrogance and fury. He fails to recognise the Supreme Lord in Krishna.

Lord Indra pulls out His celestial weapon and shouts, "I am the King of Gods. I am the most powerful person in Heaven. How can a mere mortal and that too, a small Child, challenge me?"

He instructs his commanders, "Blow strong winds and a typhoon over Goverdhan and the surrounding areas."

Saying this, He starts towards Goverdhan. Using His thunderbolt and clouds, He creates havoc with heavy rains and thunder storm. The villagers run helter-skelter. Even the animals begin to run in panic. Many houses collapse. The entire village is flooded because of the incessant rains. People try to find protection, but to their dismay they see that there is not a single place where they can hide from the fury of the rains. Until this year, Gokul had never had floods and heavy rains so the village does not have the facilities to deal with the situation. They are lost and helpless.

The villagers cry, "Oh Kanha! Please help us from the wrath of Lord Indra. He is upset because we are not worshipping Him."

Krishna sees Indra surveying the havoc that he has created. He decides to destroy Indra's arrogance.

He instructs the villagers, "Follow Me along with your family, your cattle, and household articles."

The villagers follow Him obediently. Krishna takes them to Goverdhan Hill. He tells them, "I will protect you under Goverdhan Hill."

With effortless ease, the Supreme Lord lifts the huge Hill using just the little finger of His left hand.

He instructs all the villagers, "Come and stand below the Hill. You will be protected from the fury of the thunder and rain."

The rain-drenched villagers rush below the Hill. Indra is furious. He lashes them with even more severe rains. He continues this for a week, but to no avail. All the villagers and their cattle stand below the Hill and are completely protected from Lord Indra's fury.

Krishna begins to play his flute with His right hand, while holding aloft Goverdhan Hill with the little finger of His left hand. All the villagers celebrate this turn of events. Indra is both astonished and crestfallen. He soon runs out of resources. He realises that He has to accept defeat!

He asks the sages, "Oh Holy Sages! Please tell me what to do? Why am I, the mighty Lord of the Heavens, unable to overpower a mere Child?"

The sages reply in unison, "We had warned you that Krishna is no ordinary Child. He is the incarnation of Lord Narayana Himself. He is the Supreme Lord of the three worlds. Seek forgiveness from Him."

In the meanwhile, the rain has stopped in the areas surrounding Goverdhan. Lord Krishna asks His people, who are standing below the hill, to proceed towards their respective towns. Once everyone leaves, He puts down Goverdhan Hill in its original spot.

Lord Indra, humbled and humiliated, realises His folly. He prays to Krishna, "Oh Krishna! Oh Vasudeva! Oh Supreme Lord! My arrogance blinded me. I failed to recognise who You are. You are the Lord of all of us. You are the Protector against all evils. I bow to You. Please forgive Me as a parent forgives an errant child."

Krishna tells Him, "As a King, it is Your duty to protect Your people. However, You have violated this basic principle. Forcing the people of Brij to worship You is nothing short of blackmail and it is like taking a bribe from the villagers. How can I forgive You for such a terrible sin? It does not befit the King of Gods to stoop to this level."

Saying this, Krishna refuses to forgive Indra. Lord Indra is helpless. He calls the divine Cow, Surabhi to come and help Him.

He tells Surabhi, "Lord Krishna is Govinda, the Protector of all Cows. He loves cows and will never harm any of them. Since You are the most sacred of cows, I know that He respects You and Your words considerably. He is not ready to forgive Me but I am sure You will be successful if You intercede for Me."

Surabhi too prays to Lord Krishna, "Oh Supreme Lord. Lord Indra is highly repentant of His actions. He has realised His folly. Please forgive Him. I agree that He did not behave like the King of Gods. He has shown His immaturity. Though everyone advised Him against challenging You, He committed the grave sin of confronting the Supreme Lord. However, now that He has realised His folly and is repentant, please forgive Him. Please give Him an opportunity to correct Himself."

Lord Indra begins to weep and the tears begin to accumulate. Krishna is moved by Surabhi's words and Lord Indra's plight. He takes pity on His devotee and says, "I have forgiven You. Please return to Your holy land."

Surabhi advises Lord Indra, "Please perform the Abhisheka of Lord Krishna before you return to Your Holy Abode."

Lord Indra agrees. He bathes Lord Krishna with water, milk, and Tulsi. The water is from the holy Ganga and the milk is from the holy cow, Surabhi. A kund is formed from the flowing water, milk, and Tulsi. He decorates Lord Krishna with flowers and applies sandalwood paste on His body. After this, all the other Gods also come and worship Lord Krishna.

Since the *kund* was formed when Lord Indra performed the Abhisheka of Lord Govinda using Tulsi, milk, and the holy waters of Ganga, this *kund* is known as Govinda Kund. Near Govinda Kund is a building where the 13th *baithak* of Sri Vallabhacharya was held. A *baithak* is a congregation that is held for narrating the *Srimad Bhagavatam*.

APSARA KUND AND PUNCHARI KUND

These two *kunds* are at the farthest end of Goverdhan Hill. As I went past Govinda Kund, after a few kilometres on the right I saw the Punchari Ka Lautha Baba Temple. There is a small lane adjoining this temple. After a short walk, I came across two *kunds*,

Apsara Kund on the left and Punchari (Naval) Kund, on the right. To the left of Apsara Kund is the Apsara Bihari Temple. Naval Kund is also known as Punchari Kund because this *kund* is at the farthest tip of Goverdhan, resembling the tail of a peacock. *Punch* means 'tail'. Hence this is known as Punchari Kund.

Apsara Kund

After Lord Indra finishes bathing and worshipping Lord Krishna, many Gods and Goddesses come down from Heaven and bathe and worship the Supreme Lord. The seven Apsaras also descend from Heaven and bathe Lord Krishna. The water that is collected results in the formation of a kund.

Since the Apsaras bathed Lord Krishna, this *kund* is known as Apsara Kund.

Punchari Kund

KADAMBA VAN

I took a turn after Apsara and Punchari Kund towards the road that headed back in the direction of Goverdhan Town. I soon saw a lane to our right. This was a muddy and narrow road that broadened into a huge field. The field turned gradually into a forest as I proceeded. This is the famous Kadamba Van, which has been the venue for many of Lord Krishna's and Radha's meetings.

Since I was not sure of the exact location of the three *kunds* in Kadamba Van, I thought it would be good to park the car on the main road and walk through the lane and the fields. I had walked a few metres and had just reached the field, when a bull came out of nowhere and stood in front of me. He looked at me and snorted. I retreated a few steps. The bull was in no mood to leave me alone. He snorted once again and began to furiously rub his hooves on the ground, throwing dust at my face. I realised I was no Lord Krishna to tackle Aristasuras! I beat a hasty retreat back to the main road. My driver saw me panting. I leapt inside the comforts of my car and narrated what had transpired between me and the bull! My driver said, "Saab! It is safer to visit Kadamba Van in the car. Let me drive you there." I went by car this time into the narrow lane and entered the huge field. The bull was still there but now he appeared calm and composed. He now resembled the Divine Nandi rather than the ferocious Aristasura!

As I proceeded, I saw three *kunds* in the middle of the thick woods. These were Surabhi Kund, Indra Kund, and Airavata Kund.

AIRAVATA KUND

This was the first of the three *kunds*. It was on our right as I walked further down the Kadamba Van. This *kund* had a flight of steps along one side to walk down and bathe. There was very little water in this *kund*, unlike the past when it was a huge tank created by Airavata.

Lord Indra has completed bathing and worshipping Lord Krishna. He is joined by the divine cow Surabhi who also performs Abhisheka of the Supreme Lord. All the Gods and Goddesses who have come from Heaven also bathe the Supreme Lord in the holy water. After this, it is now the turn of His elephant Airavata to worship Lord Krishna. Airavata takes the holy water in his trunk and pours it on Lord Krishna. He lifts garlands of flowers with his trunk and places them around the neck of the Lord. The water collects in the form of a kund.

Since the water collected was formed by Airavata, this *kund* is known as Airavata Kund.

SURABHI KUND

This was the second of the three *kunds*. I came across a red sandstone building and right next to it was Surabhi Kund. Monkeys seemed to make up the bulk of the population here. This was the best maintained among the three *kunds* of Kadamba Van. The kund had steps on all sides for the devotees to go down to the water. There were

Surabhi Kund

many devotees taking a holy dip in this sacred tank. Since Surabhi had helped Indra receive Lord Krishna's forgiveness and a *kund* was created by the *Abhisheka* performed by Surabhi, this *kund* is known as Surabhi Kund.

INDRA KUND (CHARANA KUND)

This was the farthest among the three *kunds* in Kadamba Van. Like the other two, this one was also on the right side of the dusty road. This was about half a kilometre from Surabhi Kund. Compared to Surabhi Kund, this one was very small and not well maintained. Most of the locals were neither aware of the name, nor the legend related to this *kund*, so it took a considerable amount of time to locate it. There were a few people sitting and chatting near this *kund*. They noticed that I was a tourist and immediately asked me to pay some donation for visiting the sacred *kund*. As it is, I was quite upset to see how badly they had maintained the *kunds*. Watching a couple of buffaloes swimming in the *kund* was the proverbial 'last straw'! I blasted the locals for the poor maintenance of a place where one of the most divine incidents had occurred. I told them that if they really wanted people to donate money for visiting this sacred place, they should first learn to maintain it properly.

Since the *kund* was formed by the tears of Indra, it is known as Indra Kund. Since his tears washed the feet of Lord Krishna, this *kund* is also known as Charana Kund (*Charana* meaning 'feet').

KUSUM SAROVAR

Kusum Sarovar

Kusum Sarovar comes on your right while travelling from Radha Kund to Goverdhan. *Kusum* means 'flowers' and *sarovar* means 'lake'. This place is known as Kusum Sarovar, because the gopis used to pluck flowers here and offer it to Surya Deva (Sun God). Kusum Sarovar has a beautiful monument made of sandstone. This was built by Jawahar Singh of Bharatpur in 1764 A.D. He built it in memory of his late father Suraj Mal. It has exquisitely carved *chhatris* — the cenotaphs of the members of the royal family of Bharatpur, who died while fighting against the British during the 18th century. The architecture of this place is very impressive.

Kusum Sarovar is famous for many legends associated with Lord Krishna, the most famous being *Kilakinchita Lila.*

The Surya Deva (Sun God) Temple is located nearby. Radha Rani and the gopis arrive at Kusum Sarovar to pluck flowers for Surya Deva. Krishna disguises himself as a gardener and shouts at them, "I am the gardener here. How dare you pluck the flowers without my permission?" Radha replies, "I know you are not the gardener. These flowers do not belong to you. They belong to Goverdhan Hill." Krishna laughs, "Would you mind telling Me why are you plucking these flowers?" Radha replies, "We are going to Surya Deva Temple. We intend to use these flowers to worship the Sun God." On hearing this, Krishna immediately vanishes. He and His friend Madhumangala disguise as priests and sit near the altar of the Surya Deva

Temple. In the meanwhile, Radha and the gopis have finished plucking flowers. They slowly walk towards Surya Deva Temple. They are thrilled to see the priests waiting for them at the altar. Little do they know that these two priests are not what they seem! Radha and Her gopi friends offer the flowers and sweets to the priests. The priests promise to perform the puja. They close the altar doors. Seeing the mouth-watering sweets, Krishna and Madhumangala are unable to control themselves! They devour all the sweets meant for Surya Deva. After some time, they open the altar doors and announce, "We have performed the prayers to the Sun God. You may leave now."

Radha asks innocently, "Oh Holy Priests! Please tell us what happened to our sweets? Where are they?" Krishna smiles, "Oh Beautiful Maidens! The Sun God was extremely pleased with your devotion and to express His gratitude, He has eaten all of them!"

To the left of Kusum Sarovar is the Sri Radha Vana Bihari Temple. This is the place where Krishna braided Radha's hair. This temple has an elegant mantapa on top of it. It is also said that Krishna killed the demon Shankuchuda at Kusum Sarovar. Behind Kusum Sarovar is Narada Kund where Sage Narada sat and wrote verses of the *Bhakti Sutra*.

UDDHAV TEMPLE

Adjacent to Kusum Sarovar is a temple dedicated to Uddhav. Uddhav was Krishna's first cousin. He was Vasudeva's brother's son and was as old as Krishna. This temple was built by Krishna's great grandson, Vajranabha, about 4800 years ago.

Uddhav Temple

The main altar is to the right of the temple entrance. There are two pairs of Radha-Krishna idols. The left pair of idols is made of white marble. Of the right pair, Radha is made of cream coloured stone and Krishna is made of blue coloured stone. On the left side of the inner courtyard are the Goverdhan Shilas. Next to them is a door that leads to a pond known as Uddhav Kund.

It is believed that Uddhav lives here in the form of a creeper so that He may be blessed by the dust from the gopis' feet when they walk over him!

Krishna and Balarama complete Their studies at Sandipa Muni's Ashram and return to Mathura. The people of Mathura celebrate the return of the two Princes with pomp and joy. Balarama quickly settles down into His princely lifestyle at Mathura. However, Krishna begins to feel the pangs of separation from Brij Bhoomi. He misses His foster parents, Yashoda, and Nanda Rai. He remembers the days He spent with the gopis at Vrindavan, Barsana, and Nandagaon. He recollects the sweet memories of His pastimes with Radha. He remembers His childhood days at Gokul and Vrindavan. He remembers His Ras Lila with the gopis and Radha in the forests of Brij Bhoomi near the banks of the River Yamuna. He also remembers His last meeting with the gopis when He had promised to return after completing His duties at Mathura. He feels sad remembering Radha's gloomy face when They had met for the last time. Krishna is unable to sleep in His palace rooms, inspite of all its heavenly comforts. He keeps pacing aimlessly in the corridors of the dark empty palace in the middle of the night. The voices of the gopis fill the corridors of the palace and He finds it very disturbing. He feels guilty that He is leading such a luxurious life in the palaces of Mathura and they are leading such a simple life in the villages of Brij Bhoomi. Various faces and voices ask Him if He has forgotten them and the dusty villages after settling into the luxurious life at Mathura. He feels as if all the gopis are imploring Him to leave Mathura and return. This plunges Him into a moral dilemma. The only face that seems to watch Him silently is the tearful face of Radha.

In the meanwhile, Uddhav arrives at Mathura to spend a few days with Krishna. He notices the Supreme Lord's strange behaviour and restlessness. Uddhav asks, "Oh Lord! What worries you? I have been watching your behaviour during the last few days and I can sense that something is wrong. Is the world in peril? Do You foresee any calamities or disasters? Will the human race end soon?"

Krishna decides to speak to Uddhav, and tells him what He has been experiencing over the last few days.

On hearing about His dilemma, Uddhav laughs, *"You are the mighty Lord of the Universe! How can you worry about such mundane matters that would worry an ordinary mortal? You should not behave in such an emotional manner like any of us."*

Krishna explains, *"I cannot watch Radha suffer silently! It makes my heart weep. I cannot watch the gopis being listless and sad. Can you please give Me some advice? What should I do? You are a very knowledgeable person."*

Uddhav smiles and says, *"Oh Lord! You are the Supreme Lord. What advice can a humble person like me give You? However, let me assure You that I do not get swayed by such worldly emotions since I am in control of myself."*

Krishna notices a streak of arrogance in Uddhav and decides to humble him.

Krishna asks, *"How can an uneducated Boy brought up in dusty villages of Vrindavan understand such philosophical matters? Please help Me understand."*

Uddhav, swelling with pride and arrogance, replies, *"I know that You are just playing with me with Your sweet words as usual. I am also aware that God can never have emotions. In fact, I feel that what You are doing is incorrect. You are playing with the emotions of the gopis, though You are unemotional and detached."*

Krishna knows that Uddhav does not understand the importance of true divine love and decides to teach him a lesson.

Krishna asks, *"Please give me your advice."*

Uddhav says, *"Please tell the gopis that they must stop being emotional. They must not look at You as their friend but instead look at You as the Supreme Lord who can take any form as and when He likes. They should not be attracted by Your handsome youthful form. They should realise that You can take any form."*

Krishna replies, *"I have told them this many times, but they don't want to change. They do not want to give up their attachments to Me. They would rather suffer the pangs of attachment and separation, than think in a philosophical manner. They prefer divine love to the liberation of their souls."*

Uddhav laughs sarcastically and asks, *"How can anyone prefer divine love to liberation? I can't believe this."*

Krishna smiles and replies, "This is the reality. What can I do?"

Uddhav replies, "The only way to free them is to remove them from the clutches of emotions, attachments and divine love."

Krishna smiles, "They want love even if it causes them suffering, since it gives them happiness."

Uddhav says, "You must go to the villages in Brij Bhoomi and educate them."

Krishna puts on a sad face and says, "I do not have the courage to face them and their power of divine love. Can you please accomplish this task on My behalf?"

Uddhav replies, "I will take up this challenge and educate them. I will tell them not to believe in love and instead concentrate on the Supreme Lord and try to reach Him. Let me proceed right away to Vrindavan and begin."

Krishna pretends that He is happy to hear this, and thanks Uddhav.

Uddhav suddenly stops in mid-stride and says, "I am a stranger to the gopis. They have never seen me. They will not believe the words of a stranger. My task would be very simple if they were to realise that I am Your messenger."

Krishna replies, "Oh that should not be a problem. I will write to them explaining the purpose of your visit and your views on how to reach God."

Uddhav readily agrees, thinking his job has become much more simplified.

Krishna writes a letter to the gopis explaining to them that they must forget Him in His current form of a handsome village Boy and get rid of all emotions and instead, concentrate on the form of the Supreme Lord. This is the only way to achieve liberation. They can achieve this by listening to Uddhav's advice.

Uddhav is thrilled when Krishna reads out the contents of the letter.

He begins to think, My work is already half done. Let me go to Brij Bhoomi and read out this letter to the gopis.

Krishna hands over the letter to Uddhav who immediately heads towards the dusty villages of Brij Bhoomi.

Uddhav travels to Vrindavan in his chariot. As his chariot approaches the quiet dusty town, the noise of the wheels of his chariot seem to be too loud. *The gopis hear the approach of the chariot and assume that their Krishna has returned. They stop whatever they are doing and rush towards the chariot. As they reach the open fields, they see the face of the youth who is sitting in the chariot. A look of disappointment crosses their face. It is not their beloved Krishna, but some other stranger. With a resigned look on their faces they turn back. Uddhav calls out to them. He introduces himself as a messenger of their beloved Lord. The faces of the gopis light up. They notice Uddhav holding a letter and ask him if it is a letter from Krishna. Uddhav nods his head. All the gopis rush towards him and each one begins to pull at the letter, saying, "Let me read what Krishna has written about me. Let me see where my name is written."*

Uddhav tries his best to stop them from pulling at the letter, but he does not succeed. Because of everyone pulling at the letter from all sides, the letter is torn up into small pieces. Each gopi hugs and kisses the piece of paper murmuring, "A letter from our Beloved Lord is like meeting Him. We do not need anything more."

Uddhav gets very upset and scolds them, "I was holding a very important letter written by the Supreme Lord Himself. He has explained the great philosophy of life that any saint would die to hear."

The gopis scold him, "We are all uneducated. What is the use of such a letter? We are content to hug and kiss the paper than read about philosophy which we cannot comprehend."

Uddhav is stunned to see such divine love and devotion.

The gopis implore, "Please show us where He has written our names. When is He is returning?"

Uddhav, who is beginning to lose his patience at their innocence, replies, "Krishna has neither written your names nor has He written about His return from Mathura. He does not intend to return to Vrindavan."

He slowly explains to them the contents of the letter.

He says, "Krishna wants you to forget His physical form and instead think of Him in His form as the Supreme Lord. He does not want to return to Vrindavan so he asks each of you to get rid of your attachments to Him and give up all emotions."

The gopis ask Uddhav innocently, "Is your Supreme Lord also as handsome looking as our Krishna? Does he have lotus shaped eyes like our Beloved? Does He have beautiful hands and legs like our Krishna? Does He

175

also play melodious tunes on His flute?"

Uddhav replies, "My Lord does not have any particular form. He can take any form and He can be present anywhere. He does not have a physical form like us. He is omnipresent and omnipotent. No one can touch Him."

The gopis unanimously reply, "If your Lord has no form, then we are not interested in meeting Him. We want to love a Person who has a physical form. We want to hug and hold our Beloved. What is the use of life, if it does not have the joys of meeting and the pangs of separation?"

Uddhav says, "If you give up all your materialistic attachments, you will not suffer from the pain of separation from your Beloved. Your mind will be at peace."

The gopis say, "We would not like to have peace like that akin to a night in the graveyard. We enjoy the experience of separation. Since you don't know what true love is, you cannot understand all this. You should first love a person to understand the joys and sorrows of attachments."

The gopis take Uddhav to where Radha is sitting near a pond. Uddhav finds Radha all alone, looking dejected and sad, lost in the thoughts of Her Lord.

The gopis tell Her, "Uddhav has come from Mathura. He is the cousin of Krishna and he has brought some news for You from Krishna."

Radha is ecstatic. She jumps up and turns to Uddhav, "Oh Uddhav!! Please tell Me what message Kanha has sent for Me. Please tell Me when He is returning."

Uddhav does not know how to react. He has no answers to Her questions. He himself does not know when Krishna will again step on the soil of Vrindavan and the other dusty villages of Brij Bhoomi. He looks helplessly at the gopis. There is a long silence.

Finally, one of the gopis replies. She informs Radha that Krishna is not planning to visit Vrindavan. She also tells Radha about the contents of the letter that Krishna had written and given to Uddhav. Uddhav now picks up the courage to preach his philosophy. He tells her to think of the Lord in a philosophical manner and worship Him as the Supreme Lord without getting involved in materialistic attachments, love, and bondage.

Radha smiles at Uddhav and says," I am an innocent village girl. I cannot comprehend your philosophy. For Me, the true worship of My Lord is in the form of divine love. I do not want to see My Lord in the form that you have just described. I want to see My Lord in the form of a young, handsome cowherd Boy. For Me, Kanha is My Lord. I want to rest in His arms, listening to His divine melodies from His divine flute. I want to hug My Lord. I want to play and dance with Him."

Uddhav replies, "Oh Radha! Please give up such attachments and bonds. Please think of Him as the Supreme Personality. Please look at Him with reverence and not love. Only if You do all this, You will be freed from the materialistic world. Only then would You be freed from the cycle of birth and death. Only then would You achieve mukti (liberation from the cycle of repeated births and deaths). You can always be at the Lotus Feet of the Lord."

Radha tells him, "The definition of happiness and pleasure is different for different people. Your conception of love need not be applicable for Me and the other gopis."

Uddhav says, "What I have preached is the universal truth. There is no truth higher than this one. Just accept my words and you will also be happy."

Radha replies, "I am already happy."

Uddhav asks Her, "You are feeling the pain of separation. You constantly think of Him and the times You spent together with Him. So how can You be happy?"

Radha replies, "Constantly thinking of My Lord gives Me happiness. There is no higher happiness than sitting here the whole day and thinking about Kanha. To me this is divine and eternal bliss."

Uddhav asks, "Are you not feeling frustrated because of the separation?"

Radha looks surprised. She asks, "Separation? What separation? Whose separation?"

Uddhav gets impatient. He says, "Your separation from Krishna."

Radha smiles again and asks Uddhav, "Whatever makes you think that I am separated from My Beloved. We are never separate. We are always together."

Uddhav laughs sarcastically and asks Her, "You mean Your Krishna is with You right now? Can I see Him?"

Radha says, "Of course He is with Me. You can see Him if you wish to. He is sitting right beside Me."

Uddhav turns around and looks. Immediately, he sees Krishna sitting there, right next to Radha, holding Her hand.

Radha asks Uddhav, "Now, please tell me. Can you see Him?"

Uddhav is too stunned to reply. He just nods his head.

Radha again questions him, "Do you think We are really separated?"

Uddhav falls at the feet of Radha and Krishna and begins to weep with ecstasy.

He tells Radha, "Oh Beloved of My Lord Krishna! Please do not humiliate me further. It is my fault that I failed to understand You. I was drowned in the arrogance of my knowledge. I had false pride about myself. You have opened my eyes and taught me the definition of divine Love. I salute both of You. Please bless me."

Both Radha and Krishna smile at Uddhav and They raise Their right hands and bless him. Uddhav touches Their feet with his right hand and then takes his right hand and touches his head with it in reverence.

Krishna says, "Oh Uddhav! Please get up. You are My greatest devotee, however you had become very arrogant. This is why I decided to play this 'Lila' on you."

Uddhav asks Krishna, "I had seen You off in Mathura. How is it You are here, in the midst of the forests of Brij Bhoomi?"

Krishna replies, "I am omnipresent. A true devotee can find Me anywhere, everywhere. If a person can light the spark of love then the darkness disappears and he can see Me."

Uddhav now begins to understand the definition of true divine love. He also realises that the best way to reach the Supreme Lord is through pure, uncomplicated, and selfless love. He once again falls at Their feet and begs for forgiveness.

Uddhav feels blessed to be watching this Lila. He realises the greatness and the depth of Radha's love for Krishna. He realises that though he used to regard himself proudly as the most knowledgeable person when it came to spirituality and philosophy, he was nothing compared to Radha. He begins to chant the Holy Name 'Radhe Radhe' and he begins to dance with joy. He stands at the very place that Radha had walked and sees Her footprints.

Uddhav collects the sand from Her footprints and puts it on his head and says, "Radha Rani is the most beloved of Lord Krishna. The only way to reach Krishna is through Radha. I am indeed blessed to have the dust from Her feet on my head."

Uddhav is aware that Radha and the gopis come every morning to Kusum Sarovar to bathe and pluck flowers for Krishna. Uddhav feels that Radha and the gopis are the greatest devotees of the Supreme Lord and they are the only ones who truly love their Lord. If anyone had to reach Krishna, it had to be through Radha and the gopis. When Radha and the gopis walk across Kusum Sarovar, the dust from their feet would fall on the grass and the creepers lying on the ground.

Uddhav thinks, Let me become a creeper, and lie on the ground near Kusum Sarovar. When Radha and the gopis walk on me with their dusty feet, the dust from their feet will cleanse my soul and I will get blessed.

He prays, "Oh Radha! I would like to be born in my next birth as a creeper at this very place. You and the gopis will walk on this path every day and bless this place. The sand of this place is blessed when Your feet touch the ground."

Radha blesses Uddhav and tells him, "Your wish will be fulfilled. You will be born as a creeper at Kusum Sarovar in your next birth."

People believe that Uddhav is still at Kusum Sarovar in the form of a creeper. They also believe that if you sing the musical *Nama sankirtan* with great love and affection for the Supreme Lord then you can see Uddhav. It is also at this spot where Uddhav narrated *Srimad Bhagvatam* to Vajranabha and Krishna's wives much before Shuka narrated it to King Parikshit.

As I went to the other side of the temple, I saw a beautiful pond. There were lots of shrubs and creepers surrounding this pond. I looked intently at them. Was one of them Uddhav, as a creeper? As I walked past the creepers, I felt I heard the sounds of *Radhe Radhe* emanating from them!

12

Barsana

...

"Ananyachetah satatam yo mam smarati nityashah,
Tasyaham sulabah Partha nitya yuktasya yoginah."

("For the devotee who constantly thinks of Me without
deviation of mind, to him I am easily attainable, Oh Partha,
because of his constant devotional service to Me.")

(*Bhagavad Gita* 8.14)

Barsana is situated about 50 km to the north-west of Mathura and
about 20 km to the north-west of Goverdhan. It is located at
27.65^0 N latitude and 77.38^0E longitude. This place is also known
as Varsana.

Many people think that Radha was born and brought up at
Barsana. There are others who believe that Radha was born in
Raval, but subsequently spent Her childhood at Barsana. So it is
quite natural that the most important temple here is the Radha
Rani Temple, also known as the Ladliji Temple. Some people
believe that Radha's father, Vrishabhanu was an ordinary cowherd
while others believe that he was a king and Barsana was his
capital. Barsana is surrounded by eight villages, each belonging to
one of the *Ashta Sakhis* (Radha's eight gopi friends)

Barsana is also famous for the unique way in which it
celebrates Holi since the Laatmaar Holi is unique to this town.
Holi is played differently by the male residents of Nandagaon and
the female residents of Barsana. The women of the village beat

181

the men with wooden sticks when the men try to spray them with coloured powders, or coloured water. It is believed by the locals that Laatmaar Holi (*laat* means 'stick' and *maar* means 'to hit') was prevalent even 5000 years ago during the times of Lord Krishna. They believe that Radha, along with the gopis of Barsana, used to play Holi in this manner with Krishna and the menfolk of Nandagaon.

RADHA RANI (LADLIJI) TEMPLE

Radha Rani Temple (old)

Radha Rani Temple (new)

This is the biggest and the most beautiful temple in Barsana. The Radha Rani Temple is also known as Ladliji Temple. *Ladli* is an affectionate way of addressing a young girl and *Ji* is a respectful way of addressing a person. So this shows the love, affection, and respect the people of Brij Bhoomi have for their beloved daughter Radha.

The Radha Rani Temple is atop a hill. There are about 180 steps leading to the temple. Climbing up these steps can be quite a tough task for children and old people. There are lots of *palkiwallas* who carry the devotees up on a *palki* and bring them back after the *darshan*. They charge Rs. 80 for the entire trip. For a trip to Radha Rani Temple and Maan Kutir, they will charge double the amount.

As I reached the top of the hill, I saw a huge open courtyard. It reminded me of the huge courtyards that we normally see in ancient palaces. The courtyard offered one of the most spectacular views. I could see the entire town of Barsana and the other peaks from here. There were two temples here in front of this courtyard. The one on the right was the older of the two. It was a white temple built by Raja Bir Singh in 1675. The one on the left was a sandstone-coloured temple which was built later.

The new temple has a huge door, reminiscent of the huge gates seen at the entrance of cities in ancient Rajput kingdoms. There are about 10 steps that lead to this door. The door opens into another open courtyard. In front of this is the inner courtyard that leads to the main altar. The main altar has idols of Radha and Krishna. The Krishna idol is the customary black and the Radha idol is golden in colour. In front of these idols, a fan has been installed with a rope tied to it. The other end of the rope is kept outside the altar, in the inner courtyard. The devotees sitting in the inner courtyard can pull this rope which will fan the idols of Radha and Krishna. The walls have huge paintings depicting the times Radha and Krishna spent together. The ceiling has one very huge painting that depicts the Rasa Leela of Radha and Krishna.

As in many other parts of Brij Bhoomi, here also a few self-appointed guides began to harass us. They kept forcing themselves upon us. I tried to argue, but in vain. Finally, I hit upon a great idea. When one of them asked me what I was writing down, I told them that I was a senior government official and I had been sent here by the Chief Minister to study the ambience and facilities of all the places in Brij Bhoomi. I told them that I planned to write in my report that all the temples are very beautiful, however the ambience is spoilt because of these guides and touts. I also told them that since they were misbehaving with me, I intended to put all this in my report. Needless to say, within a few seconds, all of them had fled the scene!

PILA POKHAR KUND

Pila Pokhar Kund is quite close to the foot of the hill that houses the Radha Rani Temple. This *kund* is well maintained and many devotees bathe in it. In Hindi, *pila* means 'yellow'. Radha Rani once washed her turmeric-coated hands here, and the water turned yellow, thus giving the *kund* its name.

Pila Pokhar Kund

Radha has gone to Nandagaon to visit Yashoda. Yashoda is delighted to see Radha. She always dreams that her son Krishna should get a bride as beautiful and sweet as Radha. She is also aware that Krishna likes Radha. Yashoda takes Radha's hands and applies turmeric paste on them. Radha is stunned to see this because turmeric paste is normally applied on a girl's hand just before her marriage. Radha realises that if She returns to Her house in this condition, then Her parents will be suspicious and ask Her about Yashoda's intentions.

As Radha walks back towards Barsana, She keeps thinking about what to tell Her parents if they notice Her turmeric-coated yellow hands. She does not have the courage to face Her parents like this. She suddenly gets an idea. She notices a kund *on the way to Her house in Barsana. She quietly heads towards this* kund *and dips both Her hands in the water. Immediately, all the water in the* kund *turns golden yellow.*

JAIPUR TEMPLE

Jaipur Temple is on a hillock adjacent to the Radha Rani Temple. Like the Jaipur Temple of Vrindavan, this one too looks more like a palace than a temple. The entrance resembles a fort. As I walked past the outer courtyard, I came across another huge gate with exquisite carvings. This led me to the main altar which had idols of Radha and Krishna. The entire outer courtyard was surrounded by beautifully carved arches.

It is believed that when Radha and Krishna descended on Earth, Lord Brahma, Lord Vishnu, and Lord Shiva also decided to come down to Earth and watch the pastimes of these two divine souls. Lord Vishnu took the form of Goverdhan Hill. Lord Shiva took the form of Nandishwara Hill at Nandagaon. Lord Brahma stayed at Barsana

Entrance of Jaipur Temple

and each of His four heads took the form of a hillock. The first hillock has the Radha Rani Temple and the second hillock has Jaipur Temple. The other two hillocks have Mor Kutir and Maan Kutir.

MOR KUTIR AND MAAN KUTIR

Mor Kutir and Maan Kutir are on adjacent hillocks. As we drove from the foot of the hill that housed the Radha Rani Temple, we arrived at an intersection. The road on the right took us to a hill that had Mor Kutir on its peak. The road on the left leads to another hill that has Maan Kutir at the top.

Mor Kutir is also known as Mayur Kutir. Both the words, *Mor* and *Mayur*, mean the same — 'peacock'. Like the Radha Rani Temple, this temple is also on a hillock, adjacent to the hillock that has the famous Radha Rani Temple. The two hillocks are separated by a couple of kilometres by road. The temple *Mor Kutir* got its name because it is believed that Lord Krishna had disguised as a peacock, to appease an upset Radha.

Though Mor Kutir Temple has fewer steps to climb than the Radha Rani Temple, my guide Mathuresh and I found this climb tougher since the steps were very steep. When we reached the top, we saw a board which said 'Mandir Shri More Bihariji More Kuti' written in Hindi. This temple looked more like the ancient residence of a hermit. We found the main door bolted. After knocking for a while and calling out 'Radhe Radhe', (the Brij way of asking 'Is anyone there?') we waited for a couple of minutes. Since no one responded, Mathuresh pushed at the main door. The door opened and we walked inside. We found ourselves inside a small room. To our astonishment, we found all the walls completely filled with paintings of peacocks and Lord Krishna! There were hundreds of peacocks painted on all the walls. I had never seen so many peacocks in my life!

To the left was the main altar. I saw a picture of Radha, Krishna and a dancing peacock. In front of the picture, were two brass peacocks. I could hear the continuous chants of 'Radhe Krishna'.

Mathuresh and I were curious to know the legend associated with this place. We saw an old priest sitting on the floor wearing a small wet dhoti. It appeared as if he had just finished his morning bath and had sat down for his morning prayers. He opened his eyes and looked at us. Mathuresh seized this opportunity and requested him to tell us the legend of this place. The priest shook his head and refused politely. Both of us were quite disappointed. Mathuresh got up to leave. However, I continued to sit. I waved at Mathuresh and asked him to come and sit next to me. In the meanwhile, the priest had finished his holy chanting of the Supreme Lord's Names. He had now got up and gone inside the main altar. He performed the *puja* of the deities. He did not use a lit lamp. Instead, he used *agarbathi* to perform the aarati. He turned around and noticed that we had continued to sit patiently for him. I really do not know the real reason for his sudden change of heart, but probably it was our patience and perseverance that did the trick. He realised that we were willing to wait for a long time to hear the legend associated with this place. He sat down next to us and began his narration in pure, but simple Hindi.

Radha and Krishna are resting on a hill in Barsana. Krishna suggests to Radha, "Let us dress up and decorate each other."

Radha agrees. After Krishna dresses up Radha, She asks Krishna, "Kanha! How do I look?"

Krishna replies, "Radhe, You look as beautiful as the full moon."

Radha feels insulted because She considers Herself to be more beautiful than the full moon and does not like to be compared to it. She thinks that even the full moon has a few flaws in it, but She has none. She angrily walks away. She climbs another hill and sits in a house on top of the hill. This is Maan Kutir (Maan means 'anger', describing the mood of Radha. The hill is known as Maan Gadh).

Krishna is sad when Radha leaves Him. He continues to stay on the hill where He and Radha had met and dressed each other up.

The next day Krishna thinks, By now Radha's anger would have subsided. Let Me go and meet Her.

He heads towards Maan Kutir. He knocks at the door. One of Radha's sakhis opens the door.

She asks, "Why have You come? Radha is still upset with You."

Krishna replies, "Please inform Radha that I have come to meet Her."

The sakhi goes inside and comes back after a few minutes and tells Krishna, "I am sorry but Radha is still angry and She does not want to meet You."

On hearing this, Krishna walks away feeling dejected. He climbs His hillock contemplating His next move.

Some days pass by. Each morning, He uses a different disguise and goes to Radha's house, only to be turned away by one of Her sakhis.

A few more days pass by. He sees Radha's sakhi, Lalitha, calling out to and collecting all the peacocks that are near the hill.

Krishna asks Lalitha, "Why are you gathering all these peacocks?"

Lalitha replies, "Radha Rani is very fond of peacocks. She is feeling lonely and bored. She wants to entertain Herself by watching the peacocks dance. I am taking them to the hill where She stays."

Krishna continues to watch. Soon He sees many peacocks dancing on the opposite hillock where Radha resides. Radha is happy watching them dance and claps Her hands gleefully. She is thrilled and totally immersed in watching the peacocks dance. As Krishna watches this spectacle, he gets an idea, "Let me hide all the peacocks tomorrow!"

The next day Lalitha comes to collect the peacocks. She is astonished to *find that Barsana, that boasts of so many peacocks, does not have a single one this day!*

Krishna meets Lalitha and tells her, "I will disguise as a peacock. Please take Me to Radha. I will dance and entertain My Beloved."

Lalitha is thrilled and agrees immediately. She helps Krishna disguise Himself as a peacock and takes Him to the hillock where Radha is.

Radha has been sitting outside her house, waiting for a long time. She notices that there are no peacocks that day. She wonders, where have all the peacocks gone? What has happened to them today?

As She is lost in these thoughts, She hears Lalitha arrive.

She asks Lalitha, "Where have all the peacocks gone today?"

Lalitha smiles, "Today I managed to catch only one peacock. Though I could get only one, let me assure you that He is the most beautiful peacock in all of Brij."

Saying this, she shows Her Krishna, disguised as a beautiful peacock.

Krishna opens His wings and dances more enchantingly than any peacock that Radha has ever seen. Radha claps and cheers, watching the peacock dance.

The dance is over. The peacock comes and stands near Radha. Slowly and gently, the peacock rubs its beak against Radha's legs and nudges against Her dress. Radha is surprised. She begins to wonder why the peacock is tugging at Her dress this way.

Radha asks Lalitha, "Why is this peacock tugging at My dress like this?"

Lalitha is amused at Radha's innocence and she thinks, The Lord of the three worlds is at Her feet and She asks me Who it is!

She tells Radha, "The peacock is none other than Your beloved Kanha!"

At that instance Radha realises that the peacock is none other than Her beloved Krishna. She hugs the peacock which immediately transforms into Krishna. As She hugs Her beloved Kanha, She also realises that it was Her Kanha who had been visiting Her house each morning disguised differently everyday. Her anger melts away immediately and She weeps with joy.

The priest narrated the story using simple words. However, the impact it had on both of us was so strong that we felt we had been transferred back in time, to the era of Radha and Krishna. Hearing about Krishna's humility and patience and the Radha's innocence filled our hearts with joy. Both of us bowed to the priest and took our leave. As I walked down the steps of the hillock, I could see Krishna disguised as a peacock and dancing in front of His beloved Radha, who was clapping Her hands gleefully.

PREM SAROVAR

Prem Sarovar is loca-ted between Barsana and Nandagaon. While going from Barsana towards Nandagaon, Prem Saro-var is on the left, about 100 metres off the high-way.

Prem Sarovar

Prem Sarovar has pink-coloured steps built around it in the shape of an octagon. Each side of this sacred tank has a narrow pathway that leads towards the centre of Prem Sarovar. The eight pathways look like the eight tentacles of an octopus. I did not find many visitors at this quiet little place. It is a pity that this sacred tank is badly maintained, despite it being the Divinne Couple's favourite meeting place.

Radha and Krishna are resting with Their friends. Suddenly a bee begins to encircle Radha. Radha feels scared. Krishna, tells His friend, "Can you please send this bee away?" His friend chases the bee away with a small stick. In the meanwhile, Krishna hides Himself. His friend returns to where Radha and Krishna were sitting. He finds Radha alone now.

He tells Radha, "Madhu has gone."

Madhu means 'bee', but it is also one of Krishna's names. So Radha assumes that Krishna has left Her and She starts weeping. Krishna, from His hiding place sees Radha crying. He feels sorry for Her and He also begins to weep. The tears of Radha and Krishna get mingled and form Prem Sarovar.

Next to Prem Sarovar is a small temple with the idol of Lord Shiva in it. Next to this temple is another temple, much bigger in size. This is a temple for Lord Rama, with the inscription outside 'Janaki Vallabho Vijayate'. This white temple is adorned outside by a huge bow pointing upwards, towards the Heavens.

KHADIRAVANA

Khadiravana is a forest located about 10 km from Barsana. It is believed that Krishna used to meet Radha here along with the gopis. Due to its proximity to both, Barsana (the town where Radha stayed) and Nandagaon (the town where Krishna resided), this was an ideal meeting place. This forest is also famous because the bird demon, Bakasura and his younger brother Aghasura, were killed here by Lord Krishna.

King Kansa is getting desperate. All his plans to kill Krishna have failed. He had sent the biggest and the most powerful demons to kill Krishna, but they had all failed and in the process had been killed themselves. He calls his demon friend Bakasura to his court.

Bakasura, in the form of a gigantic bird, arrives and bows to Kansa, "Oh mighty king! Glory to you! Please tell me how I can serve you."

Kansa replies, "I have tried my best to kill Krishna, but failed. Many demons have come forward to help me, but they have themselves gotten killed."

Bakasura laughs, "Cowards! How can they get killed by a mere Boy!"

Kansa says, "Can you help me?"

Bakasura once again laughs, "I will swallow the young Boy. Let me go to His village."

Saying this Bakasura leaves Mathura and flies away.

The cowherds are playing on the banks of River Yamuna. Krishna is sitting near a tree playing His flute. Suddenly they hear a loud quacking sound. The cowherds look around. They see a huge duck-like bird on the banks of the river. The cowherds are fascinated. Innocently, they begin to move towards the bird to take a closer look. Krishna stops playing His flute. He notices His friends standing very close to the huge bird and admiring its body. His Divine Vision tells Him that the huge bird is the demon

Bakasura. He also realises that the lives of His friends are in danger.

He thinks, before the demon Bakasura attacks My friends, I should kill him.

He rushes towards the big bird. Bakasura too notices Krishna and shifts his focus from the cowherd boys to Krishna. He opens his gigantic beak and rushes towards Krishna. In one huge gulp, he swallows Him.

Bakasura is thrilled. He was quite arrogant because of his immense strength and had no doubts that he would emerge victorious in this challenge. However, he had never realised it was going to be so easy. He tries to crush Krishna. However, he has underestimated the power of the Supreme Lord. Lord Krishna begins to grow inside Bakasura's body. Bakasura begins to feel his stomach bulging. He also realises that Krishna has moved from the stomach and is now in his mouth. Bakasura tries his best to keep his beak shut, but in vain. Krishna, using His might, presses the lower part of the beak downwards and the upper part of the beak upwards. Bakasura's mouth is now wide open. Krishna comes out. He holds the beak of Bakasura and pulls them apart. Though Lord Krishna is a small Boy, he is the Supreme Lord. He is able to break Bakasura's huge beak just as a child breaks a small twig. Bakasura shrieks out loud and falls dead.

All the cowherds rejoice and shout, "Glory to Kanha! Glory to Kanha! He has saved us once again from the demons."

The news of Bakasura's death reaches Kansa. He is terrified. Could this Boy really be an incarnation of the Supreme Lord? Is He the one destined to kill him?

He asks his men to invite another demon — Aghasura.

Aghasura, the giant snake demon crawls into his court.

King Kansa says, "The news about the death of your elder brother Bakasura must have reached you."

Aghasura replies, "Yes Mighty King! Please tell me who has killed my brother, Bakasura. I want to avenge his death. Was he killed by a God or a Gandharva or some celestial being? Bakasura was too powerful to be killed by ordinary human beings."

Kansa says, "Unfortunately, he was killed by a mere Boy."

Aghasura is stunned, "A mere Boy, you say! Who is He?"

Kansa says, "He is Krishna, who lives in the villages of Brij Bhoomi.

People consider Him to be an incarnation of the Supreme Lord. He is destined to kill me."

Aghasura says, "Don't worry, Oh King! He won't live that long. I will go now and finish Him off. Please grant me leave."

Aghasura reaches the banks of River Yamuna. It is a familiar sight. The cows are gazing in the green fields. The cowherds are playing on the banks of the river. Lord Krishna is playing His flute. The birds are enjoying the sweet melodies.

Aghasura opens his wide mouth and sits still. The cowherds see the snake lying on the ground. However, owing to its huge size and its stillness, they do not know what it is. The lower part of the mouth rests on the forest, covering a few miles whereas the upper part of the mouth touches the skies! The inner portion of the mouth resembles a huge dark cave.

The cowherds shout, "Kanha! Come and see! We have found a huge cave with a dark tunnel inside. Let us go inside."

Saying thus, they enter the body of Aghasura through the open mouth. Krishna senses the danger and He too rushes inside. As soon as they enter, Aghasura closes his mouth. He decides to kill his enemies by crushing them. He begins to coil his body. Krishna realises that time is running out. His cowherd friends are suffocating and fall unconscious. Aghasura's closed mouth ensures that the cowherds do not get any fresh air to breathe. Krishna begins to expand inside Aghasura's stomach. Aghasura, like any other python, has a flexible and expandable stomach, which naturally expands when he swallows his victims. However, Krishna is expanding and enlarging at such an alarming rate and to such an extent that Aghasura's stomach is unable to cope with the Supreme Lord's huge form. Krishna rips open Aghasura's stomach and marches out. The gigantic demon snake Aghasura breathes his last.

And then they see a divine glow emanate from Aghasura's body. A divine soul comes out and bows before Krishna and says, "Oh Supreme Lord! I was a God dwelling in the Heavens. One day I saw Ashtavakra walking in the forest. Proud of my handsome body, I failed to recognise the great learned Sage Ashtavakra. I mocked and made fun of his body which was bent at eight places. I also laughed at his gait, handicapped as he was owing to his deformed body. Sage Ashtavakra cursed me and said that since I was so proud of my handsome body and limbs, I would lose them immediately. He cursed me to become a snake and live on Earth. I fell at his feet and begged *for forgiveness. I acknowledged that I had committed a grave sin. Sage Ashtavakra took pity on me and said that he could not reverse his curse, but could mitigate it. He said that I would live on Earth for many years. One day, Lord Krishna, the incarnation of Lord Vishnu, would kill me and I would achieve moksha and go back to the Heavens. Now the time has come for my moksha. I thank you for liberating me."*

Saying this, he bowed in front of the Supreme Lord, who blessed him. The divine soul starts its upward journey towards the Heavens.

Krishna suddenly realises that He needs to wake his sleeping friends up.

He calls out to His cowherd friends who had fallen unconscious due to lack of air. They slowly wake up and rub their eyes. They ask Krishna, "Oh Kanha! What happened to us? Where are we?"

Krishna smiles, "You are all safe with Me. It is getting late and dark. Our parents will get worried. Let's head back to our village."

The images of the gory killings of Bakasura and Aghasura flashed in front of my eyes as I stood watching the trees. Only a divine Child like Krishna was capable of killing these mighty demons. It was also ironical that these demons were granted *moksha* since they had been killed by the Supreme Lord.

There were not many visitors here since most of the tourists are unaware of the divine incidents that took place here. I began my journey towards Nandagaon, the last place where Krishna resided before departing to Mathura.

13

Nandagaon

...

"Karmajam budhiyuktha hi phalam tyaktva manishinah,
Janma bandha vinirmuktah padam gacchhantyanamayam"

("By performing devotional services to the Lord, great devotees free themselves from the fruits of action. They get freed from the bondage of birth and death to achieve liberation and a blissful state."

(*Bhagavad Gita* 2.51)

Nandagaon is approximately 50 km to the north-west of Mathura and 10 km to the north of Barsana. It is located at 27.72^0 N latitude and 77.38^0E longitude.

This place has been named after Krishna's foster father, Nanda Rai. Yashoda and Nanda were too scared to live in Vrindavan owing to the frequent attacks launched by demons on their Son, Krishna. They knew that Kansa was responsible for these acts of violence. They decided to move to a town that was further away from Mathura and also less accessible to Kansa and his men. Hence, they chose to go to Nandagaon that was 50 km away from Mathura, compared to Vrindavan which was only 10 km from Mathura.

PAVAN SAROVAR

This is close to the foothills of Nandishwara Hill. It is 50 metres off the main road, and the road leading to Pavan Sarovar is

Pavan Sarovar

not in a good condition. At first glance, it looks similar to Prem Sarovar. Both are not well-maintained in spite of being places with such a divine history. Both have pink-coloured stone ghats on all sides of the *sarovar*.

However, as I approached the *sarovar*, I noticed subtle differences between the two. Prem Sarovar had eight pathways leading from the edge to the middle, like the eight tentacles of an octopus. Pavan Sarovar had about 25 such pathways. Each pathway was around 25 feet long. Prem Sarovar was shaped like an octagon, whereas Pavan Sarovar is rectangular. The steps leading to the water are fewer in number at Pavan Sarovar than at Prem Sarovar.

Nanda Rai and his family are fed up with the constant attacks from various demons on their Sons Krishna and Balarama. They had left Gokul precisely for this reason and had moved to Vrindavan. However, they have found Vrindavan to be no better than Gokul. Nanda Rai decides that he and his family must stay as far as possible from Mathura. Vrindavan is approximately 10 km from Mathura, so it is still quite accessible and close to Kansa and his men. Nanda Rai knows that one of the farthest towns from Mathura in Brij Bhoomi is a town near Barsana. This town is 50 km from Mathura and hence not easily accessible to Kansa and his men. Nanda Rai, along with his family and many fellow Vrindavan residents leave Vrindavan and head towards the dusty town which was later named after him and became famous as Nandagaon.

Nanda Rai and his family load their household articles on their bullock carts and leave Vrindavan. Since the bullock carts travel at a very slow pace, it takes many hours to reach Nandagaon.

Krishna asks His mother Yashoda, "Vrindavan was such a beautiful town surrounded by thick forests and Yamuna. Why did We leave such a beautiful place and move to a town which is at the farthest end of Brij Bhoomi?"

Yashoda replies, "My dear Son! There were lots of demons attacking You and Your brother Balarama. Vrindavan is a very unsafe place for us to stay, so we decided to shift to a place which is far away from Mathura."

Krishna smiles at His mother's innocence. She does not know that her Sons do not need any protection from these demons. They were born to slay all of them.

Nanda Rai and his family reach their destination by afternoon. It is very hot and the long arduous journey has made them tired and hungry. They decide to bathe. The villagers advise them to go to the sarovar which is close to the foothills of Nandishwara Hill. Nanda agrees. Along with Yashoda, Balarama and Krishna, he goes to Pavan Sarovar. They all bathe in the cool waters of the sarovar. Krishna and Balarama find the bath very refreshing since the journey under the scorching sun had made them tired and exhausted.

They ask Nanda, "Can we come here everyday for Our bath?"

Nanda agrees and from that day onwards, Pavan Sarovar becomes Their daily bathing place.

A few days pass by. Krishna decides that Pavan Sarovar would be the ideal place to bathe His cows. He and Balarama begin to bring the cows here everyday to bathe them and give them water to drink.

NANDA RAI TEMPLE

Nanda Rai Temple is built atop a hillock known as Nandishwara Hill. Since Lord Shiva had stayed there in the form of a Hill, it is known as Nandishwara Hill. The house where Nanda Rai stayed has now been converted into Nanda Rai Temple. The hillock is on the outskirts of Nandagaon. There is a narrow dusty road in

Nanda Rai Temple

front of Pavan Sarovar that leads towards this divine hill. This narrow road was in the midst of sunflower and mustard fields, so we almost missed it.

Lord Shiva is very eager to watch Radha and Krishna at Brij. With this desire, He approaches Lord Vishnu.

He tells Lord Vishnu, "Lord, I have a request."

Lord Vishnu asks Him, "Please tell me what You want from Me."

Lord Shiva tells Him, "I know that You have incarnated for the eighth time on Earth, this time as Lord Krishna. I would like to watch Radha and Krishna from Brij Bhoomi. Please give Me an opportunity to watch Them."

Lord Vishnu replies, "Very soon Nanda Rai and Yashoda will arrive at Nandagaon. They will begin to look for a place that is safe for Krishna and Balarama. You can go there in the form of a hillock. Nanda Rai does not want to stay in the middle of the town. He prefers to reside at a place which is far away from the town and difficult to access; hence, he will find the hillock an ideal place to reside. He will build a house on top of the hillock."

Lord Shiva is very happy.

He replies, "Oh Lord! I would be blessed to have such a house atop Me. It would be like carrying the Lord of the three worlds on My head."

Lord Shiva immediately heads towards Nandagaon. He takes the form of a hillock and awaits the arrival of Nanda Rai and his family.

Soon, Nanda Rai comes there with Yashoda, Krishna and Balarama. As predicted by Lord Vishnu, he begins to look for a safe place. He sees the hillock and notices that the road to it is virtually inaccessible.

He thinks, Just as I find the road to reach the top of this hillock very difficult to climb and almost inaccessible, I am sure, even the demons will feel the same. I think this is a safe place to bring up Krishna and Balarama.

With these thoughts, he builds a house on top of Nandishwara Hill.

When I reached the top of the hillock, I saw a few steps leading us to a huge wooden gate. Only a small portion of the huge door was open. This was similar to the Gokulnath Temple at Gokul. When I crossed the gate, I came across a huge outer courtyard. A walk to the left led me to the inner courtyard of the temple. The temple was made of white marble. The courtyard was surrounded by lots of arches on all sides, reminiscent of the

Moghul era. The inner courtyard walls had numerous paintings, depicting the life and pastimes of Lord Krishna.

The main altar had idols of the entire Nanda Rai family, kept in a golden *mantapa*. At the extreme left was a golden coloured idol of Radha. Next to it was a golden idol of Yashoda. Black idols of Krishna and Balarama were to the right. Surprisingly, both of Them were playing the flute. To the right of Balarama was an idol of Nanda Rai. To his right were idols of Mansukh and Dhansukh, both friends of Krishna. These idols were installed by Krishna's great grandson, Vajranabha. There were steps in the outer courtyard that lead to the first floor of the temple. The first floor has a huge outer courtyard, surrounding the temple below.

Nanda Rai stayed in this house for many years with his family till, one fine day, Akroor visited them and requested Nanda Rai to send Krishna and Balarama along with him to Mathura.

Kansa is worried He has tried every possible method to kill Krishna, but in vain. Putana, Trinavarta, Bakasura, Aghasura, Dhenukasura, Kesi, Aristasura, and many others have been unsuccessful in carrying out his orders and have gotten killed in the process.

He calls his ministers and asks them, "What should we do now? We have failed so far in our endeavours. Is there no one in the entire Mathura kingdom who can kill Him?"

There is a long silence in the court. Everyone knows that when Kansa is upset, silence is the best option. Kansa looks around and sees blank faces.

Finally one of his ministers replies, "The only way to kill Him is to invite Him to Mathura and kill Him. He should be asked to participate in a wrestling match. In the wrestling match, let us make Him fight the strongest wrestlers of Mathura. He is no match for them."

Kansa ponders over the idea and replies, "Sounds good, but how do we make Him come to Mathura? Krishna is a very clever Lad. If we invite Him then He will suspect foul play and refuse to come."

The minister replies, "Yes. We should ensure that He does not suspect any foul play. I have a plan. Let us plan to perform some religious events here in Mathura. We will inform Him about this and invite Him. As part of the events, let us organise a wrestling match. We will invite all the top wrestlers from Mathura and nearby kingdoms. We will force Krishna to participate and get Him killed."

Kansa thinks over for a while. He looks at his Kul Guru (head priest) and asks him, "Is it possible to organise a religious event to which we can invite Him? We need to invite Him under some pretext like this. Otherwise, He will not come to Mathura."

The Kul Guru says, "Let us perform Dhanush Yagna (Bow Sacrifice) where we worship the divine bow."

Kansa says, "Let it be so. We will perform Dhanush Yagna. Now the question is, who will invite Him? It has to be someone who is a close associate of Krishna. It should be someone whom He trusts."

His minister replies, "The best person is Akroor. He is Krishna's close friend. Krishna will never refuse an invitation from Akroor."

Kansa thunders to his guards, "Call Akroor right now to the court."

His guards return with Akroor in a few minutes.

Akroor asks, "Oh King! Please tell me what your wish is?"

Kansa says, "Akroor! I am planning to conduct Dhanush Yagna. Go to Nandagaon and invite Krishna to participate in the celebrations."

Akroor looks at Kansa. He immediately suspects foul play. He knows Kansa has some diabolic plan to kill Krishna.

He asks Kansa, "Why are you inviting Him to Dhanush Yagna celebrations? What are your real intentions?"

Kansa laughs, "After the Dhanush Yagna celebrations, I want Him to witness the wrestling matches. I want to honour Krishna when He comes here to participate in the week-long celebrations."

Akroor now guesses that the Dhanush Yagna is just a pretext to call Krishna. He is sure that Kansa will try to kill Krishna during the wrestling match.

He replies, "Forgive me, O King! Keeping His safety in mind, I would not like to invite Krishna to Mathura."

Saying this, he walks out of the court angrily.

Kansa is stunned. How dare Akroor insult him like this?

Kansa visits the prison cell and asks Devaki and Vasudev, "I am asking you for the last time. Tell me if Krishna is really your Son."

Both of them remain silent.

Kansa angrily shakes his head and says, "If you don't tell me the truth,

I will kill Vasudev."

Kansa's men come and tie up Vasudev. Kansa pulls out his sword and threatens to kill Vasudev.

Devaki starts to weep. She cries, "Yes! Yes! Yes! Yes! Krishna is my Son. Please free my husband."

Kansa laughs loudly and says, "This is just a part of my deal. There is one more condition which you must agree to. Otherwise, I will have him thrown into a pit of poisonous snakes."

Devaki begs Kansa to free her husband, but Kansa continues to laugh.

He says, "I will free Vasudev only if he invites Krishna to Mathura, so that I can kill Him."

Devaki rejects his request. Kansa says that in that case, she has to sacrifice her husband's life. She finally agrees to invite Krishna.

Kansa says, "Krishna will come to Mathura only if He is invited by Akroor. I want Akroor to visit Nandagaon and invite Krishna to Mathura. I will send Akroor to you now. You must convince Akroor to go to Nandagaon and meet Nanda Rai."

Devaki has no choice but to agree.

Kansa makes arrangements for the Dhanush Yagna. His men get the divine bow and keep it before him. This was the bow that was gifted by Lord Shiva to Lord Parshurama, who in turn had gifted it to Kansa's ancestors. Kansa has been told that if anyone breaks the divine bow before the Dhanush Yagna, then that person would ultimately be his killer. Knowing this, Kansa wants to take no chances so he asks his men to guard the bow with great care.

In the meanwhile, Kansa sends Akroor to the prison cell.

Devaki tells Akroor, "Please invite Krishna to Mathura. I want you to leave for Nandagaon immediately."

Akroor is very reluctant since he knows of Kansa's intentions. He tries his best to convince both of them not to invite Krishna to Mathura, but he is unsuccessful.

Finally he bows to them and says, "I have tried my best to convince you, but have failed. I know Kansa's intentions. He will try to kill Krishna."

Devaki says, "If I don't invite Krishna, then Kansa will kill my husband. How can I sacrifice his life?"

201

Akroor asks her, "Are you not sacrificing Krishna's life?"

Devaki replies, "I have heard many stories over the years of how Krishna has been able to overcome demons and evil spirits. I also hear from the guards that people believe that He is none other than the Supreme Lord Himself. I am sure He can take care of Himself."

Akroor realises he has no choice. He bows and says, "As you wish. I will leave for Nandagaon right away."

Akroor reaches Nandagaon and goes to Nanda Rai's house. Since they are about to start eating lunch, they ask Akroor also to join them. Both Balarama and Krishna greet Akroor and seek his blessings.

After lunch, Krishna and Balarama go out to play. The ladies of the house get busy with their household chores. Nanda Rai takes Akroor to another room and asks him the reason for his sudden visit.

Akroor remains silent. He does not know how to start the conversation. Finally, Nanda Rai breaks the silence. He asks, "Tell me, O Brave One! What brings you from the rich palaces of Mathura to my humble cottage in the dusty villages of Brij?"

Akroor answers, "Kansa is about to perform a Dhanush Yagna. He said there would be many festivities in Mathura. He has invited Krishna and Balarama to participate in the festivities. He also wants to honour both of Them."

Nanda Rai is not able to understand what Akroor is saying, since he does not know the truth about Krishna's birth. He asks Akroor once again the reason for the invitation.

Akroor says, "Kansa wants to honour all great warriors and he wants to honour Krishna also."

Nanda Rai is not convinced and he refuses to send Krishna.

Krishna enters the house and hears part of the conversation.

He says, "Balarama and I will come to Mathura and watch the festivities. Please thank Kansa on Our behalf and inform him that We will come."

Krishna knows why Akroor has come. He knows the moral dilemma that Akroor is facing and so He invites Himself.

Nanda Rai however is adamant. He says, "I know Kansa's real intentions. He will try to kill my innocent Children. He must have a diabolic scheme in his mind to get Them killed."

Akroor says, "This is the order of the King and hence none can refuse him."

Nanda asks him, "Why was decision taken without consulting us? We are Krishna's parents."

Akroor says that Krishna's parents were consulted. Nanda Rai does not understand. Akroor tells Nanda, "What I am going to tell you will shock you... Krishna is not your Son."

Nanda is stunned and begins to shout at Akroor.

He screams, "Go away from here. I will kill you if you do not leave my house. Now!"

Hearing his screams, Yashoda rushes in and asks, "Why are you screaming like this?"

Nanda narrates what Akroor has just told him. Yashoda is equally shocked to hear that she is not Krishna's mother.

Nanda and Yashoda ask him why he would tell them such a big lie, but Akroor reiterates that Krishna is not their Son.

Akroor says, "The truth is known to very few people. I did not want to reveal the truth to you, since I knew it would hurt all of you. However, Nanda Rai was adamant. He refused to send Krishna to Mathura. I had no choice but to tell the truth. The truth was hidden till now, and it has come out."

Yashoda still refuses to believe Akroor. Akroor narrates the entire story of the birth of Lord Krishna. He also narrates the story of the birth of Balarama, shocking Rohini also in the process. Akroor says that the entire episode was told to him by Vasudev who is the most truthful person on Earth. He also tells them why he had to tell them the truth.

Akroor says, "Even if Krishna has to be sacrificed, we must ensure that at least Balarama is saved. Since Kansa's spies are watching us, we should take Balarama away at night when the spies are not watching. Since the spies would be following the movements of Krishna, He can be taken to Mathura the next day in broad daylight. If you do not send Krishna to Mathura, Kansa will massacre the entire village and you will be responsible for this."

Finally Nanda, Yashoda, and Rohini agree to send Krishna with him to Mathura the next day.

Rohini wakes up Balarama at midnight. Balarama is told that He has to go with Akroor secretly.

He asks her why. "Why should I go alone and not with Krishna?"

She tells Him, "You will go secretly to Mathura, escorted by Akroor's spies, who have come to Nandagaon disguised as ordinary villagers."

In the meanwhile, Akroor's spies inform him that all arrangements have been made to take Balarama out of the town secretly. Akroor comes to take Balarama.

Balarama asks him the same question that he asked Rohini, "Why should I go alone to Mathura with your spies?"

At this point, Akroor says that both He and Krishna are children of Devaki and Vasudev and narrates briefly the story of Their birth. He tells Balarama that since Kansa has found out about Krishna, he wants Him at Mathura. However, since Kansa does not know about Balarama, He has to be safely escorted to a different place. Krishna, who is listening to all this, comes in.

He tells Akroor, "You are worrying too much, unnecessarily. Both of Us will go to Mathura together."

Akroor is upset that all his plans are going awry. However, he has no choice but to agree. Krishna comforts Yashoda that she need not worry about Him since He is strong enough to protect Himself against Kansa. He asks her to promise that she will not cry after He leaves for Mathura.

On the first floor, there are two mantapas, known as Radha Krishna Baithaks. It is believed that these are the same places where Radha and Krishna used to sit together and chat. This *baithak* was also witness to the last meeting of Radha and Krishna at Nandagaon.

Krishna says, "Radha, I will be leaving tomorrow morning for Mathura. I have been invited to participate in the Dhanush Yagna."

Radha closes Her eyes and thinks of all that has happened in the past few hours. The entire Nanda Rai household was in a sombre mood. Yashoda, Rohini, and Nanda Rai were dejected after hearing the truth about Krishna's and Balarama's birth and their plan to visit Mathura. The information had reached all the gopis — Lord Krishna would be leaving for Mathura. Radha had heard about it too.

Radha, in Her dreams, saw Krishna leaving for Mathura. She had woken up and was filled with sadness. She knows that what She saw was not just a dream, but would soon be reality. He had requested Her to bid Him goodbye before he left. She had agreed. Krishna had brought Her to the first floor. They are facing each other, near the two mantapas.

Radha now opens Her eyes and breaks the silence, *"If you are just going for the Dhanush Yagna, then why don't you return after the week-long celebrations?"*

Krishna replies, *"The Dhanush Yagna is just an excuse to get Me to Mathura."*

Radha is puzzled and Krishna realises that the time has come to explain everything to Radha. He tells her everything, starting from the truth about His birth right up to the reason for Akroor's visit to Nandagaon.

Radha listens to the whole story in awe. She had never realised Her beloved cowherd Krishna, whom She affectionately called Kanha, was a prince by birth and the future king of Mathura.

She begins to cry and says, *"Kanha! Oh Kanha! I will not be able to survive this separation."*

She cries and begs Him to stay back. *"All My thoughts, words and actions are immersed in You. I will not be able to bear the pangs of separation."*

Krishna comforts Her, *"Even I will miss You dearly, Beloved Radha."*

Radha says, *"You will not miss Me much because You will be busy with wars, politics, taking care of Your people and kingdom. I will be alone and My only thoughts will be about You."*

Radha wipes away Her tears, looks at Him and asks, *"Will You listen to Your devotees' pleas?"*

Krishna says, *"Yes. I will definitely listen to My devotees, no matter who they are."*

Radha pleads, *"I am Your greatest devotee and I beg You to stay back."*

Krishna's heart melts, seeing Radha's tears forming a puddle near Her feet.

He promises, *"I will not leave this town without Your permission."*

Heaven reverberates with these words. The Gods and the Goddesses are *shocked. They had been waiting for Lord Vishnu to manifest Himself on Earth in the form of Lord Krishna to annihilate evil forces. He was destined to kill Kansa and later, many other evil forces. If Krishna was going to stay back in Nandagaon as a cowherd, then the whole purpose of His birth would be defeated.*

All the Gods and Goddesses come down from the Heavens and pray to Radha and ask Her not to stop Krishna from going to Mathura. They tell Her that Krishna has to go to Mathura and protect the world from evil. They say that each person in the entire world is Her child and She should ensure their protection.

Hearing this, Radha realises that She needs to sacrifice Her own pleasure keeping the interest of the world in mind.

She sighs, "As usual, You have won Kanha. You have managed to have Your way!"

Krishna assures Her, "Don't worry Radha. As soon as I complete My mission of killing Kansa and freeing the citizens of Mathura, I will come back and take You. I will make You the Queen of Mathura."

Radha smiles, "I know that this can never happen. I can never be the Queen of Mathura."

Krishna asks, "Why not? Why can't I make You the Queen of Mathura?"

Radha replies, "I am an innocent and uneducated village milkmaid. What will I do in Mathura?"

Krishna replies, "You will be by My side. I will never leave You alone, even for a moment."

Radha replies, "Oh Kanha! I like Your noble intentions, but I do not think this is feasible. When You were in the villages of Vrindavan and Nandagaon, You were leading the life of a cowherd. You did not have many responsibilities. While the cattle were grazing, You spent Your time playing the flute, playing with Your friends and playing with Me. Please think Kanha, will this be possible in Mathura? It will not. You will be busy performing Your tasks as a Prince. You will not have time for Me. I would feel miserable if You are busy the whole day and I have to just sit alone in the huge empty palace. I have been brought up in the open spaces of Barsana. I like to run and play around in the open fields. I would not like to be confined to the walls of a palace. I want to be a free bird and not live in a golden cage. "*Krishna comforts Her,* "*Oh Radha! Don't worry. I promise to meet You whenever I find the time. I am sure you will start liking life in Mathura.*"

Radha tearfully replies, "*Oh Kanha! For me, You are a cowherd of Vrindavan. You are a naughty Boy playing pranks on everyone. You are the handsome Prince of Vrindavan with whom I fell in love! I think of You wearing peacock feathers in Your hair and playing the divine flute. In my image of You, I can see Myself singing and dancing with You, carefree in the jungles of Brij Bhoomi. The sweet tunes from Your flute fill the air and My dreams. I cannot imagine You wearing princely clothes and seriously working in Mathura. I cannot see my Kanha as the Prince of Mathura. To me, the Kanha of Vrindavan and the Krishna of Mathura are two different persons. I will be a misfit in the palaces of Mathura. I want to stay in the dusty villages of Brij Bhoomi. I want to dance in the forest. I want to swim in the Yamuna. I want to jump around in open spaces. Closed palaces are not for Me.*"

Krishna thinks for a while. He takes a deep breath and says, "*Yes, Radha. As usual, You are right. I too want to see My Radha happy. I do not want to imprison You within the four walls of a Mathura palace. You are the Queen of Brij Bhoomi and You will continue to remain so. People of Brij will worship You before they worship Me. They will always have Your name on their lips.*"

Radha is now weeping. She cries, "*I will sit near the lake and call out Your name. I will wait for the day when I can see the reflection of Your face in the water. I will stroll everyday on the banks of Yamuna calling out 'Kanha! Kanha!' I will sit on the grass in the forest, waiting for You to come and meet Me. I will speak to the trees and the plants. I will narrate to them the story of Our eternal love.*"

Krishna says, "*Oh Radha! Please don't feel so sad. I will come and meet You in Vrindavan one day. Please tell me what You wish for.*"

Radha asks Krishna to make two promises, "*Firstly, You must always reside in My heart and secondly, You must meet Me once before I leave this world.*"

Krishna agrees. He says, "*I promise You that I will always reside in Your heart. Radha and Krishna are one and They are inseparable. Just as the sun and sunlight cannot be separated, Radha and Krishna cannot be separated. People will realise that the only way to win My heart is through You. They will worship You as the means of approaching Me. All the gopis are dear to Me and among them, You are the most dearest to Me."*

Radha is unable to control Her tears. She turns away and swiftly runs out of the door. Krishna watches Her disappear into the thick woods of Nandagaon.

Unable to bear the separation of Radha and Krishna, I walked away and went to the other side of the courtyard. I now realised why the name of Radha always precedes that of Krishna; I also realised the true meaning of the name 'Radhakrishna'.

As I stood on the other side of the courtyard, I could see a narrow muddy road on the other side of the temple. I was told that this was the same road that Akroor used when he took Krishna and Balarama to Mathura.

Krishna and Balarama take leave of Their parents. They fall at their feet and seek their blessings. They hug and bid goodbye to Their friends. Everyone in the town comes to meet Them. The people cry inconsolably, as they watch Them bid goodbye and slowly mount the chariot. The gopis tell Radha that She should stop Krishna from leaving the town. Radha refuses to do this since She has already promised Krishna that She will not stop Him. As the chariot begins to leave town, Krishna and Balarama notice that the path is blocked by the gopis of the town. They refuse to allow the chariot to proceed. All the gopis ask Akroor to leave Krishna alone. Krishna gets down from His chariot and tells the gopis that if they really love Him, they must not prevent Him from proceeding to perform His duties. He tells them that those who genuinely love should support the lover and help Him accomplish His goal and not become an obstacle in His way. He says that supreme love should be selfless love and it should be above all mundane needs. Hearing all this, the gopis make way for Them.

Radha is standing behind a tree and watching this. She knows that She may never meet Her Beloved Kanha again. Her eyes are full of tears, but She does not cry. However, all the birds and animals are unable to bear the separation of Radha and Krishna and they begin to cry. Radha silently walks back alone towards Barsana, never to set Her foot again in Nandagaon.

As I stood watching the muddy road leading to Mathura, I realised that even a Divine Couple like Radha and Krishna had to respect destiny. My mind was filled with thoughts about how They experienced the pangs of separation and tried to overcome it. Thoughtfully, I slowly walked back towards my car.

14

Mathura Revisited

...

"*atasya hi dhruvo mrutyur dhruvam janma mrutyusya cha,*
Tasmadapariharye arthe na tvam shochithumarhasi"

("One who is born is sure to die and one who dies is sure to take rebirth. In matters that are inevitable, you should not lament.")

(*Bhagavad Gita* 2.27)

AKROOR GHAT

Akroor Ghat is on the Mathura-Vrindavan highway, on the outskirts of both towns. While going from Mathura to Vrindavan, just before Pagal Baba Mandir, we saw a signboard indicating a right turn for Akroor Ghat. Once we took the turn, we found the temple on our right. As in the case of many other Vrindavan ghats, here too, the Yamuna

Idols of Krishna, Balarama, and Akroor

had moved away by a few kilometres, so there was no water at the ghat.

The temple has an idol of Akroor, flanked by idols of Krishna and Balarama. This temple is dedicated to the famous incident that took place here 5000 years ago.

Krishna and Balarama are accompanying Akroor in his chariot from Nandagaon to Mathura. They have just tearfully waved goodbye to Yashoda, Nanda Rai, Rohini, and hundreds of villagers in Nandagaon.

Akroor notices that Balarama is asking him many questions regarding the distance that they need to cover, the kind of reception They may receive at Mathura, the speed of the chariot, and the breed of the horses. These are questions that are worthy of a prince. However, Krishna is talking about how much He misses His parents Yashoda and Nanda Rai. How much He misses Radha. How much He misses the gopis.

Akroor keeps wondering, is this Boy really the Supreme Lord? Is He the same person who has killed numerous demons? Is He the same person who is destined to kill Kansa and free the people of Mathura from his tyranny? He seems to be more immersed in materialistic attachments and bonds. His older Brother talks like a real prince. He asks me questions worthy of a prince. However, Krishna seems to be more of a lover than a warrior. Is He really the Supreme Lord?

Krishna, who is omniscient, knows what is going on in Akroor's mind and smiles at him.

Akroor talks about the tough days ahead in Mathura and the Supreme Lord smiles and asks him not to worry. Akroor does not feel comforted, in spite of Krishna's reassuring words and wonders if this young Boy is really the Supreme Lord and if He can kill Kansa. Krishna continues to smile, knowing very well the thoughts that are crossing Akroor's mind.

Just before reaching Mathura, they reach the banks of River Yamuna. The hot sun has taken its toll on Akroor who feels very exhausted. He decides to refresh himself with a bath in the river.

He asks Krishna and Balarama, "I am going for a bath, would You also like to join me?"

They both reply in unison, "No. We will wait for you in the chariot while you bathe."

Akroor gets down from the chariot and proceeds to the banks of the river. He steps into the waters and takes a dip. As he lifts his head, the scene in front of him stuns him. He sees the river has turned into a huge ocean and Lord Vishnu is reclining on a huge Serpent (Lord Seshanag). He notices that the face of Lord Vishnu is the same as that of Lord Krishna and the face of Lord Seshanag is the same as that of Lord Balarama!

Akroor thinks, something must be wrong. I have just left Them in the chariot on the dusty road. How can They be now in this lake? Moreover, how did the river transform into such a huge ocean? Am I in Mathura or in Vaikunta, the Holy Abode of Lord Vishnu?"

He decides to verify this and so comes out of the river. In his dripping wet clothes, he rushes to his chariot and sees Krishna and Balarama seated, waiting for him to return. Both of Them smile at him innocently. Akroor is relieved. He is convinced that he was just imagining things. He goes back to the river to complete his bath. He once again immerses himself in the water. As he lifts his head, he sees that once again the river has turned into a huge ocean and a huge snake (Lord Seshanag) is floating on the water while Lord Vishnu reclines on it. He notices once again that the face of Lord Vishnu is the same as that of Lord Krishna and the face of Lord Seshanag is the same as Lord Balarama. He decides to once again verify the truth of what he is seeing, so comes out of the lake. He rushes to his chariot and sees Krishna and Balarama still seated. Both of Them once again smile at him. By now, he is absolutely bewildered. How could two people be present at different places at the same time? Why is Lord Vishnu's face the same as that of Lord Krishna? Why does the Serpent King Seshanag have the face of Lord Balarama? What's happening?

He goes back to the river to complete his bath. He is convinced that he was hallucinating. He immerses himself in the water once again. As he lifts his head, he notices that for the third time, the divine spectacle has occurred! This time Akroor begins to pray to the Supreme Lord and asks him to remove the mask from his face and mind. Lord Vishnu smiles at Akroor and says that He will show him all His avataras (incarnations). He shows Akroor all His different incarnations Matsya, Kurma, Varaha, Narasimha, Vamana, Parashurama, and Rama and finally, Krishna. Akroor is stunned to see all the avataras of the Supreme Lord in quick succession. The divine light emanating from each avatara and the power displayed by them dazzles him. He realises that the two Boys sitting in his chariot are no ordinary Children, but the Supreme Lord and the Lord of the Serpents. He immediately rushes towards the chariot. Krishna and Balarama are still sitting in the chariot.

Krishna innocently asks him, "Oh Akroorji! I noticed you coming out of your bath and rushing towards Us three times. Please tell Me what is bothering you. Why did you interrupt your bath thrice?"

Akroor begins to weep. He bows and falls at the lotus feet of the Lord.

He says, "Oh Supreme Lord, You know everything. Why do You ask me this? You knew what was going on in my mind during the journey from Nandagaon. You knew the doubts that I had about You and this is Your way of removing the mask from over my eyes. You are the protector of the entire universe and I was stupid not to realise who You are. All along, I doubted Your capabilities and was trying to protect You. Please forgive me, Oh Divine One!"

The Supreme Lord affectionately smiles at Akroor and blesses him. The chariot resumes its journey and proceeds towards Mathura. This time, Akroor is very confident. He knows Mathura will soon be in safe hands.

Can you think of a place on Earth where a more divine incident took place? A place where Lord Vishnu showed his devotees all his divine incarnations? You would feel sorry that such a holy place has been forgotten by most of the locals, and devotees. This place is not only deserted, but also poorly maintained. There are many wild plants and weeds growing on the hillock. For an ignorant traveller passing by, this is just another hillock in Brij Bhoomi.

RANG BHOOMI

Rang Bhoomi was where Lord Krishna killed His maternal uncle Kansa and freed the residents of Mathura from his tyrannical rule. In Kansa's time, there was a huge wrestling arena here. Today a temple stands here. The temple is appropriately known as Rangeshwar Temple. I saw lots of devotees sitting here and singing *bhajans*. I slowly closed my eyes in reverence. Shouts of 'Kanhaiya ki Jai! Baldev ki Jai' filled the air.

'Kanhaiya ki Jai! Baldev ki Jai', these chants fill the skies of Mathura. Krishna and Balarama have arrived in Mathura. Their arrival has aroused the interest of everyone here. People want to see what their Saviour looks like. As Krishna and Balarama enter the town, all the villagers flock outside and watch Them. Kansa asks his men to inform Akroor that arrangements have been made for Krishna and Balarama to stay in a palace built for visiting

kings and princes.

Kansa tells his minister, "Now that Krishna has reached my kingdom, He is in my clutches. I will kill Him tonight in His sleep."

His minister says, "Oh Mighty King! Let me take the liberty and courage to differ. The people of Mathura are looking up to Krishna as their Saviour, so killing Him would provoke them. The best thing would be to make someone else kill Him so that you would not be blamed, and the people will not be suspicious."

Kansa nods his head. He says, "Now that you have given me this idea, tell me also how to implement it. Who can kill Him?"

His minister says, "Kuvalayapida is the biggest and the strongest elephant in your kingdom. It should be made to drink intoxicating juices through the whole night. In the morning, the barn door should be opened and Krishna should be made to stand at the entrance. The elephant, in an intoxicated state will attack the first person he sees when he comes out of the barn door. He will trample Krishna to death."

Kansa laughs, "Ah! This sounds like a great idea! Instruct your men to carry out this at once."

The whole night, the royal bodyguards feed the elephant intoxicating food and drinks. They hope that by the next morning, the elephant, in its inebriated state, will attack Krishna.

The next day Akroor meets Krishna and Balarama and leads Them through the streets of Mathura. The whole town is singing loudly and cheering on Krishna and Balarama. The royal guards open the barn door that houses the intoxicated elephant, Kuvalayapida. It is let loose and it begins to attack everyone in the streets. It proceeds to where Krishna and Balarama are walking. Krishna runs swiftly towards the intoxicated elephant and attacks it. The elephant counter-attacks, but it is no match for the Supreme Lord. They struggle with each other and the elephant lifts Krishna and tries to throw Him down, but it does not succeed. Krishna lifts the elephant up and with one heave, throws him into the sky. The elephant soars high into the sky and falls down with a heavy thud. The intoxicated elephant Kuvalayapida is dead. The spectators bow to the Supreme Lord and shout, "Glory to Lord Krishna! Glory to Lord Balarama!"

Krishna and Balarama decide to take a walk. They come across a *woman with a hump. Her name is Trivartaka. The lady is carrying different kinds of perfumes to the palace. Krishna stops her. He says, "Oh beautiful lady! Please tell me who you are and where you are going."*

Trivartaka slowly turns around. Her hump prevents her from turning swiftly. She sees Krishna and Balarama standing close by. Behind them there are hundreds of residents of Mathura. She becomes angry. She thinks, who are these two young Boys? How dare they make fun of me. They look so handsome and divine, but utter such mocking words.

She tells Him, "Both of You look like princes. However what you say does not befit You. How can You call such an ugly person as myself beautiful? You are in no way different from the other residents of Mathura."

Krishna replies with His usual innocence, "Oh Beautiful Lady! I mean what I said. People look at the exterior self and call you ugly. I look at everyone's inner soul. You have a beautiful soul. However, you have an unfortunate hump on your back because of a curse."

Trivartaka stands still, wondering who this handsome Boy is to speak with such authority.

Krishna asks her, "Where are you going?"

She replies, "I prepare the royal perfumes. I go to the palace everyday to give them the perfume that I have prepared."

Krishna says, "Why don't you apply some perfume to My body?"

She agrees. She applies the perfume to Krishna's body. As soon as her hand touches His divine body, her hump vanishes. She turns into a beautiful woman. She falls at the lotus feet of the Lord.

She cries with joy and asks Him, "Oh Lord! You are no ordinary Soul. Please tell me who You are."

Krishna informs her, "I am Krishna, Son of Devaki and Vasudev. You were born as Shabari in your previous birth. You were my devotee during My incarnation as Lord Rama."

In the meanwhile, Kansa is making arrangements for the Dhanush Yagna. His men fetch the divine bow and keep it in front of him. This was the bow that was gifted by Lord Shiva to Lord Parshurama, who in turn had gifted the bow to Kansa's ancestors.

Kansa looks at the head priest and asks him, "Oh Holy One! Where should we keep this bow?"

The head priest replies, "Oh Emperor! You need to ensure that the bow is not broken before the Dhanush Yagna. It is said that if anyone breaks the bow before the auspicious event, the person who breaks it will be the ultimate destroyer of the person performing the Dhanush Yagna. Today, you are forming the Yagna."

Kansa ponders over this for a while and then thunders to his guards, "Put up a pedestal near Rang Bhoomi. Keep this bow on the pedestal. Let security guards surround it. I want the bow to be closely guarded through day and night. Keep a tight vigil over it."

The security guards carry out the king's instructions. The bow is kept on a newly built pedestal. The entire place is cordoned off, security guards patrol every inch of the grounds.

Krishna and Balarama are walking in the streets of Mathura. Krishna tells Akroor's men, "I have heard a lot about the bow that is going to be used for the Dhanush Yagna. I have heard that this was gifted by Lord Shiva to Lord Parashurama who ultimately gifted it to My ancestors. Can I take a look at it?"

Akroor's men bow and say, "Oh Lord! This may not be possible since the bow is heavily guarded. It is believed that if the bow is broken before the Dhanush Yagna then the person who breaks the bow will kill the person performing the yagna. So Kansa is scared."

Krishna laughs, "Let us see! I would like to go to where the bow is kept."

Akroor's men lead Krishna and Balarama to Rang Bhoomi where the bow is kept under heavy guard.

They manage to enter the hall and stand before the bow. They pay their respects to the idol of Lord Shiva nearby. Krishna asks the security guards, "May I lift this bow?"

The security guards laugh. One of them mocks Him, "Oh Young Boy! Who are You? How dare You come inside? How can You even dream of lifting this heavy bow? It took more than twenty strong security guards just to lift it and carry it to this spot."

Krishna smiles at them. Even as the guards watch Him, He walks towards the bow and lifts it up in one swift action. He bends the bow till it breaks into two. He keeps the two broken pieces in front of Lord Shiva and bows. There is a stunned silence inside the hall. The guards panic. They know that they will have to face Kansa's wrath for allowing trespassers inside and *not protecting the bow. They attack Krishna and Balarama. A big fight ensues but the security guards are no match for Krishna and Balarama. They are defeated in a matter of a few minutes. The news of the broken bow spreads. All the people are now more than convinced that their Saviour has arrived.*

Kansa also hears this news. He is very angry. He has also heard about Kuvalayapida's death. He has heard people narrate how the young Boy easily overcame the mightiest of all elephants.

He shouts at the security guards, "You fools! I assigned you to such a simple task. All I asked you to do was to guard the divine bow from everyone. You could not even accomplish this!"

His head priest says, "Oh King! As the head priest of your kingdom, it is my duty to advise you on matters that are critical to you and your kingdom. Keeping in mind your safety, I would like to make a suggestion."

Kansa glares at him "Go ahead. What do you suggest?"

The head priest says, "Oh King! Please do not continue to foster this enmity with Krishna. Instead, take His protection. Since Krishna has broken the divine bow, He must be the one who is destined to kill you. Lord Krishna is the incarnation of Lord Vishnu. Oh King! Please recognise Him and take refuge in His lotus feet. He is the all merciful Lord. He will forgive your sins. He will pardon you."

Hearing this, Kansa is furious.

He shouts to his security guards, "This person is a traitor. Anyone speaking against the king is a traitor. Throw him into the prison."

It is another bright day in Mathura. People are excitedly talking about the broken bow and about the way Krishna cured Trivartaka of her ugly hump. No one has the courage to discuss all this openly, fearing Kansa and his men. So, small groups in different parts of the city are discussing the events of the past few days.

"He has broken the bow. He is destined to kill Kansa and free us from his tyranny."

"I heard that He is the incarnation of none other than Lord Vishnu."

"I heard that He killed the strongest elephant in Mathura with one mighty blow."

"Do you know he cured Trivartaka's hump? Just by a mere touch."

"Will He become the King of Mathura after He kills Kansa?"

Kansa too is getting ready for the big day. He is feeling apprehensive since he has heard many stories about Krishna. He has heard about Krishna killing Putana, Kakasura, Trinavarta, Bakasura, Aghasura, and many other strong demons. The list of his victories seems to be endless.

Kansa arrives at Rang Bhoomi, the quadrangular arena for the wrestling match. Kansa enters the special area from where only the king and his royal family will watch the match. This has bigger and better seats. The seats here are decorated with flowers. Kansa takes his seat and looks around him. Krishna and Balarama also arrive at the arena, followed by many of their followers chanting 'Glory to Lord Krishna', 'Glory to Balarama'. Every one in the arena sees Lord Krishna in a different form. The wrestlers see Him as a warrior. The young girls see Him as a handsome Boy. The older women see Him as an Infant. His devotees see Him as Lord Vishnu. And Kansa? He sees Him as the God of Death!

Kansa asks Krishna, "I have invited many wrestlers from different parts of my kingdom. With whom will you fight?"

Krishna remains silent. He turns around and finds hundreds of strong wrestlers standing at one end of the quadrangle. Many of them are flexing their muscles and showing off their well-toned bodies.

Kansa and his men ask Him the same question repeatedly. Krishna still remains silent.

Kansa taunts, "You are supposed to be the greatest warrior of Brij Bhoomi and it is rumoured that you have killed many demons, but it looks like You are scared now. You do not have the courage to pick any of these professional wrestlers."

Krishna knows that He is being provoked by Kansa and his men.

He replies, "Oh Kansa! I am a small Boy, how can I fight the greatest of your warriors?"

At once, a big debate ensues. The followers of Lord Krishna agree with Him that He is a small Boy so He must not fight with such warriors. However Kansa's men think otherwise. A fight starts between Krishna's followers and Kansa's men. Krishna, seeing this, decides to put an end to this fight. He steps forward and says, "I am ready to fight with any warrior."

A warrior steps forward and attacks the unarmed Krishna with all his might. They exchange hefty blows. However, the wrestler is no match for the Supreme Lord Krishna who overpowers and defeats him with great ease. Instantly, another warrior steps forward and attacks Balarama. Balarama shows the audience why He is believed to have the strength of a thousand elephants. With one mighty blow, He subdues His opponent. Krishna and Balarama both emerge victorious. Kansa keeps sending more wrestlers into the arena. However, one by one, they are all defeated by Krishna and Balarama. Each time a warrior is defeated there is a huge roar from the audience, followed by chants of 'Glory to Lord Krishna! Glory to Lord Balarama!'

The only wrestlers left now are Chanur and Musthika. They are the royal wrestlers who have been pampered by Kansa. Unlike the other wrestlers who stood at one end of the crowded quadrangle, these two are sitting in the 'Royal Box' reserved for the king and his family. Unlike the other wrestlers who wore only a loin cloth, these two are draped in the finest shawls, embroidered with gold and silver threads. Kansa has taken good care of them. It is now their turn to return his favours.

Both of them throw the shawls off their mighty shoulders. The audience takes in the sight of their muscular bodies. Both of them step into the arena.

Chanur roars at Krishna, "I will fight You and finish You off."

Akroor and his men begin to protest.

"He is too young."

"Fight someone your own size."

"He is not a professional wrestler like you."

Chanur is enjoying this. He glares at Krishna, "Do You agree with what they say? Don't You have the courage to face me?"

Akroor pleads with Krishna, "Please don't get provoked. Please do not fight him."

Krishna turns around and notices Chanur approaching him like a wild beast approaching its prey. Krishna lifts His head defiantly and looks at the mighty figure standing in front of Him. He looks into his eyes and says, "I will fight you."

Musthika, who has been watching all this, does not want to miss out on the fun. He approaches Lord Balarama and asks Him, "What about You? Do You want to fight me? Are You scared? Why don't You return to Vrindavan and play with Your cowherd friends?"

Lord Balarama is wild with fury. He is upset to hear Chanur taunting His brother. Now Musthika is taunting Him. He shouts, "Oh Haughty One! I am ready to fight you. Be ready to get killed."

Krishna dashes towards Chanur and Balarama towards Musthika. It is a sight to behold. Krishna and Balarama are small Boys in sharp contrast to the huge and burly figures of Chanur and Musthika. Krishna locks His arms with Chanur's. Chanur tries to push Krishna down, but cannot move Him an inch. He tries to crush Krishna in his mighty arms, but this is impossible. Suddenly Krishna begins to run around.

Chanur roars in anger, "You coward! Where are You running off to? Are You going to Gokul? Or Vrindavan? If You have the courage to wrestle, come and fight me."

Saying this, Chanur rushes towards Krishna. He bends his head and tries to ram against His stomach. However, Krishna is too swift for him. He evades this blow. Chanur goes crashing into the wooden barricades and falls down. There is a huge roar of appreciation from the audience.

In the meanwhile, Lord Balarama has caught hold of Musthika. He twists his arms back in a knot. He aims one mighty kick on Musthika's back; Musthika goes crashing down. The spectators are now clapping wildly and cheering the two Boys on. "Krishna! Balarama! Glory to both of You!"

Chanur has fallen down near the wooden barricades. He tries to get up but the weight of his body prevents him from doing so easily. Krishna is standing close to him. Before Chanur can get up, Krishna is on him in a flash. He is sitting on Chanur. He delivers powerful blows all over Chanur's body, not allowing him to recover. He holds Chanur by his neck and bends it with such force that the entire wrestling arena reverberates with the sound of the breaking bones. Chanur's dead face sends shivers down Kansa's spine.

Balarama, not to be outdone, rains mighty blows on Musthika's chest. Using His divine strength, he pulls at Musthika's limbs which come apart. Mushtika is unable to bear the pain and screams in agony. Balarama lands one final punch on his head. Musthika falls dead to the ground.

The audience once again screams with joy, "Victory to Lord Krishna! Victory to Lord Balarama!"

Kansa, finding that he is the only person left, challenges Krishna to a fight.

Krishna says, "You are my maternal uncle. I am still ready to forgive you if you seek My refuge."

However, the arrogant Kansa is beyond reason. He jumps from his seat into the arena and attacks Krishna. Krishna proves to the people why He is the Lord of the three worlds. Kansa tries his best to hold Krishna's arms, but he is no match for the Supreme Lord. Lord Krishna delivers one mighty blow after another. He throws Kansa to the ground and jumps on him. He twists his mighty arms and breaks his limbs. Kansa can see death approaching him in the form of Lord Yama, the God of Death.

He tells Kansa, "Oh King! You have led a tyrannical life. You have caused great grief to the citizens of Mathura. You have brought grief to your father. You have imprisoned him, Devaki and Vasudev. How could you dream of avoiding punishment for such unforgivable sins? You have committed the biggest of all sins in not recognising who Lord Krishna is. He is the incarnation of Lord Vishnu, the Supreme Lord of the Universe."

Saying this, Yama, the God of Death folds his hands and bows respectfully to Lord Krishna. Lord Krishna blesses Him.

Kansa begins to see the face of Lord Vishnu in the face of Lord Krishna. He realises that Lord Krishna is none other than the Supreme Lord Narayana. Alas, he has realised his mistake too late, and he takes his last breath. Gods and Goddesses from the Heaven arrive and worship Lord Krishna and adorn Him with garlands of flowers. Lord Krishna blesses the people in the arena. The air is filled with loud chants of 'Kanhaiya ki Jai! Baldev ki Jai'.

I opened my eyes.

The *puja* was over and the priest was distributing *prasada*.

He smiled at me and asked, "Where were you lost?"

I smiled back, "Kansa is dead. Kanhaiya ki Jai! Baldev ki Jai!"

The priest laughed, "Then, it is time to rest at Vishram Ghat." And he walked away.

VISHRAM GHAT

Vishram Ghat is considered to be the most important among

the 25 ghats in Mathura. It is at Vishram Ghat that the traditional Parikrama of Brij Bhoomi starts and ends. This sacred ghat is on the banks of River Yamuna. Each evening, aarti is performed and hundreds of devotees light and place small oil lamps in the river. These floating lamps look like twinkling stars in the sky on a clear night. Vishram Ghat is lined with many

Devotees at the entrance to Vishram Ghat

temples on one side and the River Yamuna on the other.

As I walked towards Vishram Ghat, I was still trying to comprehend the priest's parting remark. What had Kansa's defeat have to do with Vishram Ghat, I wondered.

The news of Kansa's death has reached the streets of Mathura. People come out of their houses and for the first time in many years, rejoice openly and speak against the tyrannical king. There are shouts of joy everywhere.

"The evil Kansa is dead."

"Long live Lord Krishna."

"Long live Lord Balarama."

"Glory to Lord Krishna and Lord Balarama."

Krishna knows that His mission is not yet accomplished. Along with Balarama and the bodyguards, He rushes to the prison cell where Devaki and Vasudev have been imprisoned. Both of Them bow before Devaki and Vasudev and free them from their handcuffs and chains.

Krishna says, "Please forgive me. I know that I am the cause of all your grief and hardships that you had to bear all these years."

Devaki and Vasudev do not reply, but hug their two children and weep.

Krishna and Balarama now head towards the prison where Their grandfather Ugrasena has been imprisoned by Kansa. They enter the cell and bow to Their grandfather and free him from his chains.

Ugrasena asks Krishna and Balarama, "Oh Handsome Boys! Please tell me who You are? How were You allowed to come inside the prison cell? Didn't Kansa's men prevent you from entering?"

Krishna introduces Balarama and Himself as the seventh and eighth Sons of Devaki and Vasudev. He narrates the events of the past few days, including the killing of Kansa. Ugrasena is surprised to hear this, since he has been under the impression that all of Devaki and Vasudev's sons had been killed. Krishna narrates to him the events that followed Balarama's and His birth. He narrates how both of Them grew up secretly in different towns in Brij Bhoomi at Nanda Rai's house to escape the clutches of Kansa. Ugrasena is overjoyed. His Grandchildren, whom he had assumed dead, have come back! He hugs Them and They seek his blessings.

Krishna is now feeling contented. He has accomplished His mission for which He had visited Mathura. His evil uncle Kansa is dead. Ugrasena has become the king once more. His parents Devaki and Vasudev have been freed. It has been a hectic week for Him. He decides to go to a quiet place and rest. As He walks along the banks of River Yamuna, He finds a secluded ghat with no one around. It is far away from the dusty roads and noisy lanes of the town. He is away from the jubilant men, women, and children who are still rejoicing the recent turn of events. He sits on the banks of the Yamuna and rests. The Gods and Goddesses from Heaven bow in reverence and chant the holy names of the God. They shower Him with garlands made of celestial flowers.

Since this is the ghat where Lord Krishna rested after killing Kansa, it is known as Vishram Ghat. *Vishram* means 'to take rest'.

It is also believed that Lord Vishnu, in His third incarnation as Lord Varaha, the boar, rested here after killing the demon Hiranyaksha. This happened thousands of years before He incarnated for the eighth time as Lord Krishna.

The 12 ghats to the north of Vishram Ghat include Ganesh Ghat, Dashashwamedh Ghat, Saraswati Sangam Ghat, Chakratirtha Ghat, Krishnaganga Ghat, Somatirth (Swami) Ghat, Ghantagharan Ghat, Dharapattan Ghat, Vaikunta Ghat, Navatirtha (Varahakshetra) Ghat, Asikunda Ghat, and Manikarnika Ghat. To the south, there are 11 ghats — Guptatirth

Ghat, Prayag Ghat, Shyam Ghat, Ram Ghat, Kankhal Ghat, Dhruva Ghat, Saptrishi Ghat, Mokshatirth Ghat, Surya Ghat, Ravan Koti Ghat, and Buddha Ghat.

THE JOURNEY

Jarasandha, Kansa's father-in-law is upset for two reasons. First, his son-in-law has been killed by his sworn enemy, Krishna. Secondly, Krishna has become very popular because of His mystical powers, strength, and diplomacy. He wants to avenge his son-in-law's death and so decides to invade Mathura and kill Krishna and Balarama.

Jarasandha arrives on the outskirts of Mathura kingdom with his huge army. The news reaches the court of King Ugrasena.

King Ugrasena calls for a meeting of all his ministers and Krishna.

He asks them, "What should we do now? Jarasandha has arrived on the outskirts of Mathura with his huge army. Our army is no match for his. I am afraid we will lose the battle."

Krishna tells Ugrasena, "Oh King! Please allow Me and Balarama to go and fight Jarasandha. We will return victorious."

Ugrasena agrees and blesses Krishna and Balarama.

Krishna and Balarama reach the battlefield with Their army. A fierce battle ensues. Though Jarasandha has a bigger army, he and his army are no match for Krishna. He is defeated and humiliated in the battle. Bruised and wounded, he returns to his kingdom. His army is also in disarray. The next day, he calls his ministers to court.

Jarasandha says, "I am very upset the way we lost this battle. We had a much bigger and stronger army than Krishna's. I am now even more determined to defeat Krishna. I want to avenge this defeat soon."

He prepares for another battle with Krishna. He attacks Mathura with an army bigger than the one before. However, once again he and his men suffer a humiliating defeat. He returns once again empty-handed to his kingdom.

Jarasandha thus attacks Mathura 17 times and he is defeated each time.

Jarasandha asks Shishupal for advice. Shishupal is Krishna's bitter enemy inspite of being his cousin. He is a close friend of Jarasandha whom he considers his mentor.

Shishupal arrives in Jarasandha's court and bows to him.

With folded hands, he says, "Oh Mighty King! Please give me your command."

Jarasandha says, "Shishupal! You are aware that Krishna has humiliated me 17 times. I am at a loss now. Please tell me what I should do."

Shishupal replies, "I have a plan to defeat Krishna."

Jarasandha says, "Please tell me about it immediately. Any idea to defeat Krishna would be welcome."

Shishupal asks, "Have you heard of Kal Yavan?"

Jarasandha replies, "No, I haven't. Please tell me."

Shishupal narrates, "Kal Yavan has the blessings of Lord Shiva. No weapon can destroy him. Neither God nor demon can defeat him. He is our neighbouring king and also a sworn enemy of Krishna. We must seek his help."

Jarasandha is pleased to hear this.

He says, "Please invite Kal Yavan with full honours."

Kal Yavan is invited to Jarasandha's kingdom. He arrives and meets Jarasandha and Shishupal. He is equally pleased with the prospect of having to fight Krishna.

He proudly says, "Oh Jarasandha! Have no fear when I am with you. I have the blessings of Lord Shiva. Even Krishna's Sudarshan Chakra cannot touch me."

Jarasandha is pleased to hear this. He nods his head menacingly and shouts "I am now ready to attack Mathura for the eighteenth time."

Jarasandha and Kal Yavan reach the outskirts of Mathura. Their armies camp near the border of Mathura kingdom.

The news of their arrival reaches Krishna. Krishna is also aware of Kal Yavan's blessings from Lord Shiva. He realises that He needs a different strategy to counter Kal Yavan.

Krishna calls Akroor.

Akroor arrives and with folded hands, asks respectfully, "Oh Lord! What is your command?"

Krishna tells him, "Please ask the entire Mathura army to surround and guard the kingdom."

Akroor is puzzled. He asks, "If the entire army guards the kingdom then who will accompany you? I have asked them to get ready for battle."

Krishna smiles, "I do not need any army. I intend to go alone."

If Krishna had said this a few years earlier, Akroor would have probably argued and protested. Not any longer. He knows that Lord Krishna is Lord Vishnu Himself. He knows that He does not need any army to help Him. He knows the entire world is under His control.

Akroor just nods his head and bows respectfully.

Obeying Akroor's instructions, the entire army surrounds Mathura. Krishna walks out of the city gates alone, closing the huge city gates behind Him.

Jarasandha and Kal Yavan are standing outside the city with their huge army. They are surprised to see Krishna come out of the city all alone.

Kal Yavan shouts at Krishna, "I admire Your bravery coming out alone like this. Tell me what weapon You choose to fight me with. I will use the same weapon."

Krishna replies, "I do not want to fight using any weapons, because I know that no weapon can harm you."

Kal Yavan is surprised. He says, "In spite of knowing this, You have come to fight me! I admire Your courage."

Krishna tells him, "I have come alone to fight you with bare hands. If you are brave and courageous, you should also fight Me alone. You should not attack Me with your army."

Kal Yavan thinks for a few minutes. Finally he replies, "Yes. I agree. It is fair that we fight each other without using our armies."

Krishna says, "Good. Please follow Me. We will go to a lonely place where the army cannot watch us."

Kal Yavan agrees. He gets down from his chariot and follows Krishna.

Krishna begins to walk in the opposite direction and Kal Yavan walks a few feet behind Him.

Both have now reached a lonely place. Suddenly Krishna begins to run. Kal Yavan is taken by surprise. He too starts running, but he cannot match Krishna's speed. The distance between the two gradually begins to increase.

Kal Yavan is furious. He is unable to keep pace with Krishna. In desperation, he begins to shout, "Come back you coward. Come back. You have tricked me. You said You wanted to fight me alone, but now, I see that You are fleeing from the battlefield. You are a 'Ranchod' (One who has fled from the battlefield)."

Krishna is unperturbed by his taunts. He keeps running. After a while, he reaches a mountainous area. He runs in between the rocks and finds Himself standing in front of a cave. He enters the dark cave.

Kal Yavan too reaches the entrance of the cave. He shouts, "Oh Krishna! No one can save You now! I will block the cave entrance so that You cannot escape."

Saying this Kal Yavan enters the cave and closes the entrance from inside with a huge boulder. Once the entrance is closed, it becomes even darker inside. The cave has many rooms and Kal Yavan goes from room to room in hot pursuit of Krishna.

In the meanwhile, Krishna enters the room where Muchukunda is sleeping.

Muchukunda has a blessing from Lord Indra that if anyone disturbs his sleep and if he opens his eyes then the person who has disturbed him will turn to ashes. Krishna, the All Knowing is fully aware of Lord Indra's boon and wants to use it to His advantage.

Krishna removes a garment from His shoulder and covers the sleeping Muchukunda with it. He looks around and finds a suitable place to hide Himself.

Kal Yavan is wild with anger. He is still looking for Krishna.

He shouts, "You coward. You think You can save Yourself from me? Come out and I will spare Your life."

A long silence follows. Kal Yavan has now reached the room where Muchukunda is sleeping. He sees someone sleeping and since Krishna's upper garment covers the sleeping body, he assumes that it is Krishna Himself.

He screams with joy, "Oh Krishna! I found You at last. You thought You were very smart, didn't You?"

Saving this, he kicks the sleeper.

Muchukunda is rudely awakened thus. He falls down because of the mighty kick. He gets up and glares at Kal Yavan. Kal Yavan is stunned. He does not know what is happening. He had come here to catch Krishna. He found someone sleeping covered with Krishna's garment. However, this is not Krishna. He seems to be an aged king. Who is this? Where is Krishna?

Muchukunda asks him, "Are you the one who destroyed my sleep?"

Kal Yavan just stands and stares. Slowly, he mutters, "Yes, but...."

Muchukunda roars, "That's enough. Say no more. I curse you to death."

Within seconds, Kal Yavan is reduced to ashes. Lord Indra's boon to Muchukunda has been realised. Krishna has witnessed this. He slowly comes out of his hiding place.

Muchukunda turns around and finds Krishna standing near by. There is a golden glow surrounding Him.

Muchukunda sees the glow and realises that the Person near him is no ordinary mortal. He bows his head and asks, "Oh Holy One! You must be some God. Pray, tell me who You are!"

Krishna smiles and replies, "I am known by many names. Some call me Krishna. Some call me Vasudev. I come to Earth whenever it is necessary to protect righteousness."

Muchukunda once again bows before Lord Krishna and seeks His blessings. Lord Krishna blesses him and both of them walk out of the cave.

Krishna walks back towards the battlefield. He finds Jarasandha and his men waiting impatiently. They had seen Krishna exchange a few words with Kal Yavan. They had seen Krishna walk away from the battlefield. They had seen Kal Yavan following Him. After that, nothing had happened. They still have no clue what has happened.

Krishna knows that in spite of Kal Yavan's death, Jarasandha will not stop attacking Mathura. He feels sorry that during each siege hundreds of innocent warriors are killed.

Lord Krishna uses His divine powers to summon Lord Balarama. Lord Balarama arrives in His chariot.

He tells Balarama, "I think the time has come for Us to move on. We must leave Mathura and establish another kingdom. Jarasandha is frequently attacking Mathura because We are here. Each time, thousands of innocent soldiers from both sides get killed, or injured. There is only one solution to prevent this. If we leave Mathura, then Jarasandha will stop attacking Mathura. This way, We can save the lives of many innocent soldiers."

Balarama agrees. He says, "As You wish. Decide where You want to go. I will accompany You."

Krishna decides to establish His new kingdom in the middle of the sea. This way, His citizens can be safe from Jarasandha's attacks. He calls Vishwakarma, the Heavenly Architect.

Vishwakarma bows in front of Him, "Oh Lord! What is Your wish?"

Krishna says, "Vishwakarma! I want You to build a city for Me. It should be the most beautiful place on Earth. It should be like Heaven on Earth."

Vishwakarma bows, "As you wish, My Lord!"

Krishna stands on the seashore and calls out to the Sea God. The Sea God arrives and bows respectfully.

Krishna says, "I plan to construct a city in the middle of the sea. Please give Me some land."

The Sea God is thrilled. He says, "Oh Supreme Lord of the entire Universe! It is indeed a privilege that You have chosen Me as the spot for Your Divine Abode. I could not have been more blessed than this."

Saying this, the Sea God removes water in the middle of the sea so that an island is formed.

He says, "Oh Lord! Please use this island as Your abode. It will be very safe since it is surrounded by water on all sides."

Vishwakarma using his divine powers, builds Dwarka, the most beautiful place on Earth. The city has many palaces and beautiful houses. There is greenery everywhere. Beautiful gardens and parks soon fill the empty places.

Vishwakarma's task is now over. He meets Krishna and informs Him about His success.

Lord Krishna thanks and blesses Him. He knows there is still one more task to be completed. He calls Goddess Yogamaya.

Goddess Yogamaya comes and bows in front of Him.

Krishna tells her, "Oh Yogamaya. Jarasandha has surrounded the entire city of Mathura. I know that there are many in Mathura who want to accompany Me and stay with Me in Dwarka. However, Jarasandha and his men will not allow them to come out of Mathura. Using Your divine powers, please transport those citizens to Dwarka."

Yogamaya says, "As You wish, My Lord."

In a matter of a few seconds, She transports all the people from Mathura to Dwarka. Since She has used Her Maya (illusion) powers, Jarasandha is not aware of what has happened. Krishna's Dwarka is no longer an empty city with bare palaces and houses. It has men, women, and children; all of them transported from Mathura by the divine powers of Goddess Yogamaya.

Jarasandha suddenly notices Krishna and Balarama fleeing in a chariot. He sees no sign of his friend Kal Yavan. He immediately suspects something has gone horribly wrong. He concludes that Krishna, using His mystic powers has tricked and killed Kal Yavan.

He shouts at his men, "There They go. The cowards. Running away from the battlefield. Follow Them!"

Jarasandha and his men follow Krishna and Balarama in hot pursuit. They find it very difficult to match the speed of Lord Balarama's chariot. The chase goes on for hundreds of miles. Jarasandha and his men are unable to catch Them.

Suddenly They reach a mountainous region.

Krishna tells Balarama, "Let us get off the chariot and hide in the mountain."

Balarama agrees. Both of Them begin to run towards the mountain.

Jarasandha spots Them running away. He realises that the path is too rocky for his chariot so he too descends from his chariot and runs towards Them.

Krishna and Balarama are well hidden in the middle of the mountain. The thick shrubs and trees make it extremely difficult for Jarasandha to spot them. Suddenly, Jarasandha gets an idea.

He calls his men and instructs them, "These Two are hiding in the middle of the mountain. There is no way we can find Them. All of you surround the mountain on all sides. Then let us burn the entire mountain. They will have no means of escape, since there will be fire and soldiers on all sides."

Jarasandha's men execute the task as he wished. They surround the entire mountain and torch the dry wood. Within a short time, the entire mountain is in flames.

Lord Balarama sees fire and smoke everywhere and is worried. He asks, "Kanhaiya! There is fire everywhere. Jarasandha's men have surrounded Us from all sides. What do We do now?"

Krishna smiles and closes His eyes and thinks of His divine vehicle, Garuda. Within a few seconds, the king of birds, Garuda, arrives. Lord Krishna and Lord Balarama sit on the divine bird. Krishna instructs Garuda to take Them to Dwarka.

15

Dwarka

...

"*Yadyadacharati sreshtas tad tadevetaro janah,
Sa yat pramanam kurute lokastad anuvartate.*"

("Whatever a great leader does, that alone common people follow. Whatever example and standard he sets up, all the people follow in his footsteps."

(*Bhagavad Gita* 3.21)

Dwarka is a small town in the modern day Jamnagar district, in the state of Gujarat. It lies on the western tip of India, on the banks of River Gomti and the Arabian Sea. Dwarka is located at 22.23^0 N latitude and 68.97^0E longitude. It is one of the four Char Dhams, the others being Badrinath, Puri, and Rameshwaram. It is also one of the seven Saptapuris, the others being Varanasi, Haridwar, Ujjain (Avantikapuri), Ayodhya, Mathura, and Kanchinpuram. This gives Dwarka the unique distinction of being the only place in India which is both one of the Char Dhams and Saptapuris.

There are many who wonder why Krishna chose Dwarka for His new capital. Mathura is located in the northern part of India, in the present state of Uttar Pradesh. Dwarka is on the western tip of India, in the present state of Gujarat. Both are separated by a few hundred kilometres. Even with trains and cars, it takes a minimum of three days to travel between these places. During the Dwapara Yuga, where the common means of transport was riding a horse, or bullock cart, it would have taken a few weeks to travel from Mathura to Dwarka. So, why did Krishna choose Dwarka?

It is believed that Krishna's ancestors were from a place known as Kusasthali. Many generations and battles later, they abandoned Kusasthali and migrated to Brij Bhoomi. It was Krishna's desire to go back to His ancestral kingdom of Kusasthali. The place that He built as Dwarka was on the site of Kusasthali. So it was a journey in the reverse direction compared to what His ancestors had done.

Any story about Dwarka is incomplete without mentioning Mirabai who is considered to be one of the greatest devotees of Lord Krishna. Some consider this saint to be an incarnation of Radha, whereas others believe her to be an incarnation of Lalitha, Radha's famous *sakhi* (friend). Mirabai was a famous poetess whose songs about Lord Krishna made her a household name in India. Mirabai was born in 1498 AD in a village named Merta in Rajasthan. Her father, Ratan Singh, belonged to the Rajput community. Her family members were ardent followers of Lord Vishnu so she was under a strong Vaishnava influence right from her childhood.

One day, her mother gave Mirabai an idol of Lord Krishna. It is believed that once Mirabai asked her mother who her husband would be. Her mother, jokingly, pointed to the idol of Lord Krishna and said, "Lord Krishna is your husband." Mirabai took her word seriously. From that day onwards, she began to treat Lord Krishna as her husband and would sit the whole day talking, dancing, singing, and playing in front of the idol. Her family worried seeing her deep attachment to Krishna. They decided that getting her married would divert her mind towards familial affairs. Mirabai was married to Rana Kumbha of Mewar. However, marriage did not change her. She continued to look upon Krishna as her sole Lord and Master. Her devotion towards Krishna made her family furious. They felt it was scandalous for a married woman from their community to be singing and dancing in front of Lord Krishna's idols in the temples of their town. The story of Mirabai's troubled domestic life has different versions. There are some who believe that she neglected her family and devoted her time to praying and singing in temples. There are others who insist that she was a dutiful wife and would complete her household chores before going to the temple. Whatever the truth, several conspiracies were hatched to defame her. There were a few people who even tried to kill her, but by God's grace, she managed to survive these attempts. Her devotion to Lord Krishna was her sole pillar of strength amidst the storm brewing in her community. On the advice of some of her contemporary saints, she left Rajasthan and went to Mathura and Vrindavan to keep herself away from all controversies. After a few years, she went to Dwarka and devoted most of her time to singing the glories of her Lord. She composed hundreds of songs on Krishna which are popular even today and sung by His devotees. She spent the rest of her life in Dwarka, singing, and dancing in public. She was so immersed in her love towards Krishna that she was oblivious of what society thought of her.

It is believed that one day, in 1547 AD, she entered the sanctum sanctorum of the Dwarkadheesh Temple at Dwarka and began to pray with great ecstasy and joy, imploring Lord Krishna to take her away from this materialistic world. The doors of the temple automatically closed. Later when the doors re-opened, the priests found that Mirabai had disappeared and her sari was wrapped around the idol of Lord Krishna. People believe that this event symbolised Mirabai's union with Lord Krishna.

LOCATION OF LORD KRISHNA'S PALACE

After Krishna left Mathura, He stayed at Dwarka for 96 years. He stayed in His palace along with Goddess Rukmini and 16,000 queens whom He had rescued from the clutches of the tyrant King, Jarasandha. Apart from Goddess Rukmini, who is an incarnation of Goddess Lakshmi, His other famous queens include Satyabhama and Jambuvanthi.

Krishna's palace was built by the architect from Heaven, Vishwakarma. It is believed that Dwarka was the most beautiful city on Earth and the palaces that Vishwakarma built were the most beautiful palaces in the world.

There are different versions regarding the location of Krishna's main palace. Some believe that the main palace stood where the present Dwarkadheesh Temple is situated, in the heart of the city. They believe that Krishna's great grandson Vajranabha built this temple over Krishna's original residence.

The second version says that the location of Krishna's opulent residential quarters was where the Dwarkadheesh Temple stands at Bet Dwarka. This could be the reason why the two Dwarkadheesh Temples, one at Dwarka and the other at Bet Dwarka, are similar in many ways and compete with each other, in claiming to be the original site of Krishna's palace. Apart from this, there is a third version that says that the palace of Krishna was submerged when gigantic waves swallowed the entire city. The palace is submerged in the Arabian Sea and cannot be seen.

People have researched the history of Dwarka and each person has proof to corroborate his theory. So the exact location of Krishna's palace is still shrouded in mystery.

DWARKADHEESH TEMPLE

Dwarkadheesh means 'Lord of Dwarka', another name for Lord Krishna. The Dwarkadheesh Temple is located in the heart of the city. This is the biggest and the most famous temple in the temple town of Dwarka. Many believe that this was the original location of Krishna's palace.

Dwarkadheesh Temple

This beautiful temple is also known as Jagat Mandir and is made of sandstone and granite. It has five storeys. At a height of approximately 160 feet, the top of the temple has a beautiful conical spire. Sixty pillars support the temple.

The temple has two entrances. The one on the north side is called *Moksha Dwar* which means 'Door to Liberation'. The entrance in the south is known as *Swarga Dwar* which means

'Door to Heaven'. Most the visitors enter through Swarga Dwar and exit through Moksha Dwar.

The Dwarkadheesh Temple is not one single temple, but houses many temples within its hallowed premises. The first temple is very close to the entrance, on the right. It has a white idol of Sri Satyanarayana. To the left of this is another altar that is known as Kusheshwar Mahadev. This has a black Shiva Linga. Behind the Shiva Linga is a black idol of Goddess Parvati.

Proceeding straight towards the main temple, on the right side, is the temple of Goddess Ambaji. Next to this is the temple of Lord Purushottama represented by a black idol of Lord Vishnu. Further down is a temple that has an idol of Lord Brahma. A few metres away is the main inner courtyard. A few steps to the left leads to the main altar that has the one metre high black idol of 'Dwarkadheesh' Sri Krishna. The salient feature of the Krishna idol here, as in other Dwarka Temples, is that it shows Lord Krishna as a four-armed God, like Lord Vishnu. He is sober and erect. In His four arms, He is holding the Shanka, Chakra, Mace, and Lotus. This is quite unlike the Brij Bhoomi temples that show Lord Krishna as a handsome, playful two-armed Boy standing cross-legged and playing the flute that gently caresses His lips. Krishna is popularly known as Ranchodrai here. *Ranchod* means 'one who fled the battlefield'. Krishna had fled from the battlefield at Mathura when He was attacked by Jarasandha and He and Balarama had flown from Mathura to Dwarka and established Their Kingdom here. Hence, the name Ranchodrai. What people should understand is that Krishna fled from the battle, but He was not a coward. It was part of His plan to kill Kal Yavan and also to ensure that Jarasandha did not attack the innocent people of Mathura if He had remained in Mathura.

Right opposite the main altar is a small altar that houses a black idol of Devaki, Krishna's mother. Next to this temple is the Radha Krishna Temple. This is a temple that has idols in the typical Brij Bhoomi manner. A black idol of Krishna stands next to a white idol of Radha.

Behind the main altar is another huge courtyard. As I stepped into this courtyard, I noticed many rooms. Each room was like an altar that housed idols of different Gods. There were four rooms to my left. These housed the idols of Jambavathi, Radhika, Lakshmi Narayan, and Hanuman. There were four rooms to my right which had idols of Saraswati, Satyabhama, Lakshmi, and Gopal Krishna. The idols of Hanuman, Gopal Krishna, and Saraswati were white and the rest of the idols were black.

To the right of the main temple is a small white temple. This has a white idol of Sage Durvasa with a Shiva Linga in front of it. To the right of Sage Durvasa Temple was another huge temple, beige in colour. This is the famous Sharada Peetha. As I walked inside, I came across a huge dome structure that had the white idol of Goddess Saraswati to my left and the idol of Shankaracharya on my right. To the right of the Sharada Peetha is another temple. This has a huge black idol of Lord Balarama. Opposite the Balarama Temple is another temple with a small black Idol of Lord Krishna known as Sri Madhavaraiji. To the right of the Balarama Temple is a huge gate. This is the second entrance to the Dwarkadheesh Temple, known as Moksha Dwar.

To the left of the main temple is a small temple that has idols of Pradyumna, son of Krishna and Anirudha, Krishna's grandson. The big black idol on the left is that of Pradyumna and the small black idol on the right is that of Anirudha. This temple is opposite the Purushottama Temple. To the left of this temple is the Gayatri Devi Temple that has a white idol of Goddess Gayatri adorned with five heads and six hands. Next to this is the Kashi Vishwanath Temple that has a Shiva Linga. To the left is the shrine of Kolwa Bhagat. This four-armed idol resembles Lord Vishnu.

Hundreds of devotees arrived suddenly. They began to perform Parikrama of the main temple and kept chanting loudly 'Ranchodrai ki Jai'.

Bodana, in his previous birth, was a cowherd named Vijayanand. He had lived in Gokul and was Krishna's great devotee and friend. Krishna had been pleased with his devotion and had promised to give him another glimpse of Himself 4200 years later in Kaliyuga. Vijayanand is now born as Bodana in Dakor, Gujarat. He is an ardent devotee of Lord Krishna and worships Him daily in the form of Ranchodrai of Dwarka. He visits Dwarka often to see the deity. Since Bodana is a poor man, he cannot afford other means of travel, and hence travels on foot.

Today is one such visit. It is night time. The main door near the altar is closed. All the devotees, including the temple priests, have left. Bodana is sitting alone in front of the closed altar door. With his eyes closed and hands folded in reverence, he prays, "Oh Lord! Please have mercy on me! I would like to worship You everyday. However, the distance between Dakor and Dwarka is considerable and I am getting old. Hence, I am unable to visit You as often as I would like to."

Krishna takes pity on His devotee and says, "Ask Me for any boon. I will grant it to you."

Bodana, with his hands still folded, implores, "Oh Supreme Lord! You know everything! I would like You to come and stay with me at Dakor. This way, I can worship You daily."

The merciful Lord says, "Bodana! I will fulfil this desire. Please get up and proceed towards Dwarka. I will come with you."

Bodana is thrilled beyond words. He gets up and with a spring in his walk, begins his journey to Dakor.

The next morning, when the priest at Dwarka Temple wakes up and opens the altar door, he is shocked. The deity is missing. The news spreads. Soon all the priests arrive at the temple. They begin to discuss the theft.

One of the priests says, "I know who has stolen the idol of Ranchodrai."

The other priests look at him.

He replies, "It is Bodana."

Another asks, "Bodana?"

He replies, "Yes, Bodana. He used to visit this temple frequently. He is an ardent devotee of Ranchodrai. I have also heard him tell his friends that it is his desire to have this idol at Dakor, so that he need not walk all the way to Dwarka to worship Him."

There is a sudden buzz of excitement all around. The priests begin to discuss the next course of action.

One of them says, "Let us go to Dakor and search Bodana's house. We should verify this."

Another says, "Good idea. Let us proceed to Dakor right now."

They proceed to Dwarka and locate Bodana's house. They find Bodana sitting inside praying to Lord Krishna. The Ranchodrai idol is in front of him.

The priests are shocked.

One of them remarks, "Look at the audacity of this thief. He not only steals our idol but keeps it in the open, so shamelessly!"

Another says, "Let us take the idol back with us."

Bodana opens his eyes hearing the commotion.

He says, "Oh Holy Saints! Welcome to my humble abode."

The head priest replies, "Enough of this. We want our idol back."

Bodana says, "This is my idol. Why should I give it to you?"

The head priest replies, "You have stolen this idol from Dwarka. We want it back."

Bodana replies, "This idol has not been stolen."

The head priest asks him, "Is this idol not from Dwarka?"

Bodana replies, "Yes, Holy One! The idol is from Dwarka."

The head priest asks, "So you agree you have stolen it?"

Bodana laughs, "No! I have not stolen it."

The head priest is now losing his patience.

He says angrily, "You say it is the same idol from Dwarka. A minute later, you say it is not stolen. Can you explain what you mean?"

Bodana says, "Let me explain. The idol of Ranchodrai is from Dwarka, but it has not been stolen."

The head priest has had enough of this.

He replies sarcastically, "Oh! So you didn't steal it? So you came back from Dwarka to Dakor and the idol followed you! Right?"

Bodana replies, "Right! I prayed to Lord Ranchodrai to come with me to Dakor and He followed me. Please tell me Sir! If the Lord has followed me, then can you consider this to be a theft?"

The head priest is now boiling with anger.

He shouts, "You lying cheat! How dare you lie like this, and that too in front of the holy idol of Ranchodrai?"

Bodana folds his hands and implores him, "Oh Holy Priest! Please don't accuse me of theft. I have not stolen the idol. If you don't believe me then please ask the Lord Himself."

Bodana and the head priest continue to argue. The head priest continues to accuse Bodana of theft and Bodana maintains that he is innocent.

In the meanwhile, one of the priests throws a spear at Bodana. The spear pierces Bodana's body and kills him instantaneously. Bodana attains moksha as promised by Krishna. The priests are not yet satisfied. They ask Bodana's widow to give them gold equivalent to the idol's weight. Lord Krishna, the ever merciful Lord, takes pity on the widow. He makes the weight of the idol so light that it weighs as much as her gold nose ring. The priests are disappointed. They once again implore Lord Ranchodrai to return to Dwarka.

The Lord replies, "Please go back to Dwarka. Go to Sevaradhan Van after six months. You will find a replica of this idol. You can install that idol as the main deity in the Dwarkadheesh Temple."

The priests are thrilled to hear this. They happily return to Dwarka. However, they are impatient and do not wait for six months. They look for the idol much earlier and therefore, though they find an idol which is a replica of the original one, it is smaller in size. The residents of Dwarka are happy to have their Lord Ranchodrai back.

RUKMINI TEMPLE

Rukmini Temple is on the way to Bet Dwarka. As I travelled a couple of kilometres from Dwarka city and headed towards Bet Dwarka, I came across a Y-intersection. I took the road on my right which led me to the famous Rukmini Temple.

This temple is dedicated to Goddess Rukmini, who is considered to be the most important among all the queens of Krishna. She is none other than Goddess Lakshmi who took birth on Earth during Krishna's

Rukmini Temple

239

presence on this planet. Though Rukmini was Goddess Lakshmi incarnate, She had to struggle in Her endeavours to marry Krishna.

Rukmini is the daughter of King Bhishmaka, the King of Vidarbha. She is the incarnation of Goddess Lakshmi, the Goddess of Wealth and Fortune. She has heard many stories of Krishna and desires to become His wife. However, Her brother, Rukmi, has other ideas. He wants his younger sister to marry his good friend Shishupal, a sworn enemy of Krishna. Rukmi knows that Shishupal was a close friend of the powerful King Jarasandha; so he hopes that this marriage would strengthen his ties with King Jarasandha and this in turn, would make him more powerful.

Rukmini comes to know of Her brother's plans. She hates the idea of getting married to Shishupala. She has given Her heart to the lotus-eyed Krishna. She writes a letter and gives it to a brahmin who had come from Dwarka to meet Her father at Vidarbha. The brahmin takes the letter from Rukmini and leaves for Dwarka.

The brahmin reaches Dwarka. He enters Krishna's palace. Krishna receives the brahmin with full honours. Though Lord Krishna is the Supreme Lord, He never forgets that He has come to earth in a human form and is living the life of a kshatriya king. He always performs all the duties of a kshatriya king to convey the message to His citizens how a dutiful king should behave. He wants to teach people the respect that needs to be given to holy brahmins. It is for this reason that when the brahmin comes to Dwarka, Krishna falls at his feet and seeks his blessings. He washes the feet of the brahmin and asks him to sit on a throne that is reserved for all brahmins visiting his kingdom.

Krishna asks the brahmin, "Oh Holy One! You have come from the land of Vidarbha. How is everyone there? How is the king of Vidarbha? How are the people? Are they happy? I hope you have only good news for Me."

The brahmin replies, "Oh Lord! Everyone is fine at Vidarbha. The people are all contented and happy. They like and respect their king who is a just ruler. He treats brahmins with respect. I also had a chance to meet Princess Rukmini."

Krishna's eyes brighten, "Oh Princess Rukmini! How is She? I have heard She is very beautiful."

The brahmin replies, "Yes my Lord! Princess Rukmini is the most beautiful Lady on Earth. People say that She is the incarnation of Goddess

Lakshmi, the Goddess of Fortune. She has given me a letter to be given to You."

Saying this, he hands over the letter that Goddess Rukmini had given him.

Krishna reads the letter. Goddess Rukmini has written,

"Oh Lord! I have heard about all Your qualities. You are the most handsome among men. You have the strength of a thousand elephants. The tales of Your killing the demons are legendary. You have captivated the heart of everyone right from Your childhood at Brij Bhoomi. It is a pleasure to be associated with You and be in Your presence. The gopis had the good fortune of spending so many years with You at Brij Bhoomi. Anyone who takes refuge at Your lotus feet achieves moksha. My Lord! I would like to become Your wife and spend the rest of My life at Your lotus feet. My brother wants Me to marry Shishupal, who is not only Your cousin, but also Your sworn enemy. I do not want to marry Shishupal since I have given My heart to You. Oh Lotus-eyed Krishna! Please come to My rescue. Please come to Vidarbha and take Me with You to Dwarka. I do not wish to stay here any longer. Rukmi has already sent an invitation to Shishupal to come to Vidarbha. He has accepted the offer and will be arriving here soon with all his friends, including his mentor, King Jarasandha. Since they are all coming here with their mighty armies, I request You to come to Vidarbha in disguise and take Me away. I know that You are the most powerful among men. I also know, You are the Supreme Lord and there is no one who can match You in strength. However, if You come with Your army and undisguised, a big battle will ensue. Thousands of innocent soldiers will get unnecessarily killed. I do not want thousands of women to become widows just to satisfy My desire to marry You.

It is our family custom that the bride should visit the temple of Goddess Durga and seek Her blessings.

This is done on the day of the marriage. I request You
to come to the Goddess Durga Temple and carry Me
away with You."

*Krishna has finished reading the letter. He looks at the brahmin and
asks him if the date of the marriage has been fixed. The brahmin tells him
the exact date of the marriage. Krishna realises there is not much time left.
He leaves immediately for Vidarbha.*

*The wedding preparations are going on in full swing in Vidarbha. The
king has received all guests, including the groom Shishupal, with full honours.
They have been given the best palaces to stay in. Hundreds of maid servants
are serving them. The palaces have been decorated with beautiful flowers. The
king, known for his generosity, has donated much wealth to the poor and
needy people on the joyous occasion of his daughter's wedding. Prince Rukmi
is also very happy. His sister is getting married to Shishupal, who is not only
his good friend, but also close to the powerful King Jarasandha. Everything is
proceeding as he had planned. He had heard rumours that Krishna might
attack his kingdom, but all that looks impossible. There is no sign of
Krishna's arrival, nor any attack.*

*It is the morning of the wedding. Goddess Rukmini has bathed in
perfumed water and is gloriously dressed. She has decorated Her hair with
flowers. She is wearing gold necklaces and gold bangles. She is indeed the most
beautiful woman on Earth.*

*Rukmini is going to the Goddess Durga Temple in Her chariot. She is
tense. She had sent a message to Her Lord but has received no response from
Him. She has neither heard from Krishna, nor from the brahmin to whom
She had given the letter. She is filled with anxiety. Did the brahmin deliver
Her letter to Krishna? Is Krishna interested in marrying Her just as She is
interested in marrying Him? Will He come and rescue Her, before Shishupal
ties the knot with Her? Her mind is filled with these worries.*

*She has reached the Goddess Durga Temple. She reaches the altar. She is
holding the aarti plate in her hand. The aarti plate contains flowers,
vermillion, and lamps used for worshipping the Goddess. She closes Her eyes
and prays to Goddess Durga, "Oh Goddess Durga! I do not want to marry
Shishupal. I have given My heart to Krishna. I want to take refuge at His
lotus feet. I am His eternal companion. I do not seek to live with anyone else.
Please send Krishna to Vidarbha."*

Saying this, She offers the flowers and incense to the Goddess. Rukmini leaves the altar of the temple and heads towards the chariot, Her mind filled with anxiety. The wedding time is approaching, but still, there are no signs of Krishna. Her restless eyes look around everywhere. Suddenly, She sees a chariot driving towards Her. The Person seated in it is the most handsome among men. Golden coloured garments decorate a radiating blue body. The blue body reminds Her of monsoon clouds. The lotus eyes, the pink lips, and the charming smile. She knows that it can be none other than Lord Krishna!

The chariot halts near Her. Krishna extends His right hand towards Her. She offers Her right hand to Him. In one swift action, He picks Her up and places Her in His chariot and drives off. The guards and the servant maids standing nearby are too stunned for words. Before they realise what is happening, Krishna's chariot is miles away down the dusty road.

The news of Krishna kidnapping Rukmini reaches the royal family. Rukmi is seething with anger. How dare Krishna come to his own kingdom and whisk away his sister like this? He goes to Shishupal's palace to convey the news. Shishupal has already heard what has happened. He is discussing the recent turn of events with King Jarasandha. Rukmi thunders, "Oh Shishupal my friend! Please don't worry. My Sister is still yours. I will pursue them with my army. I will not return till I defeat Krishna and bring back Rukmini in my chariot."

In the meanwhile, Balarama has heard that His Brother has gone all alone to Vidarbha to rescue Rukmini. Taking His own mighty army, He reaches the outskirts of Vidarbha kingdom. Shishupal, Jarasandha, and Rukmi along with their armies leave Vidarbha in pursuit of Krishna and Rukmini. They have reached the outskirts of the kingdom. They encounter the huge and mighty army of Balarama.

Rukmi tells Shishupal, "Dear friend! While you and King Jarasandha are engaged in fighting Balarama and His army, let me continue my chase. I will attack and defeat Krishna and bring back Rukmini." Saying this, he leaves the battlefield and heads towards Dwarka.

A fierce battle ensues between the armies of Balarama and Shishupal and Jarasandha. Lord Balarama is the incarnation of Lord Sheshanag. Other than Lord Krishna, an incarnate of Lord Vishnu Himself, there is no one on this Earth who can match Him in strength. Using His divine weapons, including His Plough, He humbles the mighty armies of Shishupal and Jarasandha. Both of them return to Vidarbha, disgraced and defeated. They anxiously await the arrival of their friend and host, Prince Rukmi.

The fate of Rukmi is no different. He has caught up with Lord Krishna and Goddess Rukmini, whom he has followed in hot pursuit. He screams, "Krishna! Wait! You coward! In Your childhood, You stole butter and curds from Your neighbours in Vrindavan. You have not changed much! Now You steal my younger Sister Rukmini. If You are a true kshatriya king then behave like one. Stand up and fight."

Krishna, hears these stinging words, halts His chariot and looks towards Rukmi. Rukmi, in the meanwhile, takes out an arrow and fixes it to his bow. He is about to aim and shoot, but before that, Krishna's arrow breaks his bow into two. Rukmi picks up another bow, but before he can place an arrow, Krishna breaks this bow too. Rukmi is unable to control his anger. Screaming and shouting, he descends from his chariot. With a sword in his right hand, he rushes towards Krishna. Krishna sends an arrow in his direction and breaks his sword into two. He too descends from His chariot and rushes towards Rukmi. They fight with bare hands. Rukmi is no match to the Supreme Lord, who overpowers him easily. Krishna holds Rukmi by his throat and is about to strangle him, when He hears the cries of Goddess Rukmini, "Oh Supreme Lord! Please forgive My brother. Please spare his life. He has failed to recognise who You are. Please forgive his ignorance."

Hearing this, Krishna releases His grip. He throws Rukmi to the ground and proceeds towards His chariot where Rukmini is waiting for Him. Rukmi slowly gets up. He is completely humiliated and shattered. He slowly walks back to his chariot and mounts it. He instructs His charioteer to drive him back to his palace.

Lord Krishna and Goddess Rukmini arrive at Dwarka. Lord Balarama too returns. The people of Dwarka hear about the arrival of Krishna and Balarama. They also hear the news of the wedding of Goddess Rukmini and Lord Krishna. They all decorate their homes with garlands of flowers. All the houses are worthy of the occasion. The entire city is well decorated. People are singing and dancing on the streets. Krishna marries Rukmini at the auspicious hour. Thousands of sages have come to officiate this marriage and bless the Couple. Gods and Goddesses come from Heaven and watch the marriage from the skies. They place garlands made of celestial flowers around the divine Couple. They feel blessed to have watched such a divine spectacle.

When I reached the temple entrance, I saw a flight of steps leading me to two small temples. The one on the left was the Hanuman Temple and the one next to it was the Annapurna

Temple. On my right, I saw four more steps that led me to the main shrine which had a beautiful white idol of Goddess Rukmini. On the wall, I saw a painting that depicted an incident involving Krishna, Rukmini, and Durvasa. The incident culminated in the short-tempered sage cursing Krishna and Rukmini.

Krishna and Rukmini invite Sage Durvasa to lunch during the latter's visit to Dwarka.

Sage Durvasa says, "I will come and have lunch in Your palace, but only on one condition."

Krishna says, "Oh Sage, please tell Us what your condition is. I will assure you that We will fulfil it."

Sage Durvasa makes a strange request, "I will come in a chariot that is not pulled by Your horses, but pulled by both of You. Are You agreeable to this?"

Krishna replies, "Yes, Holy One! We will pull the chariot Ourselves. Please take a seat in the chariot and make yourself comfortable."

It is a sunny day as Krishna and Rukmini begin to pull the chariot, Rukmini feels thirsty.

She tells Krishna, "Oh Lord! I am feeling very thirsty. I would like to drink some water."

Krishna immediately presses His toe to the ground and Ganga's water fountains up from the ground. Rukmini drinks this and quenches Her thirst.

The short-tempered Sage Durvasa sees this and becomes very angry.

He says, "Rukmini! You have drunk water before I, Your guest, have eaten food. I curse that You two are separated for 12 years. I also curse that the place where You stay will be an arid land and have no water."

It is believed that this is the reason why Dwarkadheesh Temple and Rukmini Temple are at different locations, separated by around two kilometres. It is also believed that due to Sage Durvasa's curse, the area surrounding Rukmini Temple is totally dry and there is no water there. The temple authorities get water from Dwarka. According to the temple custom, after seeing the Rukmini idol, we should drink the water that the priests offer us and then perform a parikrama of the idol.

The priests allowed groups of 10-15 devotees at a time inside the main temple. All of us sat in front of the Goddess Rukmini idol. The priest narrated the story of Sage Durvasa's curse. He then asked us to descend the steps and go to the main courtyard. Here, the devotees were given water to drink and asked to perform a parikrama of the main temple.

RUKMINI KRISHNA ISKCON TEMPLE

The ISKCON Temple is in the middle of the busy market area. This is a two-storey building and the main shrine is on the

first floor. The entire place has white marble floors. Unlike most ISKCON temples that have idols of Radha and Krishna, this temple has idols of Rukmini and Krishna, probably keeping the local sentiments in mind. Both the idols are white. The idol of Goddess Rukmini is to the right and that of Lord Krishna, playing His flute is on the left.

Rukmini Krishna ISKCON Temple

Most of the temples in Dwarka do not show Krishna holding His flute; however this temple seems to be an exception.

On the left side of the room is a *diwan* with a statue of Srila Prabhupada in a sitting posture. Though this ISKCON Temple is quite small compared to the other bigger ISKCON Temples across the globe, it is worth a visit to look at the exquisitely carved idols of Goddess Rukmini and Lord Krishna.

GOMTI GHAT

The Gomti is considered to be one of the most sacred rivers in this part of the country. The River Goddess Gomti is worshipped here just as Ganga is worshipped in Varanasi. It flows just behind the Dwarkadheesh Temple. On the banks of the river, there are numerous steps that stretch for more than a mile. These steps form the Gomti Ghat and allow the devotees to take a holy dip in the sacred river. It is believed that anyone who takes bath at this Ghat attains salvation and reaches the Abode of God.

As I came out of the back entrance to the Dwarkadheesh Temple, I could see the Samudra Narayan Temple on the far right and Gomti Temple on the far left. On the opposite bank of the Gomti was the Panchanada Teerth.

The entire stretch of Gomti Ghat has a tiled walkway of about a kilometre. As I walked from Samudra Narayan towards Gomti Temple, on the right hand side, I saw a flight of steps throughout the stretch of Gomti Ghat. On the left side, I found numerous temples, next to each other. All these temples are known as Gomti Ghat Temples.

SAMUDRA NARAYAN

The Samudra Narayan Temple is at the farthest end of Gomti Ghat. This temple is located at the confluence of the Gomti and the Arabian Sea. Samudra Narayan Temple is at the farthest tip of Dwarka, and Dwarka, in turn is at the western tip of India so you can say that Samudra Narayan Temple is at the 'westernmost' tip of India. Three sides of the temple are surrounded by the Gomti

Samudra Narayan Temple

and the Arabian Sea. Ferocious waves beat the rock the whole day, even during early morning. This is quite unusual because in most places, the high tide comes in only during the evenings and it is during such times that the waves lash against the rocks. The waves here seem to be beating the rocks to the tune of 'Srimad Narayan

Narayan Hari Hari' that I heard continuously from the temple.

The temple building is painted beige and white. There are five steps leading to the temple entrance. As I entered, on the left side, I saw a small cave-like room that had an idol of Goddess Gomti. Here, the locals worship the Gomti in the form of a Goddess. Goddess Gomti sits on a lion, reminiscent of Goddess Durga.

As I walked straight past the temple entrance, I came across a room that had a sand-coloured idol of Lord Samudra Narayan. The Lord here is known as Samudra Narayan, which means 'Narayan residing in the Sea'. This is probably because the temple is located at the tip of the Arabian Sea. To the left of this idol is an idol of Goddess Gomti.

GOMTI TEMPLE

I walked from Samudra Narayan Temple towards the opposite end of Gomti Ghat. When I reached the end of the walkway, I took the narrow path on the left and then the next right turn. I found the Gomti Temple on my right.

This temple has different altars, each in the form of a small room. The one in the centre houses the idol of Sri Gomti Mataji which is a white coloured marble idol. On the right is a white marble idol of Sri Mahalakshmi Mataji. On the left is a sand-coloured idol of Sage Vashishta. Between the Sri Gomti Mataji idol and Sri Mahalakshmi Mataji idol is a black idol of Sri Dwarkadheesh. An orange-coloured idol of Lord Ganesha is kept above the altar door of Gomti Mataji. The River Gomti was brought from Heaven to Earth by Sage Vashishta and his idol has been placed here to commemorate that incident.

Opposite the Gomti Temple, there are many steps that lead to one of the entrances of Dwarkadheesh Temple. It is believed that devotees must first visit Gomti Temple before visiting Dwarkadheesh Temple.

SRI KRISHNA TEMPLE

Behind the Gomti Temple is the Sri Krishna Temple. While walking from Samudra Narayan Temple along Gomti Ghat, this temple is at the opposite end. The temple building is white and the altar has a black idol of Lord Krishna. An orange idol of Lord Ganesha adorns the door of the altar. As in most temples of Dwarka, here too, the Lord is four-armed, sans the flute. Behind this temple is the Hari Kund where Lord Krishna and Goddess Rukmini had a bath.

In front of the idol, there is a huge weighing scale fixed from the ceiling. For a first time visitor, this may appear odd. Though it is quite common to see weighing scales in temples, they are generally kept in the back courtyard or at one end of the temple premises. Generally, in most temples, the weighing scales are for the *tulabhara* of the devotees. *Tulabhara* means the devotee gets weighed against items of his/her choice (this could be bananas, coconuts, jaggery, etc). After the *tulabhara*, the items weighed are given away. However, here, in this temple, the weighing scales commemorate an episode that happened 5000 years ago. That's the reason why they take centrestage here.

Satyabhama is one of Lord Krishna's queens. She is also one of the most beautiful women in the whole world. Like most beautiful people, she is also very conscious about her beauty and vain about it. She is constantly jealous of Goddess Rukmini, the incarnation of Goddess Lakshmi and the first wife of Lord Krishna. Though Krishna pampers her, she thinks He is partial towards Goddess Rukmini. She finds out that Krishna has given Parijata, the celestial flower, to Rukmini. She is jealous.

She thinks, Let me ask Krishna for a bigger gift and see what He does.

She thinks of a plan to test Krishna's love for her.

Krishna enters Satyabhama's chambers. She is sitting on her bed, sad, and forlorn.

Krishna knows the reason for her grievance very well. However, as usual, He does not show it. He sits next to her and asks, "Satyabhama, please tell Me why you are upset."

Satyabhama replies, "Oh Lord! I want the Parijata tree."

Krishna, with a shocked look, replies, "Parijata tree? This does not grow anywhere on Earth! It is a celestial tree that grows only in Heaven."

Satyabhama is adamant. She repeats her request, "You have given a Parijata flower to Rukmini, so why not to me?"

Krishna laughs, "I have given Her just the flower. I can give you the Parijata flower as well. However, I am afraid I can't get you the tree, since it belongs in Heaven."

Satyabhama is adamant and sticks to her demand.

Krishna says, "Ask Me for anything that is feasible and I will get it. I can get you the most precious gems from the deepest oceans. I can get you fruits or flowers that grow on the tallest mountains. The Parijata is something I have no access to."

Satyabhama says, "I want to perform a special puja that will make You love me more than ever. I need the Parijata tree to perform this puja."

Krishna says, "The Parijata tree grows only in Heaven. It is under the custody of Lord Indra, the king of Heaven."

Satyabhama says, "Please wage a war against Lord Indra. Once You defeat Him, You should be able to bring the celestial tree for me."

Krishna realises the moment has now come to make Satyabhama feel humble.

He smiles, "Oh Satyabhama! I will do what you wish. I will now proceed for a battle with Lord Indra."

Krishna goes to Heaven and requests Lord Indra to give Him the celestial Parijata tree, knowing very well what Lord Indra's answer will be.

As expected, Lord Indra is shocked, "How can I give You the Parijata tree? It grows in Heaven and should not be taken away from here."

Krishna smiles, "If You do not hand it over then I am afraid I will have to wage a war against You."

A fierce battle ensues. As expected, Lord Indra suffers a humiliating defeat at the hands of the Supreme Lord.

He bows to Lord Krishna, "Oh Supreme Lord! You deserve to take the tree with You. You have won it. I have only one request Oh Lord! Please return it to its rightful place, once Satyabhama finishes her special puja."

Krishna agrees to his request and promises to bring it back.

Krishna returns to earth triumphantly. Satyabhama has already received the news of Krishna's triumph. She rushes out to receive Him as he enters the palace gates, holding the Parijata tree.

Krishna greets her, "Oh Satyabhama! I have defeated Lord Indra and *brought the celestial tree for you."*

Satyabhama is ecstatic. She says, "Thank You, My Lord! I will now proceed with my puja. Please tell me who can help me perform the puja."

Krishna thinks for a moment and says, "Since it is a very special puja involving the celestial tree Parijata, the priest should be none other than the celestial sage Narada."

Krishna closes His eyes and within a second, Narada arrives.

Narada bows before Lord Krishna and says, "Oh Lord Narayana! What is your command for me? Please tell me why You have remembered me."

Krishna explains to Narada about the special puja that Satyabhama wants to perform. Narada, using his divine vision, realises the reason why Krishna has called him and no other sage. He understands that Krishna wants him to play an important role in His desire to break the arrogance of Satyabhama.

Narada bows before Lord Krishna, "Oh Lord Narayana! I will help Satyabhama perform her puja, as per her desire."

He takes Satyabhama to the celestial tree and helps her perform her puja. Satyabhama is very happy. She thinks, The puja is successful. Now Krishna is all mine.

Narada reads her thoughts.

He tells her, "Satyabhama! There is one very important task you still need to perform. Only after that, can you consider the puja to be successful."

Satyabhama is puzzled, "Oh Holy One! Please tell me what else I need to do."

Narada, waiting for this moment, says, "You need to give me a dakshina (a fee in the form of a gift)."

Satyabhama asks him, "Please tell me what you need."

Narada asks her, "What is the most important thing for you in this world?"

Satyabhama replies, "Lord Krishna!"

Sage Narada is quick to answer, "Normally, you should give the brahmin what is dearest to you. Since it is Krishna in your case, I want you to give Him to me."

Satyabhama is shocked to hear this.

She asks him, "How can I give Him? He is My Lord!"

Narada replies mockingly, "I don't care who your Lord is. All I know is that you need to give Him since He is mine."

Satyabhama has no choice, but to agree to the sage's request.

Krishna, in all humility, bows to Narada and asks him, "Oh Sage! What is your wish for Me?"

Narada, with pretended arrogance replies, "You are now my slave. I want You to go to the royal kitchen and cook a delicious lunch for me. I am very hungry."

Lord Krishna goes to the kitchen and begins to cook for Narada. Satyabhama is unable to watch what her Lord is being subjected to.

She tells Narada, "I am unable to watch this humiliation. Please release Him."

Narada acts adamant, "I have acquired Him by officiating at your puja. Moreover, if I release Him then you will not get the fruits of this puja."

Satyabhama cries, "I do not want any outcome of any puja. I want to be left alone. I want Krishna to be left alone."

Narada thinks it over and says, "I have one idea. You should compensate me suitably. In that case, I don't mind giving you back Krishna."

Satyabhama, yet to realise the true worth of the Supreme Lord, readily agrees. She says joyfully, "I will perform tulabhara. I will weigh Him against all my riches. I will give you my precious gems, silver, and gold."

Narada nods in agreement. He organises for a huge weighing scale that can seat Krishna. The ever smiling Lord takes His position in one of the weighing scales. The weighing scales immediately tilt to His side. Satyabhama calls her guards and instructs them to bring out her precious gems. The guards return with loads of precious gems. They put them in the other scale. Satyabhama is shocked to find that the balance has not moved even a bit. She asks the security guards to fetch more gems from her treasury. The security guards return with more gems and place them on the scales. However, there is still no difference. The treasury has now run out of gems. Satyabhama asks them to get the gold. The security guards return with all the gold and place them on the scales as well. However, the scales haven't titled at all. Now she instructs them to load the silver. They load the silver too, but there is no change in the position of the scales. Satyabhama is now desperate. She has exhausted her treasury of all the gems, gold and silver. Yet the balance has not tilted in her favour.

She looks desperately towards Goddess Rukmini for help. Goddess Rukmini looks at Her Lord. Through divine powers, Lord Krishna asks Goddess Rukmini to help Satyabhama. Goddess Rukmini calls Satyabhama to Her side. Satyabhama weeps, "Oh Sister! Please help me! I am at a loss for ideas."

Goddess Rukmini advises her, "You have been weighing the Supreme Lord as a commodity. You are thinking of Him as equivalent to precious gems. Please think of Him as the Supreme Lord. Please weigh Him with all your love. If you perform the task with a clean heart, He will bow even for a light item like a Tulsi leaf which is precious to Him."

Saying this, Goddess Rukmini plucks out a Tulsi leaf from the plant and hands it over to Satyabhama. Satyabhama accepts the Tulsi leaf. With her eyes closed, she prays to the Almighty and places the Tulsi leaf on the weighing scales. Behold! The weighing scales tilt in her favour!

Satyabhama, by now, is completely humbled. She realises her selfishness. She realises too that Lord Krishna is the Supreme Lord and belongs to everyone and that He is not her property. She also realises that you cannot equate the Supreme Lord with even the most precious gems. With the right spirit and utmost devotion, you can win over the Supreme Lord's heart even with a Tulsi leaf!

GOPI TALAV

Gopi Talav is located about 12 kilometres from Dwarka, on the way to Bet Dwarka. *Talav* means 'lake' in Gujarati. This place is known as Gopi Talav because this is the lake where the gopis met Krishna and had their final bath before attaining moksha to return to the spiritual world.

Gopi Talav

The gopis are restless. When Krishna left the dusty villages and green forests of Brij Bhoomi, He had promised them that He would return from Mathura after accomplishing his duties. Years have rolled by, but He has not returned. They decide, "If our beloved Krishna does not come and meet us, then let us go to Dwarka and meet Him."

They head towards Dwarka. They meet their Lord on the outskirts of Dwarka.

The gopis request Krishna, "Please build a lake here so that we can take bath in the holy waters of the lake created by Your Blessings."

Krishna immediately heeds their request and in a moment, creates a lake right in front of them.

The gopis make their second request, "Oh Lotus-eyed One, please come and bathe with us."

Krishna, along with the gopis, bathes in this lake.

After the bath, Krishna asks the gopis, "Oh gopis, you all have come from so far away to see Me. Please tell Me what else you need from Me."

The gopis reply, "Oh Lord, our wish was to just come and meet you. We have been blessed with our visit. We have no more desires. We would like to leave our material bodies here after this holy bath. Please allow us to depart from here."

Krishna is overwhelmed by the devotion and love of the gopis for Him.

He blesses them, "I bless that all of you leave your material bodies here and depart to Vaikunta. You will achieve salvation and liberation from the repeated cycles of birth and death. This is something that all of you have achieved through your love and affection for Me, something that even many sages have not been able to achieve in spite of their austerities and prayers. I also bless this land that has become holy with your presence. The mud here will be known as gopichandana and all My devotees will apply this holy mud to their body. Whoever applies this, will achieve peace of mind along with good physical and mental health."

People believe that anyone who has a bath in this holy lake will attain liberation of the soul just as the gopis attained it. I found many people selling *gopichandana* (the holy mud) in small packets. It was available in the form of small cuboids.

Opposite Gopi Talav, is a temple known as Gopi Krishna Temple. This has white marble idols of Radha and Krishna. There is also a painting depicting the incident at Gopi Talav involving Lord Krishna and the gopis. Next to this is the Rukmini Temple that houses a white idol of Goddess Rukmini. Next to Rukmini Temple is the Lakshmi Narayana Temple. This has black idols of Goddess Lakshmi and Lord Narayana. This temple also has idols of many other Gods and Goddesses.

In front of Gopi Talav is another temple that has idols of Lord Rama, Goddess Sita, and Lord Lakshmana. A salient feature of this temple is that it has a floating stone with *Sri Rama* written on it. It is believed that this floating stone was one among the many stones used in Treta Yuga by the monkey army of Lord Rama, to build a bridge from India to Lanka.

GITA TEMPLE

Gita Temple is a little away from the heart of the city, closer to the beach. There is a gate at the entrance that leads to a huge field. The temple is located at one end of this field. The appearance of the building is hardly that of a temple. I almost mistook it for a government building from afar.

The temple depicts Lord Krishna narrating the *Bhagvad Gita* to His favourite disciple, Arjuna before the commencement of the battle of Kurukshetra between the Pandavas and the Kauravas. The blue idol of Lord Krishna is standing erect, holding His conch in His left hand and the Sudarshan Chakra in His right hand. Arjuna is kneeling down to his left, listening intently to the sacred verses emanating from the divine mouth of Lord Krishna. All the surrounding walls are made of white marble with Sanskrit inscriptions from the *Bhagavad Gita* on them.

'Gitopadesha'

BET DWARKA

Bet Dwarka is an island located approximately 30 km to the north of Dwarka city. I travelled from Dwarka to Okha by road. The duration of the journey was 45 five minutes. From the port town of Okha I had to take motor boats, which leave every half hour for Bet Dwarka. The boatman refused to depart till his boat was packed completely with people. He made people sit everywhere in the boat, since there was no single designated area for passengers. This made the movement of the boat highly unsteady as it sailed through the quiet backwaters of the Arabian Sea. I could see most of the passengers praying desperately to Lord Dwarkadheesh for a safe voyage!

Thankfully, the boat ride from Okha to Bet Dwarka lasted only about 20 minutes. In fact Okha and Bet Dwarka are so close that Bet Dwarka island can be seen from the shores of Okha.

When I alighted from the ferry at Bet Dwarka, there was no need to ask anyone for directions to the Dwarkadheesh Temple, the main attraction of this Island temple town. The entire crowd started to walk towards the Dwarkadheesh Temple and I just had to follow them.

DWARKADHEESH TEMPLE

The people of Dwarka and Bet Dwarka seem to vie with each other in asserting that theirs is the 'real' Dwarkadheesh Temple, which had earlier housed the Lord. The similarity between the two temples is quite striking. Incidentally, these are the only two temples in the entire Dwarka region where cameras and mobile phones are not permitted. However, they have made very good cloakroom arrangements at the entrance for keeping these items safely.

When I reached the temple premises, I came across a huge gate. Opposite the main gate was the temple of Lord Kusheshwar. To the right of the main gate was a Ganesha Temple that had an orange-coloured idol of Lord Ganesha. Next to the gate was the main courtyard. The courtyard had eight rooms and each room had an altar. Each altar contained idols kept in silver mantapas. As I entered the courtyard and turned to my left, I saw three small rooms. The altar at the centre was obviously that of Sri Dwarkadheesh. There was a black idol of Lord Krishna, the Lord of Dwarka. The altar had a silver door with silver idols of Lord Vishnu on either side. The altar to the left was Sri Kalyan Rai and the one on the right was that of Sri Trivikrama. To my right, I saw two more altars. The one on the left was Sri Garudaji and the one on the right was a white idol of Sri Ambaji. Behind me, there were three more rooms. The one at the centre housed a black idol of Devaki, mother of Lord Krishna. To the right, was a black four-armed idol of Lord Purushottama. On the left, was a black idol of Sri Madhav Rai. This entire courtyard, with eight adjoining rooms, reminded me of the identical scene at the Dwarkadheesh Temple in Dwarka.

I proceeded to the left of this courtyard and reached the Goddess Lakshmi Temple which has a black idol of the Goddess. Next to the Goddess Lakshmi Temple was another courtyard. As I walked ahead, I reached the altar of Sri Seshavatar Dauji, there is a black idol of Lord Balarama, who is the elder Brother of Lord Krishna and also the avatara of Lord Seshanag. On my right was a white idol of Lord Satya Narayana. Next to it was the altar of Sri Goverdhanji, which had many gold-coloured idols of Lord Krishna. Opposite the Goddess Lakshmi temple is a temple with an enclosed courtyard. The altar has a black idol of Goddess Radhika.

I came back to the main courtyard (the one with eight altars) and proceeded to the right. This led me to another smaller courtyard with a temple that housed a black idol of Goddess Satyabhama. To the left of the Satyabhama Temple was another temple with two altars — the one on the left was that of Goddess Jambavathi and the one on the right had a shrine of Lakshmi Narayana.

16

Porbandar (Sudamapuri)

•••

"*atram pushpam phalam toyam yo me bhaktya*
prayachchathi,
Tadaham bhaktyupahrutamashnami prayatatmanah"

("If a person offers Me a leaf, flower, fruit or water with
devotion, I will appear in person and accept it with love.")

(Bhagavad Gita 9.26)

Porbandar is located between Dwarka and Somnath. It is
approximately 95 km from Dwarka. The drive from Dwarka to
Porbandar was breathtaking. During most part of the journey, we
were driving next to the Arabian Sea. The gigantic waves of the
blue sea made such a pleasant sight that we repeatedly stopped the
car and stood transfixed by the beautiful sight. The sound of the
waves lashing against the rocks had a soothing effect on our
nerves and tired bodies. As was the case in most parts of Gujarat,
the roads were well-maintained and driving was a pleasure.

Porbandar was formerly known as Sudamapuri during the
Dwapara Yuga. It was named after Sudama, Krishna's childhood
friend.

SUDAMA TEMPLE

Sudama Temple is in the heart of the city and quite well-
known among the locals. Though it was in the middle of the busy
city, parking our car was not a problem because there was a huge

Sudama Temple

parking area reserved for people visiting this temple. It was a fairly long walk from the gate to the temple. Near the entrance, I came across a spot where there were hundreds of pigeons. The pigeons were very friendly and did not seem to mind the presence of visitors.

The temple was a cream-coloured building with a vast courtyard that had plenty of trees. The inner courtyard had many carved pillars and arches. It had black and white tiles so arranged that it made me feel as if I was standing on a gigantic chessboard.

Since this temple was dedicated to Sudama, he took centrestage here. There is a big idol of Sudama at the centre. To the left are idols of Radha and Krishna and to the right is the idol of Sushila, Sudama's wife. There were many paintings that depicted the friendship of Krishna, the Lord of Dwarka, and Sudama, His poor brahmin friend.

Sudama and Krishna are childhood friends. They had studied together in Sandipa Muni's ashram. Many years have passed since then. Lord Krishna is now Lord Dwarkadheesh, the Lord of Dwarka. Sudama is a brahmin living in abject poverty. He lives with his wife, Sushila, and four kids in a small hut. Like a true brahmin of that era, he spends his time chanting the holy names of the Supreme Lord. He begs for alms to feed his family. His entire village is affected by drought. Most of the farmers are themselves struggling to feed their own families so how can they donate anything to this poor brahmin? Though Sudama has no money to buy good clothes for his wife and children he leads a contented life since he is not interested in materialistic pleasures. Inspite of not being able to afford two meals a day for himself and his family, he is a very happy man. He is a strong believer in destiny and believes that what he has is what he deserves, based on the actions of his previous birth.

His wife tells him, "Lord Krishna, who is the Lord of Dwarka, is your childhood friend. Why don't you meet Him and seek His help?"

Sudama laughs sadly, "Lord Krishna is my childhood friend. I am also His devotee. If I consider myself His true friend then how can I go and ask Him for help? This is not a sign of friendship. I can ask Him for help if I was just His devotee, but being His friend too... I can't do this. It is against the principles of friendship."

His wife replies, "Your children have been eating only one meal per day since the past few months. There are days when you get nothing after begging for alms and on such days, they sleep on an empty stomach. They wear tattered clothes. All the other boys in the neighbourhood make fun of them."

Sudama says, "Krishna has given each of us our lives according to our destiny. We need to live accordingly."

His wife replies, "Krishna is the Supreme Lord. He is very merciful towards His devotees. He is married to Goddess Rukmini who is none other than Goddess Lakshmi, the Goddess of Fortune. She will shower you with wealth. Please go and meet them."

Sudama says, "I am a brahmin. Why should I go and chase wealth?"

His wife replies, "I am not asking you to amass wealth as some of your friends have done. I am asking you to pray for wealth that is enough for acquiring the basic necessities of life. Both of us are suffering from ill-health. This is due to improper food."

Sudama says, "If I ask anything from my childhood friend then I will be breaking the principles of friendship."

Since this conversation had taken place many times, this time Sushila is determined to have her way. She replies, "Fine. I understand your problem. I will go and meet Krishna and ask Him to help us. Since He is my Lord and not a friend, I would not be breaking any principles of friendship."

Sudama is shocked at his wife's perseverance. He realises that this time, she is determined to force him to visit Dwarka.

He agrees grudgingly, "All right. I will go. However, on one condition."

His wife asks him, "What is that?"

Sudama states, "I will visit Dwarka to meet my childhood friend, Krishna. However, I will not ask for His help."

His wife is happy that at least, he has consented to go. She is not worried

261

about this condition. She says, "That is all right. You need not ask Him for any help. If you just go and meet Him, it's enough. He is omnipotent and omnipresent. He has seen and heard our conversations many times. I know He is waiting to help you. Once you meet Him, He will give us whatever we need."

Sudama says, "I will proceed to Dwarka tomorrow morning."

His wife asks him, "Will you go barehanded like this? Won't you carry any gift for Him?"

Sudama laughs, "Gift! What gift can a poor brahmin like me give to the Lord of Dwarka, the richest Emperor in this world! He is married to the Goddess of Fortune. What gift can I give Him?"

His wife says, "He is very fond of puffed rice. Let me pack some for Him."

Saying this, she goes inside and looks in all the kitchen vessels. Sadly, they are all empty. There is not even a grain of puffed rice in the house. She goes to her neighbour's house and borrows a handful. She puts the puffed rice in a cloth. Folding the cloth tightly she hands it over to Sudama who ties it to his waist cloth.

The next morning Sudama leaves for Dwarka. He has no money to travel by bullock cart. After many days of walking barefoot in the heat, he manages to reach the city of Dwarka. Dwarka is one of the finest and richest cities on earth. The city has thousands of palaces. Sudama has not seen such opulence anywhere before. All the citizens are dressed in fine clothes. The womenfolk are adorned in fine jewellery. Sudama is the only person in the entire city wearing torn clothes. Curious onlookers wonder who this beggar is and what he is doing in this city. Sudama does not know where his friend Krishna lives. He asks a few onlookers and they laugh at him, "Look at the audacity of this beggar! He wants to meet none other than the Lord of Dwarka Himself!"

With great difficulty, Sudama manages to reach the gates of the main Dwarka palace where Krishna resides.

The security guards stop Sudama, "Halt! Who are you? Whom do you want to meet?"

Sudama replies, "I am Sudama, a friend of Krishna's. I have come to meet Him."

The security guards look at each other.

One of them asks Sudama, "Lord Krishna! Do you know who He is? He is Dwarkadheesh, the Lord of Dwarka."

He looks at his fellow guards and laughs, "He is a friend of our Lord! This beggar!"

All the security guards laugh at him.

Sudama is tired after his long journey. The heat is sweltering. He is unable to stand straight. His body is bent from exhaustion and he holds on to his stick.

He says, "Yes. What I say is the truth. I am a friend of Krishna's. Please go and ask Him if you don't believe me."

Krishna is aware of what is happening. Even Goddess Rukmini knows what Sudama is going through.

She asks Him, "Oh Lord! Just like Me, I am sure even You have noticed what is going on at the front gates of the palace. Why don't you ensure that Your security guards escort Sudama inside the Palace? Why are You watching Your friend getting humiliated this way?"

Krishna smiles at Goddess Rukmini, "I know how You feel. I am doing this with a specific intention. Let Me explain. It is very easy for Me to ensure that the security guards allow Sudama inside. However, they will never realise the love and affection that I have for my dear friend, Sudama. I want to send a message to the people of this world that friendship makes no distinction between wealth and poverty. I want to show the people that you should love poor people just as you love those who are rich and affluent. Just watch!"

Goddess Rukmini smiles, "I should have guessed that My Lord was again performing one more of His lilas (plays) to teach a valuable lesson to the world."

In the meanwhile, the argument has heated up at the front gates. The security guards refuse to believe that a poor beggar could be a friend of Emperor Lord Krishna. They try to push him out.

Krishna calls his head security guard and asks him to find out what the commotion is at the front gates. The head security guard returns a few moments later and bows to Krishna, "Oh Lord! There is a beggar at the front gate. He claims to be a brahmin and says he is Your friend. He wants to meet You."

Krishna smiles innocently and asks, "He claims to be My friend? Who is he? What did he say his name was?"

The head security guard replies, "His name is Sudama."

Krishna shrieks dramatically, "Sudama! Did you say 'Sudama'?"

The head security guard is amazed at his Lord's reaction and says, "Yes, My Lord!"

Krishna gets up from His throne and begins to run barefoot, shouting "Sudama! Sudama!"

All the guards and chamber maids are amazed to see their Lord running like this to meet a stranger. They follow Him to see who Krishna is interested in meeting so desperately. This Sudama must be a king, they think.

Krishna has now come out of the palace. Under the hot sweltering sun, he is running barefoot. His hair is dishevelled and He is running towards the front gates chanting "Sudama! Sudama!". He is followed by many of his ministers, guards, and chamber maids. He has now reached the front gates. Sudama is being pushed out by the security guards. Krishna shouts, "Stop! What are you doing to My friend?"

Saying this, He pushes aside His security guards. Sudama has fallen on the dusty ground. Krishna helps lift up His childhood friend and hugs him, "Sudama!"

Sudama is shocked at the turn of events. He had almost given up hope of meeting Krishna. He hugs his Friend and sobs with joy, "Krishna! I thought I would never be able to meet You!"

Krishna notices that everyone is watching Them. He replies, "How did you even think like this? How can I ever forget you?"

Saying this, He affectionately dusts Sudama's clothes which is covered with dust because of his scuffle with the security guards. He puts His arms around Sudama's shoulder and takes him inside the palace.

Krishna and Sudama are inside the palace. He makes Sudama sit on His royal throne. He cries out, "Rukmini, see who has come to meet Us."

Goddess Rukmini, followed by Her chamber maids, comes to the main hall. She too joins Krishna in honouring Sudama. Both of Them wash the poor brahmin's tired feet with hot water. Next, They apply sandalwood paste and different kinds of perfume to his body. They give him a set of new clothes befitting a king. He is taken to a huge king-sized bed and made to lie down.

Both of Them massage Sudama's feet. They fetch fruits and other delicacies and feed him. The onlookers are astonished to see the Lord of the three worlds and the Goddess of Fortune pampering Their friend this way. They realise the true essence and value of friendship. Krishna smiles at Goddess Rukmini and She smiles back at Him. They have both realised that They have conveyed a very important message to the people of Dwarka.

Krishna asks Sudama, "Oh Sudama! What have you brought for Me?"

Sudama suddenly remembers the packet of puffed rice. However, seeing the opulence in the palace, he hesitates. He feels ashamed to give Them the dirty bag of puffed rice.

Krishna senses Sudama is feeling uneasy. He repeats His question. Sudama bows his head down and shakes his head gently.

Krishna, the constant prankster, laughs and goes close to Sudama and pulls away the dirty bag hanging from his waist.

Sudama cries out, "Oh Lord! Please don't open that. It is not meant for You."

Too late! Krishna has already opened the dirty bag. He sees the puffed rice and screams with joy, "Sudama! You still remember how fond I am of this! Let Me eat it."

He looks at Sudama in mock anger and says, "Sudama! You have brought Me My favourite food and you were hiding it from Me? You wanted to eat this all by yourself?"

Sudama laughs, "Oh My Lord! Who can ever hide anything from You! You are omniscient. There is nothing You don't know. I was feeling ashamed to give this packet to You."

Lord Krishna is omniscient. He knows why Sudama has come to Dwarka. He knows why his wife had sent him. He also knows that Sudama is such a principled brahmin that he will not ask Him for His help, even on his deathbed. He decides that Sudama must be repaid for his devotion and friendship. He looks at Goddess Rukmini. She knows what is going on in His mind and She acknowledges His thoughts by smiling back. When Krishna eats the first handful of puffed rice, Goddess Rukmini, the incarnation of Goddess Lakshmi, the Goddess of Fortune, transforms Sudama's small hut into a huge palace. When Krishna eats the second handful, She transforms the clothes of Sudama's wife and children. Their ragged and torn clothes are replaced and they now wear the best clothes worn by princes and princesses. When Krishna eats the third mouthful, She fills Sudama's house with riches.

Sudama, in the meanwhile, is unaware of all that is happening. It has been two days since he arrived at Dwarka. He is thrilled at the hospitality shown by Lord Krishna and Goddess Rukmini. However, he is in a dilemma. He does not want to ask Them for monetary help. At the same time, he feels awkward about returning to his wife empty-handed. He remembers his wife's words, "Lord Krishna is omnipotent and omnipresent. He has been watching and hearing us all the time. He will surely help us, even if you don't ask Him." He decides not to ask Them for anything.

The next morning, Sudama bids goodbye to his Lord Krishna and Goddess Rukmini. Both of Them ensure that he leaves with full honours befitting a royal guest.

Sudama is on his way back home. He recapitulates the events of the past few days. How he was stopped by the security guards. How Krishna came out running barefoot. How Krishna and Rukmini pampered him with the best possible hospitality. He remembers the love, affection, and warmth shown by Krishna and Rukmini. He also recollects the fact that neither he nor They discussed the purpose of his visit to Dwarka. Neither did They talk about his financial status and suffering. However, Sudama is as contented as ever. "I came to meet my Friend Krishna. I was fortunate enough to see Him. I was also very fortunate to be given such a warm welcome by Lord Krishna and Goddess Rukmini. Both of Them also took good care of me during my stay at Dwarka. What more can I ask for?" So thinking, he continues his return journey.

A few days have passed by. He reaches his village. On reaching it, he notices that everything has changed! His small hut has been transformed into a beautiful palace. His children and wife come out to greet him. He notices that their torn clothes have gone, they now wear royal clothes. As he steps inside his house, he notices diamonds, gems, and gold everywhere. The opulence is similar to what he had seen in Krishna's palace in Dwarka. His children shout, "Oh Father! Look at our clothes! We have become rich! We have enough to eat three times every day!" He finds his wife smiling at him. His eyes are filled with tears. He looks Heavenwards and says, "Oh Lord Krishna! How stupid of me to think that You didn't ask about my financial condition. How stupid of me to doubt Your love and affection towards me.

How stupid of me not to realise that You need not be told anything! You know everything. You control the whole Universe!"

By now, all the villagers have assembled near Sudama's home. They describe the divine incidents that happened in his house when he was in Dwarka. Sudama once again looks Heavenwards and says, "Oh Supreme Lord! I have one more request. All the people of this village have helped me and my family during our days of poverty. I don't deserve to live in such a huge palace when they are still living in their homes. Please help them also."

Goddess Lakshmi arrives and within a flash, She transforms the entire village. All the buildings are replaced by palaces. Everyone is dressed in rich clothes. The drought leaves the village. People have enough food and grains to live happily. The villagers decide to name their village 'Sudamapuri', in honour of the man responsible for this transformation.

The story of Krishna and Sudama shows us the merciful ways of the Supreme Lord. It also shows us that the Supreme Lord does not distinguish between the rich and the poor and we can win His heart by sheer love and affection. We need not shower Him with riches like gold and silver. He does not need them. We can win Him over with humble gifts like a handful of puffed rice.

The priest gave us a packet of *poha* (puffed rice) to commemorate the incident of Sudama giving puffed rice to Dwarkadheesh Sri Krishna as his humble gift. He also narrated the story of the evergreen friendship of Krishna and Sudama for those visitors who did not know of it.

17

Kurukshetra

...

"*Karmanye vadhikarasthe ma phaleshu kadachana,*
Ma karma phalaheturbhur ma te sango astvakarmani"

("You have a right to perform your duty but you do not have
the right to the fruit of the action. You should not consider
yourself the cause for results of your activities and you should
never get attached to inaction.")

(*Bhagavad Gita* 2.47)

Kurukshetra literally means 'The land of the Kuru Dynasty' and it
has been named after King Kuru. It is associated with the famous
18-day epic war, the Mahabharata, between the Pandavas and their
cousins, the Kauravas, for the throne of Hastinapura.

The Mahabharata war is considered to be the battle that was
fought for upholding *dharma* (righteousness), the battle between
good and evil in which the Pandavas, aided by Lord Krishna
emerged victorious. The war was fought in Kurukshetra, which is
in the northeastern part of the modern state of Haryana. It is
about 160 km from New Delhi.

People consider Kurukshetra to be one of the holiest places in
India, since, this is the land where Lord Krishna preached the
Bhagavad Gita to Arjuna and also showed him His Cosmic Form
(Vishwa Roopa). The general perception is that this place became
a famous religious place because of the Mahabharata. However,
there are many who consider that it is the other way around. They

believe that Kurukshetra is one of the most ancient places of pilgrimage in the world and that it finds a mention even in the *Rig Veda*, much before Dwapara Yuga, when the Mahabharata war was fought. They believe that the Pandavas and the Kauravas decided to fight at Kurukshetra because it was one of the holiest places in the subcontinent. It is the sacred place where Sage Manu composed *Manusmriti*. It is also the place where the *Rig Veda* and the *Sam Veda* were compiled. In the *Bhagavad Gita*, Kurukshetra is described as a *Dharmakshetra* (place of righteousness).

It is a tourist's delight with numerous temples, tanks, and ghats. It is believed that if anyone dies in Kurukshetra, he attains *moksha* (liberation from the repeated cycle of births and deaths). Since thousands of soldiers were destined to die during the war, what better place than Kurukshetra to host this war?

It is believed, according to the religious scriptures, that the ancient Kurukshetra covered not only the present district of Kurukshetra, but also the present day Panipat and Jind districts in the south and eastern parts of Patiala district in the west. However, the present day Kurukshetra is only a small district in the modern state of Haryana.

Gita Jayanti is celebrated during the last week of November and the first week of December. *Bhagavad Gita* recitals, *aartis* and *Deep Daan* events are organised. The festival commemorates the preaching of the *Bhagavad Gita* by Lord Krishna to Arjuna at the start of the Kurukshetra war.

SRI STHANESHWAR MAHADEV TEMPLE

Sri Sthaneshwar Mahadev temple is in the northern part of Thanesar, which derives its name from this famous temple. Thanesar is a small town, located about five kilometres to the north of Kurukshetra town. Sri Sthaneshwar Mahadev is a famous temple dedicated to Lord Shiva. It is believed that the Pandavas, accompanied by Lord Krishna, prayed to Lord Shiva to seek His blessings before the commencement of the Mahabharata war. It is also believed that Lord Shiva in the form of a *Linga* was first worshipped here.

The roads leading to this temple were very narrow, so we had to park our car quite far from the temple and walk the rest of the way. As I walked along the narrow lanes, I saw small shops on either side of the road, selling idols of various Gods and artefacts related to Kurukshetra. When I reached the temple premises, I saw the sacred Sthaneshwara Tank on my right and the temple building

Sri Sthaneshwar Mahadev Temple

to my left. The temple consists of two buildings. The one on the left, Mandir Sri Badri Vittal Sri Lakshmi Narayan Ji, was the smaller of the two. To the right was the bigger and the more famous Sri Sthaneshwar Mahadev Temple.

The sanctum sanctorum of Sri Badri Vittal Sri Lakshmi Narayan Ji Temple had three altars. The altar in the centre had idols of Badrinath, Vishnu, and Lakshmi. An idol of Adi Shankaracharya was in the left altar. Next to this altar was a Shiva Linga. The altar on the right had an idol of the Goddess of Learning, Saraswati. Next to this was an inner courtyard which connected this temple to the Sthaneshwar Mahadev temple.

When I entered this courtyard, I saw a black idol of Bhairav on my left and a cream-coloured idol of Hanuman on my right. As I crossed the courtyard and moved towards the sanctum sanctorum, I found myself in a small room. This had idols of Radha and Krishna on my left and idols of Rama, Sita, Lakshmana, and Hanuman on my right. All these were made of white marble. As I walked further, I entered a huge room. This was the sanctum sanctorum which had a dome-shaped ceiling. There was huge black Shiva Linga at the centre. The Linga had white marble slabs along the border. On the opposite side of the room were idols of Shiva, Parvati, and Ganesha. There were many pictures on the walls surrounding the Shiva Linga. These pictures were quite unusual because the scenes depicted in these pictures were not well known incidents. One of them depicted Shiva and Vishnu playing in the water in a lake. Another had Krishna and the Pandavas pouring milk on a Shiva Linga and worshipping Lord Shiva to seek His blessings before the Kurukshetra war.

The peace talks between the Pandavas and Kauravas have failed in spite of Lord Krishna Himself being the Mediator. Duryodhana, the Kaurava prince, refuses to hand over Indraprastha to the Pandavas which he had won by deceit during a game of dice. The Pandavas have completed 13 years of exile and returned to Hastinapura to claim their rightful share of the kingdom. However, Duryodhana is in no mood to relent. He says, "Forget getting back your kingdom. I am not prepared to give you even five tiny villages."

The Kuru cousins decide to battle it out instead of coming to an agreement. Lord Balarama does not want to witness this war so He goes on a pilgrimage.

Arjuna and Duryodhana both go to meet Lord Krishna to seek His help. They reach Krishna's chambers at the same time. Duryodhana, the arrogant prince, chooses a seat near Krishna's head. Arjuna, who considers himself a humble devotee of Lord Krishna, sits near His feet.

Krishna opens His eyes. He first sees Arjuna and then Duryodhana. He says, "I know why both of you have come to meet Me. Since I saw Arjuna first, I will give him the first choice for picking one of the two options. I have decided not to actively participate in this battle. So you should either choose to have My Narayani Army or Me. However, remember that I will not use any arms during the battle so I will be available only for moral support."

Arjuna falls at Krishna's feet and says, "Oh Supreme Lord! When You are there with us, why would we need the Narayani Army? I request You to be my Charioteer during the battle." Lord Krishna readily agrees. Since Lord Krishna becomes the Sarathy (Charioteer) of Partha (Arjuna), He is also known as Parthasarathy (Charioteer of Arjuna). Duryodhana is thrilled to hear this since he was worried that Arjuna might choose the army. He says with a smile, "In that case, I will settle for the Narayani Army." Both of them return to their respective destinations, thrilled to have got what they wanted.

The date for the epic battle between the Pandavas and the Kauravas has been fixed. The Pandavas, along with Lord Krishna, reach the holy city of Kurukshetra. Though Krishna knows that the Pandavas would be ultimately victorious, He does not want the Pandavas to become complacent. He wants the Pandavas to take the blessings of the important Gods and Goddesses before the commencement of the war.

Lord Krishna and the Pandavas arrive at Sthaneshwar Mahadev Temple. They enter the sanctum sanctorum, which has a Shiva Linga at the centre. Krishna starts the proceedings by performing the Abhisheka of the Shiva Linga with milk, honey, and water. The Pandavas follow suit. They also decorate the Shiva Linga with flowers. Krishna, inspite of being an incarnation of Lord Vishnu, wants to show to the world that He leads the life of a normal human being. He bows before the Shiva Linga and seeks the blessings of Lord Shiva. The Pandavas too prostrate before the Almighty One. Lord Shiva, watching this spectacle from Mount Kailash, smiles, and blesses them.

I found it quite unusual that there was no priest performing the *puja* of the idol. Instead, devotees were allowed to go right up to the Shiva Linga and perform the *puja* themselves! I saw lots of devotees pouring milk and water over the sacred Linga. A few decorated the Linga with marigold flowers. This scene is unthinkable in the temples of south India where we are not even allowed to enter the area around the main altar, let alone touch the idols.

On the other side of the sanctum sanctorum, I saw a flight of steps which led me to a huge open courtyard. On my right, I saw another flight of steps which took me to a small room. This room too, like the one below, had a dome-shaped ceiling. The Shiva Linga at the centre of this room was the most unusual one I had ever seen in my life. A Shiva Linga usually has only one mound at the centre. However, this Shiva Linga had one huge mound at the centre and 10 small mounds surrounding the big one.

To the right of the inner courtyard of this temple, was a huge room with two altars. The altar on the left had an idol of Jagadamba sitting on a lion. The altar on the right had an idol of Santoshi Ma. Both these were huge idols and made of white marble.

The Sthaneshwara Tank was in front of the temple. This sacred tank had a huge blue idol of Lord Shiva. The tank was well-maintained and the water looked clean. There were steps, on all four sides, for devotees to descend to the tank. On the opposite side of the tank was a garden which had a huge idol. I found this idol quite unusual since the left portion of the idol showed Lord Vishnu with Garuda, and the other portion had Lord Shiva with Nandi. Was the artisan, who created this beautiful idol, trying to convey that Vishnu and Shiva are essentially one God? While standing near this idol, I gazed at the main temple building. I noticed one more unusual sight. The temple's *gopuram* did not look like the ones we see in the temples of north India. This one had a mosque-like structure with a lotus on top of that. A brass *trishul* was mounted on the lotus.

JYOTISAR

Jyotisar is five kilometres from Kurukshetra, on Pehowa road. This sacred site, along with Brahma Sarovar, is the most popular tourist place in Kurukshetra. It was at this very spot that Lord Krishna preached the *Bhagavad Gita*, the sacred text of the Hindus to Arjuna. *Jyoti* means 'light' and *sar* means 'tank' so *Jyotisar* means 'the tank of enlightenment'. This refers to the enlightenment that Arjuna received in the form of the *Bhagavad Gita*. This is also the sacred place where Lord Krishna showed Arjuna His Viraat Roop (Supreme Form) as the Creator, the Preserver and the Destroyer.

While travelling on the Kurukshetra-Pehowa highway, Jyotisar is on the right, about 500 metres off the main road. Since it is one of the most famous tourist places in Kurukshetra it was no surprise to see lots of tourists here. In the narrow lane that led to the entrance, there were shops on either side of the road, selling books and pictures related to Kurukshetra, and Jyotisar, in particular. A beautiful marble courtyard greeted me at the entrance. I found verses

The sacred 'Banyan Tree'

of the *Bhagavad Gita* inscribed on the walls. Beyond this courtyard, was an old banyan tree to the right. There are steps that lead to a small shrine which has an old Shiva Linga. I noticed that the shrine was in ruins. The priest informed me that this shrine was partially destroyed by the tyrant Moghul king, Mohammed Ghazni. Next to this was a modern Shiva Temple. To its left was an idol of Hanuman and to its right was the Kali Mata Temple.

As I proceeded, I came across an open courtyard that had two small temples on the left, namely, Gita Mandir, and Saraswati Mandir. Gita Mandir had a blue idol of Krishna. On the right side of the courtyard, there was a shrine which housed eight sets of idols. These were — Dhritrashtra and Sanjaya; Dronacharya and Duryodhana; Surya Bhagwan, Arjuna, and Krishna; Krishna showing His Viraat Swaroop to Arjuna; Narada and Krishna talking to Bhishma who is lying on a bed of arrows; Krishna preaching the *Bhagavad Gita* to Arjuna; and Shiva, as Nataraja, in His dancing posture.

As I walked further, I came to a flight of steps that led me to the most sacred spot of Jyotisar. On the left were shrines of Vishnu, Durga, and Hanuman and on the right were those of Ganesha and Vyasa. It is believed that all the idols of these shrines were found in Jyotisar lake. The priest informed me that these idols had been hidden by the priests during the times of Mohammed Ghazni to prevent desecration. Ahead was an ancient banyan tree. People believe that this was the same banyan tree, under which Krishna preached the *Bhagavad Gita* to Arjuna at the start of the war at Kurukshetra. A board hung on this tree proclaims 'Immortal Banyan Tree — Witness to the Celestial Song *Bhagavad Gita*'. White marble had been laid on the ground around the banyan tree, which made the place look very neat and clean. In front of this tree was a marble mantapa. A picture of Krishna in His Viraat Swaroop (Cosmic Form) was placed at the centre. To the left was a small white marble chariot. Marble idols of Krishna and Arjuna had been kept on the chariot. On the right were marble footprints of Lord Krishna.

I stood transfixed, my mind visualising the events that happened before the Mahabharata war started which led to the preaching of the *Bhagavad Gita*. Slowly, I shifted my gaze to my left. I saw another white marble chariot with idols of Krishna and Arjuna. Those were identical to those inside the *mantapa* but were probably 20 times bigger in size. In order to prevent miscreants from causing damage to the chariot and the idols, they are kept inside a glass enclosure. The enclosure was aptly labelled as 'Gitopadesha' since it depicted Krishna preaching the *Bhagavad Gita* to Arjuna. There was also a huge picture of Lord Krishna showing His Viraat Swaroop to Arjuna.

In front of the banyan tree I saw the Jyotisar lake. This lake was quite clean and well-maintained. It was about 1000 feet by 500 feet in size. On the other side of the lake I saw an amphitheatre. There was a beautiful garden which connected the area near the banyan tree with the amphitheatre. The amphitheatre hosted a 'Light and Sound Show' which is held every evening at 6.45 p.m. The show depicted the Kurukshetra war and related stories. Since my visit to Jyotisar was in the morning, I came once again in the evening to witness it. The show is conducted by the Haryana Tourism Department and is quite reasonably priced at Rs. 15.

The show starts only after dark, so the timings vary, depending on the season. On that day, the show started promptly at 6.45 p.m. For the next 60 minutes, we saw lights flashed from different locations of Jyotisar, accompanied by the narration of different incidents from Mahabharata. The narration was in Hindi, interweaved with *shlokas* in Sanskrit. As the Sanksrit verses boomed through the loudspeakers and filled the cold winter air, I was transported to a different era. I was in the midst of the Pandavas and the Kauravas on a huge battlefield.

The armies of the Pandavas and the Kauravas are facing each other. The Kaurava army, led by Bhishma, is the bigger of the two, with eleven divisions. Apart from the hundred Kaurava princes, it has stalwarts like Dronacharya, Karna, Kripacharya, Ashwatthama, and Kritavarma. The Pandavas, with a much smaller army of only seven divisions, are led by Dhristadyumna. They also have Satyaki, Drupada, and Abhimanyu in their midst. In both armies, there are some warriors mounted on horses, some on elephants, and some on chariots. There are also a vast majority on foot. Different weapons like bows, arrows, maces, and clubs adorn the hands of these warriors. Bhishma blows his conch which is followed by the loud beating of drums and blowing of trumpets from the Kauravas. Lord Krishna blows His conch, the

Panchajanya. This is followed by all the Pandava princes blowing conches. The twang from Arjuna's bow, the famous 'Gandiva', sends tremors across the open field.

Arjuna tells Krishna, "Please station my chariot between the two armies." Krishna does so. The chariot faces the chariots of the mighty Bhishma, the revered Drona, and Kripa. As the two armies come face to face, Arjuna looks at all the enemies. Seeing the familiar faces of Bhishma, Drona, Kripa, his hundred cousins, uncles, grand uncles and well-wishers, he begins to feel remorse. He drops his weapons to the ground and puts his hand on his head. Lord Krishna, being the Supreme One, knows what His favourite disciple is thinking. However, in His usual innocent style, He asks Arjuna, "Oh Mightiest among the Mighty! The one who has no equal in the battlefield! The one whose ability to strike with deadly arrows scares even the Gods! What has happened to you? Why did you drop your weapons?"

Arjuna replies sadly, "Oh Keshava! My hand is not able to hold the celestial Gandiva bow. My head is spinning. I do not want to fight this battle."

Krishna expresses surprise, "Oh Partha! There is no one on this battlefield who can match your skills. You have defeated each of them atleast once in your lifetime. Why are you worried now?"

Arjuna says, "I am not worried about defeat. Neither am I scared of facing the powerful enemy. I am not interested in winning a battle that requires me to kill Bhishma, Drona, Kripa, and my hundred cousins. I have played in Bhishma's lap during my childhood. I have learned to how to hold the bow and arrows from Drona and Kripa. I have played with my cousins during my childhood. How can I now kill them just to satisfy my materialistic desires? What happiness will I get, killing my own brothers, uncles, grand-uncles and teachers?"

Lord Krishna realises that now is the time for Him to educate Arjuna on the doctrine of dharma. He also decides to teach him about his duties and the differentiation between right and wrong. The conversation between Lord Krishna and Arjuna forms the Bhagavad Gita, also known as the 'Song of the Supreme God'.

The teachings of Lord Krishna in Bhagavad Gita span 18 chapters covering topics like 'Yoga of action' (Karma Yoga), 'Yoga of knowledge', (Gnana Yoga), 'Yoga of self control' (Dhyana Yoga), 'Yoga of attaining the Supreme', 'Yoga of the most confidential knowledge', 'Yoga of the divine energies and glories', 'Yoga of the Universal Form', 'Yoga of devotion' (Bhakti Yoga), 'Yoga of three modes of nature', 'Yoga of the Supreme Person', 'Yoga of the knowledge of divine and demonic natures', 'Yoga of the three modes of faith', and 'Yoga of liberation and renunciation'.

During this discourse, Lord Krishna tells Arjuna that he should perform his duty and not think of the results of the activities. He advises Arjuna not to worry about killing his kith and kin since he is waging a war against 'adharma' (injustice). He explains that during a 'dharmayudha' (war for righteousness) the objective should be to reinstall righteousness, even if it involves killing near and dear ones. Krishna also explains to Arjuna that he should not think of each person in terms of their physical body but in terms of their eternal soul. He explains that the soul is immortal and it cannot be burnt, or killed. Just as a person removes his old clothes and wears new ones, a soul sheds its present body at the time of death and takes on a new body at the time of birth. He says that people like Bhishma and his cousins may be related to him in this lifetime; however, they would have been strangers to him in his previous birth. Hence, he should not attach any importance to such relations. Krishna also tells him how to control his wavering senses and focus on the immediate task at hand, which is to vanquish the Kauravas. He says that he should focus his mind on the battle, but at the same time, he should not think of the results of his actions. Lord Krishna explains to Arjuna, the importance of achieving detachment from materialistic needs.

Lord Krishna explains to Arjuna, "I am the Supreme Lord and nothing moves in this world without My permission. I am the Controller. I am the Creator, I am the Preserver, and I am also the Destroyer." Arujna bows before Lord Krishna and says, "Oh Supreme Lord! I wish to see Your Cosmic Form (Vishwa Roopa). Please show me Your Original Self."

Lord Krishna says, "You cannot see My Cosmic Form in your present state. Let me grant you divine vision."

Saying this, Lord Krishna grants division vision to Arjuna.

Arjuna is now able to see Lord Krishna in His Cosmic Form. He sees the Supreme Lord with thousands of hands and legs. Each hand holds a different celestial weapon. The effulgence radiating from the Cosmic Form is more than that of a thousand suns. Arjuna sees the Supreme Lord with thousands of heads, each head denoting a different God. Arjuna sees Lord Brahma, Lord Shiva, and hundreds of other Gods within Lord Krishna.

Arjuna is awestruck. He bows his head and with folded hands, says,

"Oh Supreme Lord! I see all the Gods and Goddesses within You. I see that You are without any beginning or end. You have thousands of hands and feet. I see the fire blazing from Your mouth. I see all the planets and the moon revolving around You. I see the seas coming out of Your mouth. I also see You devouring all the demons."

Lord Krishna explains to Arjuna the benefits of pure devotional service to Him, the three modes of nature, the Yoga of the Supreme Person, the divine and demoniac natures and the different types of faith and finally, the act of renunciation.

After hearing and understanding the profound teachings of Bhagavad Gita from none other than the Supreme Lord Himself, Arjuna's mind is now at ease. The storm has passed and his mind is like still water in a lake. He realises the need to take up his weapons and fight his enemies. With a strong sense of duty and an equally strong sense of the need to reinstall righteousness, he takes up his celestial Gandiva bow with one hand and blows his conch with the other. The twang of the Gandiva and the sound of the conch reverberate throughout the battlefield.

The battle has just begun.......

BAN GANGA (NARKATARI) — BHISHAM KUND

Like Jyotisar, Ban Ganga (Narkatali) is also on Pehowa road. After travelling around three kilometres from Kurukshetra towards Jyotisar, we took the dusty road on our right. Another one kilometre on this road led us to Ban Ganga.

As I got off my car, I noticed a tank, surrounded by many temples. The tank had 10 red steps on all four sides. These steps were quite steep

Ban Ganga Temple

and one wrong move would have spelt disaster. It was a pity that

279

in spite of this tank's divine legend, it was not well-maintained and the water was not clean. This *kund* had been named after Bhishma, who was the grandsire of the Pandavas and the Kauravas. It is believed that Bhishma lay on a bed of arrows at this very spot during the Kurukshetra battle. It is also believed that Arjuna shot an arrow into the ground to get water for quenching Bhishma's thirst. The water that came out of the ground formed a tank which is known as Bhisham Kund.

Nine days of intense fighting between the Pandavas and the Kauravas has drawn to a close. Bhishma, at the start of the war, had taken an oath that he would not kill any of the Pandavas. Instead, he would kill 1000 soldiers every day. He has managed to keep his promise and inflict heavy casualties on the Pandava army. The Pandavas are a worried lot since they have been unable to subdue Bhishma. Arjuna too has confronted Bhishma on a few occasions, but has been unable to overwhelm him in each of those confrontations.

During one such confrontation, Bhishma smiles at Arjuna and tells him, "Son, please spend your energy on someone else. Attacking me is futile because neither of us will be able to kill the other. You can never overpower and kill me in a battle. I can kill you if I wish to, but I have taken an oath that I will not kill the five Pandavas. So fighting me is a waste of your time and energy."

It is night now. Yudhishtira is sitting in his tent with his hands on his head. He is frustrated since he feels there is no way to conquer Bhishma. He looks even more invincible as each day passes.

Lord Krishna enters Yudhishtira's tent.

He asks Yudhishtira, "Tell me. Why are you so worried?"

Yudhishtira answers, "Oh Keshava! You know everything. I am deeply troubled by our inability to defeat Bhishma. Each day he kills 1000 soldiers and an equal number of horses and elephants. Our resources are fast getting depleted. Unless we do something about this, victory will be theirs."

Lord Krishna is aware of the solution for this problem. However He just smiles and replies, "Let us go and talk to Bhishma himself. He may be able to guide you."

Yudhishtira agrees and along with Lord Krishna, he goes to Bhishma's tent. Bhishma is thrilled to see Krishna and Yudhishtira and warmly welcomes them.

Bhishma asks Yudhishtira, "My son! What brings you to my tent? How can I help you?"

Yudhishtira replies, "We have come to seek your help."

Bhishma laughs, "You have the Lord of the three worlds with you! What help would you need from a mere mortal like me?"

Saying this, Bhishma bows to Krishna, who blesses him.

Yudhishtira, with tears in his eyes, replies, "Oh Grand Sire! After nine days of fierce fighting, I have become frustrated. Is there no way to defeat you? Please tell me what to do. Otherwise, we will never be able to vanquish the Kauravas."

Though Bhishma is the commander of the Kaurava army, his heart is with the Pandavas. He is very well aware that the Pandavas stood for righteousness and they should emerge victorious for the benefit of mankind. He also knows that they would never be able to win this battle as long as he is alive. He realises that it is time to make one more great sacrifice. He decides to tell Yudhishtira how to defeat him.

He replies, "Oh Yudhishtira. I never fight against a woman in a battle. In your army, you have Shikandi, who was a woman in her previous birth. She has the boon from the Almighty to kill me. I will not attack her if she confronts me. Let her attack me tomorrow along with Arjuna. This is the only way to kill me."

Yudhishtira is greatly touched by this noble sacrifice. He once again falls at Bhishma's feet and weeps inconsolably.

It is Day Ten of the battle of Kurukshetra.

Arjuna has been told by Yudhishtira how to defeat Bhishma. Arjuna reluctantly agrees to this scheme since he feels it is an unfair way to defeat an enemy. However, after Lord Krishna convinces him, Arjuna relents.

Shikandi, as advised by Yudhishtira, rides towards Bhishma. Arjuna follows him in his chariot. As soon as Shikandi encounters Bhishma, he begins to shower arrows on Bhishma. Bhishma, realising that it is Shikandi attacking him, drops his bow and arrows. Though Shikandi's arrows pierce his body, he stands still and is unmoved. Suddenly a shower of arrows pierce deep into his body.

He smiles, "Ah! These must be Arjuna's arrows. They pierce the deepest.

It is time for me to bid farewell to this fight."

Arjuan's arrows cover his whole body and he falls from his chariot. Since his entire body is pierced with arrows, they support his body and prevent it from touching the ground. The mighty thud of his body sends shock waves in the Kaurava camp. Both the armies stop the fight and gather around Bhishma to pay their respects to him.

It is believed that if any person wants to attain moksha then he should die during the auspicious Uttarayana (summer solstice) period. Bhishma realises that it is now Dakshinayana (winter solstice). Since he has the boon from the Gods to choose his time of death, he decides to stay alive till the sun shifts to Uttarayana.

He tells his men, "I want to rest here till the beginning of Uttarayana. I will give up my mortal body on the first day of Uttarayana. Please give me a headrest to make myself comfortable."

The Kauravas fetch different types of soft pillows but he refuses all of them.

He tells Arjuna, "Can you please provide me with a headrest befitting a warrior?"

Arjuna nods his head and shoots three arrows that pierce the ground and act as support for Bhishma to rest his head.

Next, he asks for water. The Kauravas fetch various types of fruit juices but he refuses all of them. Once again he turns towards Arjuna.

Arjuna removes an arrow from his quiver and chants a mantra. Fixing the arrow to his Gandiva bow, he shoots the arrow into the ground. The arrow pierces the ground, creating a small fountain of water. The water springs from the ground and enters Bhishma's mouth, quenching his thirst.

It is believed that Arjuna brought Ganga from the ground when he shot an arrow. So this place is also known as *Ban Ganga* (*Ban* means 'arrow'). Since Bhishma had the boon to decide his date and time of death, he continued to live in spite of being grievously injured and lying on a bed of arrows. He waited for the sun to change its position and enter the *Uttarayana* phase before giving up his mortal body.

Right opposite this tank is the Sri Bhishma Pitamah Ban Shaya Temple. As the name suggests, at the centre of the sanctum sanctorum is an idol of Bhishma, lying on a bed of arrows (*Ban*

Shaya means 'bed of arrows'). He can be seen drinking water from the Ganga which has been brought from the earth by an arrow shot by Arjuna. The idols of the Pandavas are kept behind the idol of Bhishma. To the left was *Ram Darbar*, which had white marble idols of Rama, Sita, Lakshmana, and Hanuman. To the left of these idols is a pink idol of Sri Ganga Mata. The idol of Ganga was installed here to symbolise Arjuna bringing the sacred river to quench Bhishma's thirst. To the right of the idol of Bhishma is an idol of Hanuman, known as Panchmaukhi Hanuman since the deity had five heads. To its right is an idol of Sri Durga Mata. There were many pictures that presented the legend of Ban Ganga. The priest was a very generous soul who gave me *prasada* and a booklet which narrated the legend of this place.

To the right of this temple is the Sri Tarkeshwar Mahadev Temple. This temple had a black Shiva Linga mounted on a platform of white marble. Behind the Shiva Linga were idols of Shiva, Parvati, Ganesha, and Nandi. On the right is an idol of Santoshi Mata.

To the left of Sri Bhishma Pitamah Ban Shaya Temple is a very huge orange-coloured idol of Lord Hanuman. A board proclaimed that the height of the idol is 26 feet but it looked much more than that. This huge idol was kept inside an enclosure. A priest sitting in front of this idol applied a red *tilak* on my forehead and gave me *prasada* of puffed rice.

On the other side of the tank is the Sri Krishna Bhagwanji Vishwa Viraat Swaroop Darshan Temple which means the Temple of Sri Krishna which shows His Cosmic Form. This beige coloured temple has walls with *Bhagavad Gita* verses written in simple Hindi. The entire floor is covered with colourful mats. The serene atmosphere allowed me to meditate here for a long time.

The sanctum sanctorum had two blue idols of Lord Krishna. One showed Krishna holding a chariot wheel and the other showed Him displaying His Cosmic Form at the beginning of the Kurukshetra war. To the right is an idol of Bhadrakali Mata. I expressed my surprise on seeing the Bhadrakali idol in this temple.

The priest explained, "Arjuna had prayed to Goddess

Bhadrakali before the commencement of the Kurukshetra war, so this idol is installed here to commemorate that incident."

As I came out of this temple and headed towards the car park, I heard verses of the *Bhagavad Gita* in Hindi coming from a nearby shop. Hearing and seeing different events related to Mahabharata transported me back to the era of Krishna. Instead of walking towards the car park, I began to walk towards the *kund*. My driver saw me walking in the wrong direction and began to call out to me, and broke my trance!

BIRLA GITA TEMPLE

Birla Gita Temple

Birla Gita Temple was built by the late Jugal Kishore Birla. It is located quite close to Brahma Sarovar. I took one of the lanes which was perpendicular to the northern banks of Brahma Sarovar and found this temple to my left. Like the other Birla temples at New Delhi and Vrindavan, this one too is painted maroon and beige. All the temples maintained by the Birlas are known for their high degree of cleanliness and this one was no different. It was one of the cleanest temples in the holy city.

As I entered the temple premises, I saw a Ganesha idol, made of white marble. As I walked further, I came to an inner courtyard. This courtyard had seven white pillars on either side of the sanctum sanctorum with an idol of Hanuman on the right.

The sanctum sanctorum had white marble idols of Krishna and Arjuna. It depicted Krishna preaching the *Bhagavad Gita* to Arjuna, before the start of the Kurukshetra war. The walls near the altar have inscriptions from the 18 chapters of *Bhagavad Gita* in Sanskrit.

The temple was surrounded by well-maintained lawns. I took a stroll around the temple premises. To the right of the temple, I saw a huge platform, made of white marble. The platform walls had Sanskrit inscriptions from the *Bhagavad Gita*. I saw a beautiful chariot, drawn by four horses, resting on top of this platform. Inside the chariot, there was a picture of Krishna preaching the *Bhagavad Gita* to Arjuna. The chariot and the horses were also made of white marble. The entire structure looked simply breathtaking.

As I walked further, I saw another platform. This one was much smaller in size. It had a huge bell, made of white marble. An interesting story was inscribed on this bell. It is believed that Lord Krishna was strolling in this part of Kurukshetra before the start of the war. He found eggs of a *Titu* bird lying on the ground. He realised that these eggs would be crushed during the course of the war. He removed a huge bell that was tied to one of the elephants and protected the eggs by keeping the bell on top of them. After the war, Krishna returned to this spot. By then, the eggs had already hatched and the young ones of the bird were living inside the bell. When Krishna lifted the bell, all the young birds screamed with joy and flew away. Isn't this a fascinating story?

DERA BABA SHRAVANTHJI TEMPLE

This Temple is also known as the Sri Lakshmi Narayan Kaurava Pandava Mandir. It is so called because there are many idols of the Pandavas and the Kauravas in this temple. It is located close to the Birla Gita Temple. The entrance is one of the most colourful ones I have ever seen. As I stood outside the huge gate of the temple and looked at the architecture of the building and the colourful

Entrance of the temple

paintings and carvings on the walls, I wondered if this was a temple or a luxurious palace belonging to one of the rich Rajput kings. On either side of the gate, there were beautiful paintings of Radha and Krishna.

As I walked inside, I found myself in a huge courtyard. There were steps that took me to a locked room. I saw a huge idol of Lord Hanuman in the centre of the room. There were five idols to the left, namely, Shakuni, Dushashana, Karna, Duryodhana, and Guru Dronacharya. On the right were idols of Bhagwan Sri Krishna, Dharamraj Yudhishtira, Draupadi, Arjuna, Gadhadhar Bhima, Nakul, and Sahadev.

There were four paintings which depict the following incidents:

- Dushashana trying to disrobe Draupadi
- Krishna showing His Viraat Swaroop to Arjuna
- The game of dice being played between the Pandavas and the Kauravas
- Krishna and Arjuna blowing Their conches at the start of the Kurukshetra war

To the left was an altar which had idols of Lakshmi, Narayan and Durga Ma. In front of the altar, was a huge bell, kept in a glass enclosure. Lots of devotees had deposited their donations inside the glass enclosure. Some people believe that the incident involving Krishna and the *'Titu'* bird took place here and hence the bell was kept here to commemorate that episode.

BRAHMA SAROVAR

Brahma Sarovar is in the heart of Kurukshetra town. It is also the best known landmark. Whenever I asked the locals for directions to any tourist place, they would guide me using Brahma Sarovar as the 'reference point'. At the entrance was a huge parking lot. There were many shops on either side of the road, selling artefacts related to the Kurukshetra and Brahma Sarovar.

There are many legends associated with the Brahma Sarovar. The most popular legend is that Lord Brahma created the entire cosmos from this sacred place. It is believed that if a person has a bath in this lake on Amavasya (the first night of new moon), or on a solar eclipse day, he will get blessings equivalent to those received by a thousand *Ashwamedha* sacrifices and it would bring him salvation from all sins. It is believed that Krishna, Balarama and Subhadra came all the way from Dwarka and bathed here during the solar eclipse. Most of the

Sri Sarveshwar Mahadevji Temple at
Brahma Sarovar

people from Brij Bhoomi, including Nanda, Yashoda, and Radha came here on this occasion. This would be the final meeting of Krishna and Radha.

It is also believed that when Bhima killed Dushashana, he carried the latter's blood from the battlefield to this place and gave it to Draupadi to fulfil her oath of washing her hair with Dushashana's blood.

As I passed through the main gate, I saw a huge lake which was the Brahma Sarovar. This was the biggest lake in Kurukshetra, measuring 1000 metres by 500 metres. The *sarovar* had concrete walls on all four sides to prevent miscreants from polluting the lake and its surroundings. This magnificent *sarovar* had many bathing ghats, named after famous personalities associated with Mahabharata. I noticed many devotees taking a holy dip in the sacred lake.

I remarked to Vikram, "This *sarovar* must be very sacred. I see hundreds of devotees bathing here."

Vikram laughed out loud. I looked at him, surprised.

Vikram saw the look on my face and said, "Saab! This is nothing compared to what one sees during solar eclipse. Bathing in Brahma Sarovar on a solar eclipse day is equivalent to a thousand *Ashwamedha* sacrifices."

I replied, "So devotees have been coming here for hundreds of years to have a bath during the solar eclipse?"

Vikram said, "No sir! People have been visiting this sacred place for thousands of years, since the era of Lord Krishna! In fact, not only ordinary mortals but even Gods like Krishna, Balarama, and Subhadra visited this place. It was known as 'Samantapanchaka' during those days."

I asked Vikram, "Did they visit this *sarovar* during the battle at Kurukshetra?"

Vikram replied, "No, sir! They came here all the way from Dwarka to witness the solar eclipse. Nanda, Yashoda, and the gopis also came from Brij."

I was surprised, "So did Radha and Krishna finally meet, after years of separation?"

It is the day of the solar eclipse. Bathing in the Samantapanchaka is considered very auspicious. People come from distant places to bathe here. Krishna, accompanied by Balarama and Subhadra comes from Dwarka. Nanda, accompanied by Yashoda, comes from Nandagaon. The gopis too, accompanied by Radha, come to bathe here.

The news about Krishna's presence reaches the gopis. They convey this to Nanda, Yashoda, and Radha. All of them are thrilled to hear this.

Yashoda says, "I have not seen my Kanha ever since He left Nandagaon. Let us go and meet Him."

Nanda agrees.

Radha says, "May I and My friends accompany you?"

Yashoda knows Radha had been pining for Krishna's love, all these years.

She smiles, "Of course Radha! You should accompany us."

All three of them walk towards the sarovar.

Krishna, accompanied by Balarama and Subhadra, is also heading towards the sarovar. Suddenly, He hears a loud cry, "Kanha!"

He turns and looks around. He sees Nanda, Yashoda, Radha and the gopis. Krishna is thrilled to see them and He and Balarama run towards them. They prostrate in front of Their foster parents and seek their blessings. Nanda and Yashoda weep with joy. Yashoda says, "My Kanha! I never thought I would see You again! You and Balarama never visited us after going to Mathura. Did you forget us and our humble dwellings?"

Krishna pacifies her, "Oh Mother! How can We ever forget both of you? Though Devaki gave birth to Us, you are Our real mother. I might forget Mathura and its palaces, but not the villages and forests of Brij."

Yashoda wipes her tears, "Kanha! As usual, You have won me with Your words!"

Krishna and Balarama hug Nanda who enquires about Their well-being. All of them talk about what They have been doing during these years.

Krishna notices Radha, standing a few paces away, watching Them silently.

He goes near Her and says, "Radhe! How are You?"

Radha had been controlling Her emotions so far. Hearing Krishna enquire about Her, Her heart is filled with mixed emotions. She is elated seeing Krishna and recollecting the golden days that She spent with Her Kanha in the forests of Brij Bhoomi. She also feels sad, thinking of Their separation.

She looks in His eyes and replies, "Kanha! I have been waiting for You all these years. I have spent My time sitting on the banks of the Yamuna waiting for You. I have been calling out Your name and asking every bird, every animal, if they have seen You. When I see butterflies fluttering near the bushes, I chase them and ask them about Your whereabouts. When I hear the sounds of chariot wheels, I run out to see if it is You. When I hear the sound of music, I wake up, wondering if it is from Your flute. Without You, I feel like a flower without nectar. Like a river without water. Not a minute passes without My remembering You. And You ask Me how I am!"

Krishna takes Her hand and touches His heart, "Oh Radha! You always reside here, in My heart. I might be staying hundreds of miles away from You, but I always think of You. I may be living in magnificent palaces but I always remember the houses of Vrindavan. I may be riding the swiftest horses in Mathura but I can never forget the cows of Gokul. I may be spending My days with the noblemen of Mathura in My court but how can I ever forget My cowherds and gopis of Vrindavan. I may be travelling across the length and breadth of My kingdom but I will never forget the dusty towns of Brij Bhoomi. I may swim in different lakes and rivers in the country, but how can I ever forget splashing around the waters of River Yamuna with You. I may be fighting battles and conquering kingdoms, but I still dream of the Ras Lila with You and the gopis of Vrindavan. The cooks in the royal kitchens may prepare hundreds of delicacies everyday for Me but I miss the simple fare that You cooked for me on the banks of Pavan Sarovar."

Radha's eyes become moist, recollecting Her pastimes with Her beloved Kanha.

Krishna continues, "Even after I left Nandagaon, I have been spending every moment of My life with You. I am playing the flute and You are dancing beside Me. I am sitting on the foothills of Goverdhan with You by My side. I am frolicking around the groves of Madhuvan with You. I am bathing in the Yamuna with You. I might have married many Princesses from royal lineages but You will always hold a special place in My heart. How can We ever be separated, Radha?"

Radha is unable to control Her tears, they roll down Her cheeks.

She holds Krishna's hand and sobs, "Oh Kanha! I have been waiting for this day. After waiting for so many years, I had begun to think that I may never meet You again."

Krishna consoles Her, "Radhe! When I met You for the last time in Nandagaon, I had promised You that I would meet You once again before We depart. This is Our last meeting in this material world."

Hundreds of Brij Bhoomi residents, who have come to Samantapanchaka on the occasion of solar eclipse, watch Radha's tearful reunion with Her beloved, Krishna. Tears roll down their cheeks as they watch the meeting of the two divine Soul Mates. They realise that they have been fortunate to witness an emotional event that even the Gods in Heaven would have cherished. The Master of the three worlds expressing His feelings towards His beloved Radha! They prostrate before Radha and Krishna and seek Their blessings. Even the Sun God, witnessing this poignant event, hides His face in grief, causing an eclipse around the world!

I looked around and saw the sun shining brightly. There was no solar eclipse today. Had the sun forgotten the heart-rending incident? Maybe, 5000 years had lapsed since then!

I decided to further explore this famous landmark. As I walked on the pathway in the middle, I noticed that it separated the lake into two. I took the path to the left which led me to a bridge. A walk of about 50 feet across this bridge took me to Sri Sarveshwar Mahadevji Temple. This temple was an island, in the middle of Brahma Sarovar. This beige-coloured temple had a beautiful courtyard with red stone floors and also had exquisite carvings on all the walls. The entrance to this temple was from the side, so when I entered, I found the sanctum sanctorum to my right. At the entrance, on the left, was an idol of Lord Hanuman. I walked further to reach the sanctum sanctorum, which had a Shiva Linga at the centre and idols of Shiva, Paravti, and Ganesha at the back. It is believed that this Shiva Linga was installed by none other than Lord Brahma Himself. I walked to my left and found a shrine of Sri Garud Narayan, which had a white marble idol of Lord Vishnu on His carrier, Garuda.

After a visit to the Sri Sarveshwar Mahadevji Temple, I retraced my steps to the entrance of Brahma Sarovar. This time, I took the central pathway which led me to three more temples. On my left, I saw the Sri Katyayani Devi Temple. As the name suggested, this temple was dedicated to Goddess Katyayani Devi. It had a magnificent white idol of the Goddess.

As I walked further, I saw a temple which was painted a fiery red. This has an idol of Lord Hanuman. Opposite this temple was an ancient building, known as Prachin Mandir Chandrakup. The altar had a black idol of Lord Krishna and to its left were 15 steps that led to a well below.

Prachin Mandir Chandrakup

It is believed that Draupadi drew water from this well and gave it to the thirsty Pandavas. Hence this place is also known as Pandava

"Well" used by the Pandavas

Draupadi Kup (*Kup* means 'well').

The Kurukshetra war rages on. Bhima remembers the oath that he and Draupadi had taken in the court of Dhritrashtara, when Dushashana had tried to disrobe Draupadi.

His fiery oath had reverberated and shaken the entire court, "Oh Dushashana! You have dared to insult Draupadi, who is the light of the Pandava dynasty. I will break those arms of yours which pulled at Draupadi's clothes. I will detach those arms from your body, you insolent fool!"

Draupadi too had taken an equally horrifying oath, "Dushashana held my hair as he dragged me from my chamber into Dhritrashtara's court. I will not tie my hair till my husbands avenge this humiliation by killing Dushashana!"

Bhima roared, "Oh Draupadi! I will break Dushashana's bones. I will tear open his chest and drink his blood."

Draupadi told Bhima in front of a shocked court, "Please bring me his blood. I will wash my hair with his blood and only then will I tie my hair!"

Bhima recollects this fateful incident as he stands in his chariot. He asks his charioteer to take him towards Dushashana. The charioteer obeys his command.

Bhima roars at Dushashana, "Oh wicked one! Today is the last day of your life! Decide with which weapon you wish to die!"

Dushashana picks up his bow and showers arrows on Bhima who is able to split them easily with his arrows. This continues for a long time without either gaining an upper hand since they are evenly matched. Bhima now decides to use his favourite weapon, the mace. He picks up his mace and steps off his chariot. Dushashana follows suit. Both of them rush towards each other and engage in a deadly duel which lasts a few hours. Finally, an exhausted Dushashana falls to the ground. An elated Bhima realises his time has come. He lifts his mace and strikes lethal blows on Dushashana. Dushashana wriggles in pain. Bhima throws his mace away. Seeing this, Dushashana is relieved. He thinks Bhima will spare him. However, his joy is short-lived. Bhima grabs Dushashana's arms and begins to pull them. Dushashana screams in agony but Bhima continues. He severs the arms of Dushashana from his body. Bhima screams in delight as he watches Dushashana's torso wriggling in pain. He collects the blood that is oozing from Dushashana's body and begins to gulp it. Uttering a loud cry, he dances around Dushashana's dead body. He suddenly remembers Draupadi's oath. He bends down and collects the blood flowing from Dushashana's body and rushes towards Samantapanchaka.

Draupadi is sitting near an old well in Samantapanchaka. Her eyes light up when she sees Bhima, accompanied by his brothers, rushing towards her.

Bhima is ecstatic and screams with joy. He shouts, "Oh Draupadi! Your wait is finally over. I have killed Dushashana and severed his arms. The same arms that had dared to disrobe you. I have also brought his blood for you to wash your hair."

Draupadi collects the blood and washes her hair.

She thanks Bhima and says, "Finally, the day has come! Now that my oath has been fulfilled, I will once again tie my hair."

Bhima says, "Oh Draupadi! We are all very exhausted and thirsty. Can you please give us some water?"

Draupadi walks to the well nearby. She draws water from the well and quenches the thirst of the Pandavas.

GAUDIYA MATH

Gaudiya Math is located on the northern banks of Brahma Sarovar. As the name suggests, this Math has been built by Gauda Vaishnavas, ardent followers of Lord Chaitanya Mahaprabhu. They consider Chaitanya Mahaprabhu to be an incarnation of Lord Krishna.

Gaudiya Math, Shri Jayaram Vidyapeeth, and Gita Bhavan are located close by, adjacent to one another. Gaudiya Math is at an elevation and located behind a string of small gift shops that adorn the road. I would have missed this building had I not been watchful. There were about 10 steps at the entrance to this building. As I climbed these steps, I came across a ticket counter on my left. For just two rupees, I was allowed to enter a huge room full of puppets. These puppets depicted the glorious pastimes of Lord Krishna. There were 19 glass showcases, each depicting an incident.

The incidents depicted were:

1. Brahma's birth from the navel of Vishnu
2. Krishna dancing on the poisonous serpent, Kaliya
3. Krishna stealing butter from the houses of gopis
4. Chaitanya Mahaprabhu singing *Sankirtan* in the forests of Brij Bhoomi
5. Krishna killing the serpent demon, Aghasura
6. Krishna killing the bull demon, Aristasura
7. Balarama killing the donkey demon, Dhenukasura
8. Radha with Krishna
9. Vishnu taking birth as Krishna in a prison cell that houses Devaki and Vasudev
10. Vasudev carrying Krishna on his head and crossing the Yamuna
11. Yashoda giving birth to Yogamaya
12. Krishna killing the demoness, Putana
13. Krishna performing Ras Lila with the gopis
14. Krishna lifting the Goverdhan Hill
15. Krishna killing his evil cousin, Shishupala
16. Krishna meeting the gopis at Brahma Sarovar on the day of a solar eclipse
17. Krishna coming to Kurukshetra with His family on the occasion of solar eclipse
18. Krishna seeking the blessings of His foster parents, Yashoda and Nanda
19. Uddhav reading Krishna's message to the gopis

All these puppets looked so real that I felt as if I was witnessing these incidents in Dwapara Yuga. When I came out of this room, I found myself once more in Kali Yuga!

As I ascended five more steps, I reached the top of the building. I had reached the sanctum sanctorum of this Math. It had a black idol of Krishna, flanked by idols of Radha and Chaitanya Mahaprabhu. I proceeded further and reached an open courtyard. I suddenly felt as if I was in the 15th century. Cows tied to wooden stumps, kids with *gopichandana* adorning their foreheads, running around in dhotis!

Behind this courtyard is the Veda Vyas Temple. To its right were many rooms, where the residents of the Math lived. Technology and its associated modern day evils have not affected the serene ambience of this place.

SRI JAIRAM VIDYAPEETH

Sri Jairam Vidyapeeth is also located on the northern banks of Brahma Sarovar. As I stood in front of Gaudiya Math, with my back to Brahma Sarovar, I saw this Vidyapeeth on my left. The temple was built in 1973 by Sri Devendra Swaroop Bramhachari.

When I crossed the main gate of the Vidyapeeth, I saw many small mantapas on either side

Sri Jairam Vidyapeeth

of the gate. Each mantapa housed a small idol. The mantapas on the right had idols of Shiva, six of the 10 incarnations of Vishnu, namely, Matsya, Kurma, Varaha, Narasimha, Vamana, and Parashurama. Next to them were idols of sages like Gautama, Bharadwaj, Vishwamitra, Kashyapa, Jamadagni, Vasistha, Atreya, and Arundati.

The mantapas on the left had idols of the remaining four incarnations of Vishnu, namely, Rama, Krishna, Budha, Kalki, and various forms of Durga such as Siddhidhatri Durga, Maha Gauri Durga, Kaal Ratri Durga, Katyayani Durga, Skanda Mata Durga, Krishnapada Durga, Chandraganda Durga, Brahmacharini Durga, Shailaputri Durga, and Santoshi Mata Durga.

Bheeshma lying on a bed of arrows

There are white statues on either side of the path leading to the sanctum sanctorum. The one on the left depicts Karna, plucking out his golden tooth and handing it to Krishna, who comes to him in the guise of a poor brahmin. On the right is the famous incident of Bhishma lying on a bed of arrows and Arjuna bringing him the holy water from Ganga by shooting an arrow into the ground.

A walk down the path leads to the main temple. At the entrance is a huge idol of Krishna, standing in front of a cow and playing His flute. As I walked into the inner courtyard, I saw two more huge idols. The one on the left was Parashurama and the one on the right was Ganesha. As I walked further, I came to the sanctum sanctorum of the temple. This consisted of five altars. The altar on the left had an idol of Hanuman, with an inscription from the *Rig Veda* on the door. The altar on the right had an idol of Durga Ma, with an inscription from the *Atharva Veda* on its door. At the centre, there were three altars. One had idols of Rama, Sita, Lakshmana, and Hanuman, with an inscription from the *Yajura Veda* on its door. Next to it was an altar that housed idols of Vishnu and Lakshmi. To its right was an altar that had idols of Krishna and Radha. The door had an inscription from the *Sama Veda*. It is believed that each inscription denoted the direction of each *Veda*.

Behind the main temple was the Rameshwar Shiva Temple. At the entrance was a Shiva Linga. Behind this was a small room which had a glass enclosure. It had a magnificent Shiva Linga inside the glass enclosure whose base was made of silver and the mound was made of pure *mani* (gemstone). It was simply breathtaking!

To the right of the main temple was a building which had numerous puppets depicting different incidents that occurred during the Mahabharata story. An entry fee of two rupees is all that is needed to go to the basement and see those beautiful puppets! As in Gaudiya Math, here too, the puppets were enclosed in glass showcases.

The incidents depicted were:

1. Veda Vyasa dictating the Mahabharata epic to Lord Ganesha
2. Dushashana trying to disrobe Draupadi in the court of the Kauravas
3. Krishna trying to mediate with the Kauravas
4. Arjuna and Duryodhana seeking Krishna's help before the war
5. Krishna as Arjuna's Charioteer
6. Krishna showing His Viraat Swaroop to Arjuna
7. Sanjay narrating the incidents of the Mahabharata war to the blind king Dhritrashtra
8. Draupadi seeking blessings from Bhishma
9. Gatotkacha creating havoc on the battlefield
10. A frustrated Krishna trying to kill Bhishma
11. Kunti imploring Karna to join the Pandavas
12. Gandhari blessing her son Duryodhana
13. Bhima killing Duryodhana
14. Krishna performing the coronation of Yudhishtira after his victory
15. Brahma Sarovar

To the right of this building is a huge multi-storeyed building. This is the residential quarters of the students who study at this Vidyapeeth.

GITA BHAVAN

Gita Bhavan is also located on the northern banks of Brahma Sarovar. It is quite close to Sri Jairam Vidyapeeth. There is a tall Dharamshala building in front of Gita Bhavan, so I did not notice it in the first instance. There is a narrow dusty path near these buildings that led me to the Gita Bhavan. Gita Bhavan is on an elevation of about a hundred metres from the ground, so the climb can be quite tough for aged people. Gita Bhavan is a beautiful edifice but it is a pity that it is completely hidden from the main road because of the Dharamshala in front of it.

When I reached the top, I had to turn to my left and walk a few metres. The main temple was the Sri Krishna Temple. It had an idol of Krishna, flanked by idols of Shiva and Durga. To the left was an idol of Hanuman. Near by, was an idol of Ganesha and ten idols depicting various forms of Durga. On the right side of the altar was an idol of Krishna. The entire floor was covered with a white mattress and the ceiling was well-decorated with a colourful velvet cloth. The walls had beautiful carvings and pictures depicting the pastimes of Krishna.

To the left of the Sri Krishna Temple was a Shiva Temple. This had a Shiva Linga at the centre and idols of Shiva, Parvati, and Ganesha behind it. To the left of the Shiva Temple was the Vishwa Swaroop Sri Vamana Bhagwan Mandir. The idol depicted Lord Vishnu, in His Vamana Avatara, crushing King Bali. To the right of the Sri Krishna Temple was the Sri Lakshmi Narayan Temple. It had a blue-coloured idol of Lord Narayan and a white idol of Goddess Lakshmi.

SANNIHIT SAROVAR

Sannihit Sarovar, like Brahma Sarovar, is a very important bathing tank in Kurukshetra, measuring about 500 metres by 150 metres. It is three kilometres from the central point of Kurukshetra town, on the way to Pehowa. It is believed to be the meeting point of the seven tributaries of the sacred river Saraswati. When I stepped out of my car, I saw a very strange sight. At the entrance of the *sarovar*, the dates of solar eclipse for the next five years had been painted on the wall.

Sannihit Sarovar

I thought, why have they written these dates? What is the significance?

As if reading my thoughts, my guide Vikram informed me, "The belief here is similar to that of Brahma Sarovar. The devotees believe that taking a bath here at the time of a solar eclipse is equivalent to performing a thousand *Ashwamedha* sacrifices. It is also believed that all the *Tirthas* (holy rivers) assemble here on the *Amavasya* (new moon) day."

I asked him thoughtfully, "Any chance of having a solar eclipse in the next few hours? I don't mind having a bath if we have a solar eclipse soon."

Vikram chuckled, "Saab! It is not so easy. You have to wait for years. You should visit Sannihit Sarovar during a solar eclipse. This *sarovar* will be swarming with thousands of people. Hundreds of people will be bathing at the same time so you will not be able to see even an inch of water."

I reached the steps of the *sarovar*. I saw many people bathing. Near the steps of the *sarovar*, I saw a priest, along with a group of people, performing a *puja*. As I walked further, I saw similar scenes. I looked at Vikram. He explained, "Sannihit Sarovar is considered the most sacred place for performing *Shraddha* (prayers to the departed souls). People immerse the ashes of the cremated bodies and perform *Shraddha*, just as they do in the River Ganga at Varanasi."

I asked him, "Do the locals consider this place to be as holy as the Ganga?"

He replied, "When people die in Punjab, Haryana, and

adjacent areas, they find it difficult to go to Varanasi. They come to Sannihit Sarovar and perform the last rites. It is believed that if a dead person's last rites are performed here, his soul will automatically go to Vaikunta."

I was left wondering if the process to go to Vaikunta, the Holy Abode of Lord Vishnu, was so simple!

As I reached the edge of the *sarovar*, I took a turn to the left and walked towards the temples situated on one side of Sannihit Sarovar. The first one was a red temple, Sri Surya Narayan Temple. This temple had two idols of Lord Vishnu. I took the blessings of the Lord and walked to the right.

I came to another temple, Sri Nilkanta Mahadev Temple. The blue idol has only the face of Lord Shiva, also known as *Nilkanta* (He whose throat turned blue because of the poison that He drank to protect the world).

In front of this temple, I saw a Shiva Temple and a Santoshi Mata temple. I retraced our steps and walked towards the road. At the corner, to my left, I saw another temple, painted bright red. This was the Dhruva Narayan Temple. It had idols of Dhruva and his master Lord Narayan. Both these were made of pure white marble.

BHOR SAIDAN

Bhor Saidan is around 12 km from Kurukshetra, on the way to Pehowa. While travelling from Kurukshetra to Pehowa, this temple is on the right side. We parked our car a few metres from the main gate. We were disappointed to see that the gate had been locked from inside. We knocked a few times, but no one came out. My guide, Vikram, grew impatient. Vikram is a 'body builder' by profession who works as a guide in his spare time. This probably makes him behave more as a wrestler than as a guide! He flexed his muscles and began to bang the gate furiously. Hearing the loud thumping noise, one of the priests arrived at the gate. He partially opened the gate and asked Vikram why he was banging on the gate so violently. Vikram replied that we wanted to visit the temple. The priest retorted that the temple was closed till 4 pm. He asked us to come later. Vikram was wild since he was not a person who would take 'no' for an answer. He threatened to break open the gate. He also told the priest that he had 'high level contacts' and would get the priest removed from his post! The priest was a tough nut to crack. He muttered, 'Come back at 4 pm,' and walked away. I found the whole spectacle quite amusing. I patted Vikram and said, "We have not had lunch, let us go back to town and eat. We will come back later."

A couple of hours later, we returned to Bhor Saidan. This time, the gate was wide open. To my left, I saw a huge room which had many pictures of Krishna. I also saw an idol of Krishna resting in a cradle. To its right was a Shiva Linga, made of copper. As I walked further, I saw a red temple. This temple had a black Shiva Linga with a border made of white marble. The room was octagonal in shape. I heard continuous chants of 'Om Namo Shivaya'. As I performed the Parikrama of the temple, I saw a small temple dedicated to Hanuman. This was Sankat Mochan Hanuman Temple. Next to this, was a temple dedicated to Raja Rajeshwari. It had an idol of the Goddess sitting on a lion.

On the other side of the temple was a huge open courtyard. The courtyard had six *samadhis* of saints who were associated with this place. A priest, with a white flowing beard, came and struck up a conversation with us. He asked me, in Hindi, where I had come from. When I told him I was from Bangalore, he switched over to Kannada. It was a pleasant surprise! Even in my wildest dreams, I had not imagined that I would meet a fellow Kannadiga in a remote village in Haryana. The white dhoti-kurta clad priest told me that his name was Prasad and he hailed from Karnataka. He had left his family behind in Karnataka and was staying here with another priest. He waved his hand towards the other priest who was walking towards us. Imagine our shock when we discovered that he was none other than the priest who had been abused by Vikram a couple of hours ago! Vikram apologised for his bad behaviour and the priest was quite forgiving. He told us that he gets up every morning at four a.m. so he needs to rest in the afternoon. We nodded our heads in sympathy.

The priest continued, "We lock the gates because many unruly tourists come and disturb our crocodiles. We take care of them like our own children. We do not want their sleep to be disturbed."

'Crocodiles' did someone say?

I laughed and told the priest, "You won't believe this, but I thought you said crocodiles!"

The priest replied with a serious look in his eyes, "Yes, you heard right. That's what I said."

I jumped out of fear and looked everywhere in the courtyard. It was the priest's turn to laugh. He said, "Not here! Please go to the other end of the courtyard and look."

We went to the wall of the courtyard and peered at the other side. We saw a huge lake filled with weeds and plants. I could spot a few crocodiles resting on the rocks. I cried out loud, "Look at them! Won't they come and attack us?" The priest laughed, "They are our babies!"

I asked the priest to narrate the legend of Bhor Saidan.

It is the first day of the Kurukshetra war between the Pandavas and the Kauravas. Lord Krishna, while reciting the Bhagavad Gita, *tells Arjuna, 'Bhavan Bhishmascha Karnascha Kripascha samitim jayah, Ashwatthama Vikarnascha Saumadattis tathaiva cha' (There are personalities like you, Bhishma, Karna, Kripa, Aswatthama, Vikarna, and the son of Somadatta who are always victorious in battle). The 'son of Somadatta' refers to Bhurisrava, who was considered to be one of the best warriors and invincible in most of the battles that he had fought.*

It is the fourteenth day of the war. After the fall of Bhishma, Dronacharya has taken over as the Commander-in-chief of the Kaurava army. A fierce battle is raging between the two armies. Bhurisrava, the son of Somadatta, whom Lord Krishna had Himself extolled on the first day of the war, leads the attack on the Pandavas. A fierce battle takes place between Satyaki and Bhurisrava. Satyaki showers arrows at Bhurisrava who manages to shoot them down. Next, Satyaki throws a javelin at Bhurisrava and breaks his bow. Bhurisrava picks up his sword and jumps down from his chariot. Satyaki follows suit. A fierce battle ensues. Both of them are highly skilled sword-fighters, so neither is able to get the better of the other. Finally, Bhurisrava strikes one mighty blow and Satyaki falls on the ground. Bhurisrava notices that Satyaki's sword has fallen from his hands and is lying a few feet away from him. Seizing this opportunity, he raises his sword to kill an unarmed Satyaki. Arjuna reaches the spot, he shoots a shower of arrows which sever both the arms of Bhurisrava. In the meanwhile, Satyaki gets up and picks up his sword. With one mighty swing of his arm, he beheads Bhurisrava.

What a gory end to such a mighty warrior. Compared to this, playing with the crocodile seemed like child's play!

As we were chatting, we suddenly heard someone calling us. It was Prasad, the priest, informing us that tea was ready. He had earlier insisted that we should have tea and snacks with them. We went to the residential quarters and sat on a cot made of wood and coir. All of us drank the tea and munched on the biscuits that he offered us.

Seeing Vikram chatting and joking with the two priests, I wondered how a situation could change within a couple of hours. A few hours back, Vikram was at loggerheads with the priests and now, here he was, chatting with them and patting their back!

ASTIPURA AND RIVER SARASWATI

Most of the tourist books and pamphlets give the exact location of the tourist places. However, Astipura was an exception. Most of the books and websites had not even mentioned this place, leave alone specify its exact location. There was only one book which said, 'Astipura is located to the west of Thanesar'. However, there was one small problem. It did not tell us if it was one kilometre, or five kilometres, or twenty kilometres from Thanesar!

I stated this problem to Vikram, my guide. He asked many local people but none seemed to know Astipura. After spending three days with me, I noticed that my passion and enthusiasm had rubbed off on him. I decided to give up our futile search. But, he would have none of it! He said, "Sir, I have lots of contacts. I know people who know each and every spot in Kurukshetra. Give me 15 more minutes and I will locate it for you." Fifteen minutes and 10 phone calls later, Vikram was ready to eat his words!

I suddenly hit upon an idea. I told Vikram, "Let us go to Neelkanthi Yatri Nivas. Since it is a hotel run by the Haryana Tourism Department, they will surely be able to tell us the location."

Vikram agreed that it was an excellent idea. We hopped into

the taxi and sped off to Neelkanthi Yatri Nivas. Since I had taken a few meals here during the past couple of days, I was familiar with the hotel staff. I narrated my problem to one of them. He thought for a while and suggested, "I recommend that you meet Mr. Purohit, the Curator at Krishna Museum. He is the most knowledgeable person in this part of the world. If he can't solve your problem, then no one else can."

With renewed hope and enthusiasm, we drove to the Krishna Museum. At the entrance of the museum, we asked a security guard to take us to Mr. Purohit. Having been a victim of government red tapism on many occasions, I expected a long delay. I was in for a pleasant surprise! Within a couple of minutes, we were escorted to the chambers of Mr. Purohit. I had one more pleasant surprise as I entered the room. I had expected Mr. Purohit to be one of those typical government servants. However, he looked more like a corporate executive, working on his laptop. I nervously went in and introduced myself. Mr. Purohit shook hands with me and asked me about the purpose of my visit. I told him I was writing a book on Krishna. This interested him and he began to mention all the places in and around Kurukshetra that were associated with Krishna and Mahabharata. I told him that I had just one more place to visit since I had covered the rest of the places in the past couple of days. He was curious to know which was left. I replied, "I have been desperately hunting for Astipura for a long time. Do you know its location?"

"Astipura," he repeated. He looked at Vikram and asked him, "How long have you two been hunting for this place?"

Vikram replied, "Since the past two hours."

Mr. Purohit guffawed, "Two hours you said? You call that a 'long time'? My dear friends, I have been searching for it for the past two years and have not yet found it!"

He explained the kind of research that he was doing. He showed us many articles and books that mentioned his research work. He informed us that, currently, his two pet projects were the identification of the location of Saraswati and identification of the location of Astipura. I asked him to tell us more about his findings.

Mr. Purohit informed us that he had discovered the lost river Saraswati at a place behind Bhor Saidan, about 15 km of Kurukshetra, on the Pehowa road. He told us that the scientists from ISRO had taken pictures from satellites and had reported that this location possibly matched what was described in the Vedic scriptures. Excavation at the riverbed also led to the discovery of painted greyware and pottery which were used during the Mahabharat era.

He said, "If you want to look at the site, please go to Bhor Saidan village. Behind the Bhor Saidan temple, you will see a narrow muddy road. This will lead you to the riverbed." Regarding the location of Astipura, he told us that he had 'zeroed down' on two places. One was at Kaithal, which was 45 km southwest of Kurukshetra. The other possible location was Shamshipura, near Jyotisar, five kilometres from Kurukshetra. He also cautioned us that searching for Astipura may be futile since there was a strong chance that the erstwhile Astipura may have been taken over by agricultural lands.

We thanked Mr. Purohit for sharing his findings with us and bid him goodbye. We boarded the taxi with a renewed determination to locate River Saraswati and Astipura. I was quite excited to hear about this river from the curator since I had read contradictory articles and views in many books and websites. There are many who believe that this river existed during the era of Krishna. However, there are many cynics who say that this was only a mythical river which existed only in the scriptures. Though I had read that this river was supposed to have flowed through the fertile plains of Haryana, I never knew I was so close to seeing it!

We went back towards Bhor Saidan Temple and took a narrow lane behind it. Mr. Purohit had informed us that most of the houses in this village were built with bricks that belonged to the pre-historic era. Seeing them, I understood what he had meant. The bricks were very thin and looked fragile. They were less than half the size of modern bricks. We drove about 500 metres and had to halt our vehicle since no road existed beyond this point. We looked around and saw only fields. An old *Sardarji* (Sikh) was passing by, on his mobike. He realised we were tourists and stopped his vehicle. I told him the purpose of our visit.

Sikhs are supposed to be one of the friendliest and helpful people in the world and this gentleman certainly lived up to that reputation. He got down from his mobike and asked us to accompany him. We walked about 100 metres with him. He stopped and his trained eyes pointed towards a patch of wet land which was around one kilometre from the place where we stood. He asked us to focus our eyes in that direction. Suddenly, we noticed a small stream flowing near the wet patch of land. We also saw a dried riverbed, as described by Mr. Purohit. He declared triumphantly, "My friends! That is a tributary of River Saraswati. Many people say that this river never existed. It is sheer rubbish! Recently, the Government of India has also clicked photographs of these places using satellites and it has been proved beyond doubt that this river is Saraswati. The location as mentioned in the scriptures matches the location as gauged by the satellites."

He was prepared to take us much closer to the flowing tributary. However, because of the paucity of time, we had to excuse ourselves. We thanked him and hurried back to our taxi to continue our journey towards Shamshipura.

Shamshipura is a small village, five kilometres from Kurukshetra, close to Jyotisar. As I approached Jyotisar, I saw a board telling us that a right turn would take us to Shamshipura. I got down from the car and walked to my right. Soon, I arrived at Shamshipura village. I asked the locals about Astipura and none of them seemed to have heard about it. I decided to explore the surroundings and spent an hour searching for the lost Astipura. I saw only agricultural lands everywhere. I remembered Mr. Purohit's words that it was quite likely that the erstwhile Astipura may have been converted into a field.

I felt sad that a place, so rich in heritage and history had probably ceased to exist in its original form and was converted to agricultural fields to cultivate crops! *Asti* means 'remains (ashes) of a cremated body'. Did Astipura indicate a cremation ground? Whose cremation had taken place here? In the midst of the mustard crops, could I see smoke ascending towards the Heavens?

The 18-day war at Kurukshetra is finally over. The Pandavas have emerged victorious. Though both sides suffered heavy losses, the five Pandava brothers remained alive at the end of the war. After the initial euphoria and celebrations, it is time for introspection. Lord Krishna advises the Pandavas that they should express their gratitude to the warriors who fought for them and laid down their lives. Yudhisthira, the epitome of righteousness, promptly agrees. He calls his brothers and tells them, "Let us go to the outskirts of this holy city where the dead bodies have been cremated. It is our duty to pray for the departed souls of our kith and kin. This is the only way we can thank them and express our gratitude."

His brothers agree. The Pandavas, accompanied by Lord Krishna and Kunti go to the cremation ground. The Pandavas are shocked at the heartrending scenes. They witness funeral pyres still being lit. The fire from some of the pyres is still simmering. Young widows are weeping inconsolably, banging their foreheads on the wooden logs kept nearby. They see young boys light the funeral pyres of their departed fathers, who had died in the battle.

Yudhishtira, unable to bear these scenes, cries out, "Oh Keshava! A victory, but at what cost? Because of me, thousands of young girls have become widows, young children have lost their fathers. I am solely responsible for this great tragedy. The people of this great nation will never forgive me for this. How can I look up and show my face to these young widows and orphaned children? What sin have they committed to suffer this way?"

Krishna puts His arm around Yudhishtira and hugs him. Krishna comforts the grieving Pandava, "Oh Righteous One! What you fought was not for materialistic comforts. It was a 'Dharma Yudha' (war to protect righteousness). The people who died for you were great soldiers. They will be liberated from the cycle of repeated births and deaths. I assure you that each one of them will attain moksha. They were great souls who had just one more human birth left before attaining moksha. Today, by dying for the cause of righteousness, they have achieved that. You and your brothers have just been tools for them to reach the holy abode of Vaikunta."

Yudhishtira feels comforted, knowing that this is one more of Lord Krishna's Lilas. The Pandavas bathe and change into white clothes. They perform the last rites for all the departed souls who were either their relatives, or had fought for them.

Yudhishtira says, "We have finished the last rites. Let us leave and head towards Hastinapura."

Kunti continues to sit in front of the sacrificial fire.

Yudhisthira goes to her and says, "Oh Mother! Please get up. The time has come for us to leave now."

Kunti is weeping inconsolably.

Yudhishtira says, "I can understand how you feel. Even I am devastated to see the loss of lives that I have caused when I see thousands of bodies being cremated here. However, we now have a duty to perform at Hastinapura also. Since we have finished performing the last rites of our dear ones, let us go."

Kunti continues to weep. She looks at Krishna. Krishna, the omniscient God, knows what is going on in her mind. He finds it difficult to watch a weeping mother grieving for the death of her eldest son. He looks away.

Kunti wonders if she should reveal her secret or not. She had maintained the secret for the past few decades. However, she also realises that if she does not reveal her secret now then she would be doing great injustice to a person who was not only a great warrior but also a wonderful human being. She finally replies, "Oh Yudhishtira! You have forgotten to perform the last rites of one more person."

Yudhishtira is surprised. He thinks of all the departed ones whose last rites had been performed. He says, "Oh Mother! I think I have performed the last rites for everyone. Pray, tell me if I have forgotten someone."

Kunti weeps, "You have forgotten the one who is the closest to you."

Yudhishtira says, "I do not know who you are referring to."

Kunti cries out, "Karna!"

The Pandavas are stunned

Bhima is the first to speak, "Oh Mother! Karna! He is the son of a charioteer. He is not even a kshatriya, let alone being our relative. He is also the closest friend of our sworn enemy, Duryodhana. Why should we pray for his soul?"

Kunti looks at Lord Krishna and says, "My Lord! Will you clarify the reason to Bhima or do you want me to perform this difficult task also?"

Krishna narrates the story of Karna's birth. The Pandavas are shocked to know that Karna was actually born a Pandava, their eldest brother.

Arjuna begins to weep, "Oh Keshava! Why did you not tell this to me earlier? I have committed the most heinous crime, of killing my elder brother! The ages to come will never forgive Arjuna for taking the life of his own dear brother. Had I known this, I would never have killed him."

Yudhishtira says, "Had I known that Karna was my elder brother, I would never have fought this war. I would have happily given him the kingdom of Indraprasta and retired to the forest."

Kunti says, "I had begged Karna to spare the life of my sons. He had assured me that he would not kill any of the Pandavas, other than Arjuna. He had told me that either he, or Arjuna, would survive, so I would have five sons left intact at the end of the war."

Bhima recollects, "I fought with Karna prior to his death. It was a fierce duel where he defeated me. If he wanted to, he could have killed me. I was surprised when he spared my life. Now I understand the reason for his generosity."

Nakula and Sahadev too recollect similar incidents.

Yudhisthira is devastated, "We had such a generous brother whom we never recognised. Instead, we kept taunting him, calling him names. The Gods will never forgive me for this!"

Krishna comforts them, "My brothers, I know how you all feel. This is the time for us to realise what we have lost. However, you should realise that you were not fighting your brothers and cousins but enemies of righteousness. All those who oppose Dharma are your enemies and Karna, by being a staunch supporter of Duryodhana, was one of them. Had I informed you of this before the war, I know you would not have fought in it. Duryodhana would have continued his tyrannical rule. Would the people have forgiven you for that? Watching a crime being committed and remaining passive is as sinful as committing the crime."

Yudhishtira and his brothers feel comforted. They sit down and perform the last rites of their brother, Karna.

BHADRAKALI TEMPLE

This temple is also known as Sri Devi Kup Bhadrakali Mandir. It is considered to be one of the 18 Shakti Peethas. This temple has a very good parking lot but it is a long walk from the parking lot to the temple. As I walked towards the temple, I saw shops on either side of the road, selling flowers, coconuts, and small toy horses.

Toy horses? That's right. Toy horses! I was quite fascinated. What were these toy horses doing in front of a temple?

I thought to myself, *maybe the toy horses are kept for the kids who visit the temple.* I continued on my walk towards the temple.

Bhadrakali Temple

The temple looked very bright and resplendent in red. Numerous red flags, both inside and outside the temple, added to the vibrancy of the place. I was told that red is liberally used in most Devi temples, this one being no exception.

When I entered the temple, I found myself in a huge courtyard. At the centre of the courtyard, was an idol of a 'right foot'. The foot was protected by a silver umbrella on top. This *foot* rested on a lotus, made of concrete. I was astonished. What was a *foot* doing here, kept as an idol and worshipped by the devotees?

It is believed that Lord Shiva had married Sati, much against the wishes of Her father, Daksha. Once, Daksha performed a *Yajna* (sacrifice) to which he invited all the Gods and important sages. However, he did not invite his own Son-in-law, Lord Shiva. Though Sati was not invited by her father, she decided to visit him to participate in the *Yajna*. Shiva was against Her visiting Her father, but He could not stop Her.

During the *Yajna*, Daksha made disparaging remarks about Lord Shiva. Sati could not bear this humiliation so she committed suicide by jumping into a pyre. When this news reached Lord Shiva, He was furious. He arrived at Daksha's house and disrupted the *Yajna*. Next, he chopped off Daksha's head and killed him. However, all the Gods requested him to restore Daksha's life. Lord Shiva placed a goat's head and brought back Daksha to life. He was still filled with grief so He lifted Sati's body and danced with it throughout the cosmos. All the planets and other heavenly bodies trembled because of the fury of Lord Shiva. The Gods requested Him to stop but He did not relent. Finally, the Gods prayed to Lord Vishnu to save the cosmos from Lord Shiva's fury. Lord Vishnu realised that Shiva would remain infuriated as long as He had Sati's body with Him since it reminded Him of Her suicide. He decided to dismember Her body to make Lord Shiva forget His woes. He hurled His Sudarshana Chakra (Discus) which cut Sati's body into 51 pieces. These pieces fell at 51 different places in and around India and each one of them is worshipped as a sacred Shakthi Peetha. It is believed that Sati's 'right foot' fell at this spot; hence it is worshipped like an idol.

As I went closer, I noticed that the 'foot' was kept on top of a well. I had another surprise! Toy horses, similar to the ones being sold outside, were neatly lined up near the entrance of the well. I was astounded! What were these horses doing here? I felt as if I had heard the sound of hooves! Was I seeing and hearing things?

The sound of the hooves grows louder. Lord Krishna comes out from His tent. He sees the Pandavas coming towards Him. They are waving and cheering loudly. And why not? They have emerged victorious after a fierce 18-day battle with their cousins, the Kauravas.

They get off their chariots and walk towards Krishna. Yudhishtira bows to Lord Krishna and says, "Oh Keshava! This victory would not have been possible without your blessings. Though we managed to defeat great warriors like Bhishma, Drona, Karna, Duryodhana, and others, I know that You had a major role in all their deaths."

The rest of the Pandavas too bow to Krishna and seek His blessings.

Krishna smiles at Yudhishtira's humility. Blessing the Pandavas, He says, "It is not My blessings alone. Before the war started, you had been blessed by Lord Shiva and Goddess Bhadrakali. I hope you remember the vow you have taken in front of the Goddess?"

Krishna is reminding the Pandavas about the visit that they had undertaken before the commencement of the epic war. He, accompanied by the Pandavas had prayed at the Bhadrakali Temple and sought the blessings from the Goddess. Krishna had made the Pandavas take an oath that if the Goddess blessed them with victory, they would donate all their horses to Her.

Yudhishtira nods, "Yes Keshava! How can we forget that? The time has come for us to go to the Bhadrakali Temple and thank the Goddess. We will fulfil our promise."

Krishna and the Pandavas take the horses and go to the temple. They see a well at the entrance.

Krishna advises them, "Please tie the horses near this well and head towards the deity."

The Pandavas do as per His command. Having tied the horses to the barricade near the well, they go to the sanctum sanctorum of the temple. They prostrate themselves before the Goddess.

Yudhishtira, with folded hands, prays, "Oh Devi! I know that our victory would not have been possible without Your blessings. I would like to gift my horses to You."

Goddess Bhadrakali smiles, "Oh Yudhishtira! I am pleased with your righteousness. I am also glad that even in your moment of ecstasy, you did not forget your oath. Please ask Me for any boon, I will grant it."

Yudhishtira replies, "Oh Goddess! I have emerged victorious in the battle. All my brothers are alive. What more could I want?"

However, Goddess Bhadrakali insists that Yudhishtira should seek a boon.

Yudhishtira says, "I have one request. You fulfilled my wishes when I came and prayed here. In the future, You should fulfil the wishes of any devotee who comes here and prays."

Goddess Bhadrakali blesses him, "Let it be so."

A thrilled Yudhishtira replies, "When a devotee's wishes gets fulfilled, he will come to this temple and place miniature toy horses in front of the well, just as we tied our horses after our prayers were answered."

Once the priest finished narrating the story, I understood the significance of the toy horses. The priest told me, "Many devotees pray to the Goddess, seeking for favours. If their wishes are fulfilled, they visit this temple. They buy one of the toy horses sold near the temple premises and keep it near the well. This is similar to what Lord Krishna had advised the Pandavas to do when their prayers were answered. Since this well is of great importance, this temple is known as Sri Devi Kup Bhadrakali Temple."

After hearing this fascinating story, I decided to proceed further. There were steps to my left which led me to the first floor. On my left was a Shiva Linga. To the right, I saw an idol of Goddess Durga, sitting on a lion. Next to this idol was a corridor. As I walked ahead, I came out of an exit, which is shaped like a lion's head. I took the stairs and reached the ground floor once more. The sanctum sanctorum was in front of the sacred well. It had a black idol of Goddess Bhadrakali. As I performed the Parikrama, on my left I saw idols of Hanuman and Mahalakshmi. As I proceeded further, on my right, I saw an idol of Saraswati, playing Her divine musical instrument, the Veena. To the right of sanctum sanctorum were idols of Ganesha and Krishna, showing His Viraat Swaroop.

It is also believed that the *mundan* (hair removing) ceremony of Lord Krishna and Lord Balarama was performed here.

KRISHNA MUSEUM

The Sri Krishna Museum is located in the heart of the town, close to Brahma Sarovar. As the name suggests, it is centred around the multifaceted personality of Lord Krishna. It shows different episodes from His childhood and His philosophy in the form of paintings, sculptures and manuscripts. The Museum was established by Kurukshetra Development Board in 1987 and shifted to the current location in 1991. A board at the entrance of this museum states, 'The aim of setting up the museum is to think about the cultural and moral resurgence among the people through the ideas and ideals of the multi-faceted personality of Sri Krishna and to also exhibit materials concerning the Mahabharata and Kurukshetra regions.'

The museum has six galleries, spread across three floors in two blocks. Though each gallery is quite distinct from the other, the underlying theme is the same — it is Lord Krishna. Though the museum has numerous artefacts related to Kuruskhetra and Krishna, it is known as Krishna Museum because he is the Protagonist of the Kurukshetra war and the rest of the characters revolve around Him. Abundant archaeological material, unearthed from Kurukshetra and surroundings, are also on display here. These include an excellent collection of artefacts like idols, seals, coins, and pottery that date back to the era of Krishna and the Harappan civilisation.

First Gallery

This gallery is on the ground floor. It consists of sculptures made from a variety of materials like wood, bronze, and ivory. Most of these are from Karnataka, Tamil Nadu, Andhra Pradesh and Orissa. There are various idols of Krishna, Balarama, Radha, Rukmini, Satyabhama, and Yashoda. There are idols that show scenes from Krishna's life and some of the famous depictions include Yashoda scolding a naughty Krishna, Krishna killing Putana, Krishna defeating Kaliya, Krishna killing Aghasura, Krishna killing Nikumbhasura, and Krishna preaching the *Bhagavad Gita* to Arjuna. I saw many wooden doors and panels that showed scenes from Krishna's life. There was a beautiful painting of Krishna performing the Ras Lila with Radha and the gopis. Krishna had multiplied Himself into many forms and each form was dancing with a gopi in a circle, with the original Krishna dancing at the centre with Radha.

Second Gallery

The second gallery is also on the ground floor, almost an extension of the first gallery. It consists of archaeological objects belonging to the Harappan civilisation from 2400 B.C. to 1700 B.C. There is also a section on artefacts discovered during underwater excavations at Dwarka. The Kurukshetra region was on the banks of the rivers Saraswati and Dhrishadwati and is believed to be an integral part of the Harappan civilisation. The artefacts from Harappan civilisation include idols of Ganesha, Vishnu, Shiva, Bhoo Devi, Varaha, Yogamaya, Vishnu with Lakshmi, Seshashayi Vishnu, and Garuda. There are exhibits that consist of seals, coins, terracotta statues and potteries belonging to the Harappan era. One section of the hall has antiquities like carvings, pots, bowls made of painted grey ware and idols of Gods which were discovered in Sthaneshwar.

The Dwarka section has antiquities from Dwarka and Bet Dwarka, belonging to the 15th century B.C. These were discovered by the famous marine archaeologist Dr. S.R. Rao, when he conducted excavations in Dwarka and Bet Dwarka and underwater excavations in the Arabian Sea, near these two cities. For the sceptics, these archaeological artefacts provide ample evidence about the existence of Dwarka during the era of Krishna.

Third Gallery

If the first gallery has exquisite carvings and idols, the third gallery is all about beautiful paintings. As I walked the stairs, near the entrance, I saw a striking painting of Radha and Krishna, painted on a huge silk cloth.

When I entered the gallery, I saw several Rajasthani paintings. These belonged to different schools of paintings like the Mewar school, Bundi school, and Basohli school. These paintings showed scenes from Krishna's life like the Ras Lila, Krishna killing the crow-demon Kakasura, Krishna killing Aghasura, Bhishma lying on a bed of arrows, Radha and Krishna together, etc. At the other end of the room, I saw Razm Nama paintings. These were paintings done by Hindu artists who belonged to Akbar's court. At the centre of this gallery was an octagonal wall, consisting of eight paintings. I personally rate this as the best section of the Krishna Museum. These were scenes from *Srimad Bhagawatam*, painted in the Oriya style. The eight episodes shown here are: Krishna killing Sishupala, Krishna in Kurukshetra on the occasion of the solar eclipse, Krishna abducting Rukmini, Bhima killing Jarasandha, Krishna with Arjuna and Duryodhana prior to the epic war, Krishna giving life to infant Parikshit, Krishna in the court of Duryodhana performing the role of a peace mediator, and the sages cursing Samba and other Yadavas.

Fourth Gallery

This gallery was on the second floor. It had nine tableaux that depicted various incidents from Krishna's life such as, Vasudev carrying Krishna across the river Yamuna to Gokul, Krishna stealing butter, Krishna killing Bakasura, Krishna lifting Goverdhan, Krishna dancing on Kaliya after vanquishing him, the cosmic dance of Krishna with Radha and the gopis, Krishna killing Kansa, Krishna in Kurukshetra on the occasion of solar eclipse and Krishna preaching the *Bhagavad Gita* to Arjuna.

The idols in these tableaux are 'life-size' and are dressed in vibrant and colourful clothes. I felt as if I was actually witnessing these incidents.

Fifth gallery

This gallery consists of Thanjavur paintings. The unique feature of Thanjavur paintings is the use of gold and semi precious stones. Another distinctive feature of Thanjavur painting is that Krishna is normally shown in His infant form. The paintings depict different incidents from Krishna's life.

Sixth Gallery

The sixth gallery has different sections, each unique in its own way. Unlike the other galleries which contain artefacts of a particular style, here I saw a blend of Madhubani paintings, Yakshagana style tableaux, shadow puppets from Andhra Pradesh and idols depicting the Manipuri style of dancing.

At the entrance of the gallery there are leather shadow puppets from Andhra Pradesh. Next to them are idols of Krishna and the gopis performing Ras Lila in Manipuri style attire and dancing. To their right is a tableau that depicts the great Pandava warrior, Abhimanyu being killed in an unfair manner by Kaurava warriors Dronacharya, Karna, Dushashana, Duryodhana, and others. Next to this is a huge tableau that shows Bhishma, lying on a bed of arrows, preaching Rajadharma to Yudhishtira and the Pandavas. At the end of the hall, I saw the famous Madhubani paintings that depicted pastimes from Lord Krishna's life.

I spent a few hours at the Krishna Museum and found it to be an unique experience since it has mythological depictions of the life and times of Sri Krishna placed as well as scientifically studied archaeological artefacts that have been dated using modern techniques like carbon dating. I have never seen anything like this anywhere in the world.

Kurukshetra Panorama and Science Centre is situated adjacent to the Sri Krishna Museum. The ground floor has exhibits related to science and technology. The first floor has a huge cylindrical hall which depicts the epic war at Kurushetra. There are 34 paintings adorning the cylindrical walls. The front portion was covered with sand that made it appear as an open field. The various tableaux and paintings depict different scenes from the battle. The battle cries, the sound of conch shells and the chanting of the *Bhagavad Gita* transport the visitor to the battle of Kurukshetra!

18

Somnath

...

"*Aprakasho apravruthischa pramado moha eva cha,
Tamasyetani jayante vivruddhe Kurunandan.*"

("Oh Descendant of Kuru! Darkness, inactivity, madness, disinclination to perform duties and illusion get manifested when there is mode of ignorance.")

(Bhagavad Gita 14.13)

Somnath is located in Saurashtra in the state of Gujarat. It is approximately 225 km from Dwarka and 10 km from Veravel, a famous harbour close to the Arabian Sea. It is also close to Prabhas Kshetra, a place where Lord Krishna spent His last few hours on Earth before returning to His Heavenly Abode, Vaikunta. Somnath is also famous for the Shiva Temple which is one of the 12 Jyotirlingas in India.

The journey from Sudamapuri (Porbandar) to Somnath was very similar to the picturesque drive from Dwarka to Sudamapuri. Most of the journey took us close to the banks of the Arabian Sea. I saw hundreds of windmills during the journey. The view was simply breathtaking. Wind energy seemed to play an important part in generating electricity in this part of the country.

BALKA TEERTH

Balka Teerth is four kilometres from Veravel, on the way to Somnath. While driving from Veravel to Somnath, this temple

Hunter begging for forgiveness from Krishna

comes on the left. As I passed through the main gate, I saw a pond on the left. This pond is considered sacred because it has a Shiva Linga at the bottom. To the right of the sacred pond is the main temple. When I entered it, I saw a huge 'life-like' idol of Lord Krishna in a reclining pose. The idol is made of pure white marble. It looks so realistic that I felt the Supreme Lord was really sitting there! It takes a few minutes to realise that it is only an idol. His right leg was resting on a dais and the left leg was slightly raised in the air. I could see all the sacred symbols on the arch and the heel of His left foot. As in the case of many other Lord Krishna Temples in Gujarat, here as well, the Lord was four-armed, holding His Sudarshana Chakra and Shanka.

To the left of the idol of Lord Krishna is the idol of a hunter, kneeling down and with folded hands, begging the Supreme Lord for forgiveness. He is horrified that he has shot an arrow into Krishna's left toe, mistaking it to be the eye of a deer. The Supreme Lord is sitting relaxed and is smiling at the hunter. He knows that the hunter has done what he was ordained to do and he was just a 'tool' facilitating His return back to Vaikunta.

The great war of Kurukshetra has ended. Yudhistira has been crowned king of Hastinapura. Lord Krishna and Lord Balarama have long returned to Dwarka. The kings and princes of the Yadava dynasty have become arrogant. Because of wealth and opulence everywhere, the rich and the noblemen have become insolent. They have forgotten their pious duties and have stopped walking on the path of righteousness. They are indulging in vices like gambling and drinking. The princes have lost respect for saints and sages.

Samba, the son of Lord Krishna and Jambavathi, is sitting with his friends. He sees sages Narada, Vishwamitra, and others arrive in Dwarka.

Samba hits upon an idea. He tells his friends, "I will disguise myself as a woman and accompany you. As we approach the sages, you tell them that I am pregnant. Ask them if I will deliver a boy or a girl. Let us test their powers."

His friends laugh and decide to have some fun at the sage's expense. They dress Samba as a pregnant lady and take him to the spot where Narada and Vishwamitra are resting. They bow before the sages and say, "Oh Holy Sages! Our lady friend is pregnant. Please tell us if she will deliver a boy or a girl."

The sages curse them, "Oh Arrogant ones! The person standing with you is Samba, son of Lord Krishna, disguised as a pregnant lady. He wants to know what he will deliver! He will deliver an iron bolt. The Yadavas will get intoxicated. They will fight one another and the iron bolt will destroy the entire Yadava clan."

Samba and his friends are shocked. They rush to the palace and narrate this episode to King Ugrasena and Lord Krishna. Krishna knows that the inevitable cannot be avoided. He listens and smiles. However, King Ugrasena is worried. He bans the manufacture and supply of all intoxicating drinks throughout his kingdom.

The next day, as predicted by the sages, Samba delivers an iron bolt. King Ugrasena crushes it into fine powder. He realises that even the powder may have the potency to destroy the Yadava race, so he asks his men to throw the iron powder into the sea.

Lord Krishna is unmoved by this incident since He knows that His dynasty is to reach its gory end soon. He remembers the curse of Gandhari on Him and His dynasty. At the end of the Kurukshetra war, Gandhari had cursed Him, "Oh Krishna! You are the Supreme Lord of the three worlds. Not even a strand of hair can move without Your approval. Everyone and everything is under Your control. If You had so desired, You could have prevented this war. You could have ensured that my sons didn't get killed. I was a mother of a hundred sons but today not even a single son survives. My entire dynasty has been wiped out and You are responsible for that. Oh Krishna! I curse You and Your dynasty. Just as I watched my sons and dynasty get wiped out helplessly before my own eyes, so will You witness Your dynasty get wiped out before Your own eyes. Not even a single soul will survive."

The entire assembly was shocked hearing Gandhari's words and everyone felt that she had spoken too harshly and cursed Lord Krishna for no fault of His own. However, Lord Krishna had just smiled and replied, "O Gandhari! I would like to state that you have been very unfair by accusing Me of not stopping the Kurukshetra war. You and your husband Dhritrashtra have always turned a blind eye towards Duryodhana. Your son Duryodhana has been committing atrocities on the Pandavas since childhood, but you have never tried to stop him. He tried to kill them in a house of wax but you did not try to prevent that. He cheated them in a game of dice and you remained a mute spectator. He and his brother Dushashana insulted Draupadi in front of the entire court, but you watched silently. When Duryodhana refused to return the kingdom to the Pandavas after they had completed their exile, you did not intervene. I tried to be a Mediator and came to Hastinapaura to convince Duryodhana to return the Panadava's share of their kingdom. He responded by trying to get Me arrested. You once again chose to remain silent. You have always encouraged Duryodhana by your silence and inaction. However, I am ready to accept your curse. I am aware that My dynasty is the most powerful dynasty in the world and the only people who can destroy them are themselves. In a few years from now, they will be intoxicated with their own power and become arrogant. Instead of having to perform the difficult task of annihilating them, I can now allow the curse to take its course."

Today He recollects her curse. He knows that the time has come to end the Yadava dynasty and return to His Holy Abode Vaikunta. He calls His men and tells them, "The time has come for all of you to visit holy places and get rid of your sins. Let us go to Prabhas Patan."

The Yadavas travel to Prabhas Patan. After the religious ceremonies they head towards the beach. They pitch their tents on the seashore. The men begin to eat and drink heavily. Slowly, intoxication gets the better of them. In an intoxicated state they begin to insult one another. Kritavarma, Satyaki, and Pradyumna get into an argument. Satyaki attacks Kritavarma and kills him. Kritavarma's loyal followers are shocked to see this. They are also intoxicated. They struggle to get up and hold their swords. Slowly they drag themselves up and rush towards Satyaki. Pradyumna sees Satyaki being overpowered by them. He rushes to support Satyaki. A fierce battle ensues. Both Satyaki and Pradyumna get killed. The iron powder which had been thrown into the sea had reached the banks of the sea and had been converted into thick long blades of grass. The Yadava soldiers begin to uproot this grass. As soon as the blade of grass is uprooted, it transforms into an iron *bolt. The Yadavas use these iron bolts to kill one another. Lord Krishna sees His Yadava dynasty get wiped out before His own eyes. He summons Daruka, His charioteer, and tells him, "The end of the Yadava clan is near. None of the men will survive. Rush to Hastinapura and ask My dear friend Arjuna to come and take all the ladies and children to Hastinapura. The city of Dwarka will be submerged soon."*

Daruka bows to Lord Krishna and rushes towards Hastinapura. In the meanwhile, the carnage continues. Only Lord Krishna and Lord Balarama are left. All the other soldiers, noblemen, princes, and kings are dead.

Jara, a hunter by profession, arrives in search of animals. A few days earlier, he had caught a fish from the sea. When he had opened the bulging stomach of the fish, he had found a lump of uncrushed iron. He had thought, "Someone has thrown iron into the sea. This fish has swallowed a lump. The piece looks very strong and hard. Let me make an arrow out of that."

Today, he is carrying that arrow in his quiver.

Lord Krishna decides to rest under a pipal tree. He stretches His feet and puts His arms around His head and closes His eyes. Jara has arrived very close to this spot. He sees the lotus feet of the Lord and imagines that it is the eye of a deer. He removes his arrow from the quiver and lets it fly. The arrow, made from the cursed iron bolt, pierces the left toe of Lord Krishna. Jara is thrilled. He thinks he has got his victim. He rushes towards the pipal tree hoping to see a dead deer. He is horrified to see Lord Krishna lying on the ground with an injured left foot. He falls at the feet of the Supreme Lord and begs for forgiveness. Lord Krishna smiles at him and says, "Whatever you have done was already destined. Please get up and go back to your hunting." Jara is inconsolable. As he weeps, his tears wash the holy feet of the Lord. He says, "What a horrendous crime I have committed! I have hit Lord Dwarkadheesh, the Protector of the universe. I am sure I will be sent to hell."

Lord Krishna smiles and says, "No you will not, Jara. Please get up."

Jara looks surprised.

Lord Krishna continues, "In Treta Yuga, I had incarnated as Lord Rama. During that incarnation, I had performed only one wrong act. When the monkey king Vali had overthrown his brother Sugreeva and usurped his kingdom, Sugreeva met Me and sought My help. I asked them to have a fight in the forest. It was decided that if Sugreeva won then Vali would have to

321

return his kingdom. The next day, a fierce battle ensued between the two. Since they matched each other in strength and valour, it was a well-balanced fight and it did not appear that it would end soon. I was standing behind a tree, watching the fight. As time passed, I grew impatient. There were no signs of either of them losing. I slowly lifted My bow and picked an arrow from My quiver. I took aim and sent the arrow flying at King Vali. It struck him and felled him. I came out of My hiding and ran towards him.

In his dying moments, Vali looked at me and said, "I would not have felt sad if I had lost the battle in a fair manner. I am not feeling sad that I am dying. I am feeling sad that the person whom I regarded as the noblest of all men, Lord Rama, the righteous one and is known as 'Maryada Purushottam', had to stoop to this level to defeat me."

Hearing this, I felt very remorseful. I realised I had committed a grave unpardonable sin in My anxiety to help My friend Sugreeva.

I told Vali, 'I realise the crime that I have committed against you. I have killed you in an unfair manner. As part of My repentance, I want to ensure that I too suffer an end similar to yours. In My next birth as Lord Krishna, you will be re-born as a hunter and will kill Me when I am resting under a tree.'

So, as you know now, all this was destined. You were destined to be reborn as a hunter. I was destined to be shot by you. You have performed your duty as determined by your destiny. Have no sense of guilt and return to your village."

Jara feels relieved hearing this. He bows once again to Lord Krishna and departs. Lord Krishna knows His time has come. He decides to find a river or sea so that He can depart to Vaikunta, He begins to walk, with an injured foot, in search of water.

To the right of the altar is a huge Pipal tree. People believe that this is the same Pipal tree under which Lord Krishna was resting when He was hit by Jara's arrow. To the right of this tree is a Shiva Linga with a snake serving as the hood. At the extreme right side of the main hall is a white marble idol of Lord Krishna playing the flute.

As I came out of the main temple, I noticed that the entire area was filled with lots of Pipal and Banyan trees. It was quite easy to imagine that, during Krishna's time, the vegetation here would have been much thicker and the entire area would have been a dense forest. It was not difficult to understand why the hunter mistook the Lord's foot for a deer's eye. Next to the sacred pond is a temple dedicated to Lord Shiva — Shri Pragateshwar Temple. The altar has a black Shiva Linga with a serpent hood.

In the local dialect, *Bal* means 'arrow', hence, this place is known as Balka Teerth since an arrow from the quiver of Jara, the hunter, was responsible for ending Lord Vishnu's eighth avatara on this planet.

SRI PRABHAS GOLOK DHAM

This sacred place is four kilometres from Balka Teerth. It is believed that when Lord Krishna was hit by an arrow from the bow of the hunter, Jara, He walked four kilometres and reached this spot. He and His brother Balarama left their mortal bodies and proceeded towards Vaikunta which is also known as Goloka. Hence this sacred place is known as Sri Prabhas Golok Dham.

Sri Prabhas Golok Dham

When I entered the sacred Golok Dham, the first thing that struck me was the serenity and calmness here. It took me to a different era. As I visited the different sacred spots, I began to feel as if I was witness to those incidents that took place here 5000 years ago!

GITA TEMPLE

Entering Golok Dham, I noticed lots of temples on the left and River Hiran on the right. The first temple that I came upon

Gita Temple

Balarama's Footprints and
Seshavatar idol

was the Gita Temple. At the altar is a beautiful huge white idol of Lord Krishna playing the flute. This is known as Gita Temple because it has Sanskrit inscriptions of the entire *Bhagavad Gita* on the walls near the main deity.

SRI SESHAVATAR TEMPLE AND CAVE

Next to the Gita Temple is the Sri Seshavatar Temple with a cave adjoining it. As the name indicates, this is a temple dedicated to Lord Balarama who is the incarnation (avatara) of Lord Seshanag.

As I entered, on my left I saw a huge idol of Lord Balarama, made of white marble. Lord Balarama, also known as Sri Baldevji, was holding His divine weapon, the Plough, in His left hand. On the right, I saw five steps leading me to a cave below. This cave is known as *Balaramji Ni Gufa* which means 'Balarama's Cave' in Gujarati.

This cave has an orange coloured carving of a snake on the wall. The snake symbolises the sacred event of Lord Balarama leaving His mortal Body and transforming Himself into His original Self as Serpent King Seshanag, before proceeding to Vaikunta.

Like Lord Krishna, Lord Balarama had also witnessed the carnage of the Yadava dynasty at Prabhas Patan. He is disgusted to see His own men kill one other. He realises that the time has come for Him to go back to

Vaikunta. Just like Lord Krishna, he too walks towards River Hiran. He finds a cave very close to River Hiran. He enters the cave and sits on the floor and closes His eyes in deep meditation. Suddenly, a divine event takes place. A snake begins to come out of His mouth. The snake begins to grow in size. The snake is none other than Lord Sheshanag Himself. He is leaving the mortal human body of Lord Balarama and is changing into His original Self. He crawls towards River Hiran. All the Gods and Goddesses descend from Heaven and bow to the mighty Lord Seshanag. They drop garlands from the Heavens and worship Him. Lord Seshanag enters the river and begins His journey upwards towards Vaikunta. The Gods and Goddesses know that if Lord Sheshanag has left His mortal body and returned to Vaikunta, then His Lord, the Supreme Lord of the Universe can't be far behind. They welcome Lord Seshanag and await Lord Krishna's arrival in Vaikunta.

In front of the snake carving on the wall are Balarama's footprints carved on white marble to indicate His presence here. To the right is a stone idol of Seshanag.

BHAGWAN SRI KRISHNA CHARAN PADUKA (SRI KRISHNA NEEJADHAM TEERTH)

As I walked from Seshavatar Temple towards the banks of the river Hiran on the right, I came across a white mantapa-shaped enclosure, known as Sri Krishna Neejadham Teerth. The place was so quiet and tranquil that I could hear the soft and gentle sounds of the river that flowed nearby. This is the place where Lord Krishna left His mortal body and proceeded towards His Heavenly Abode, Vaikunta. Since He went back to 'His original sacred place', this spot is known as Sri Krishna Neejadham Teerth. This place is also known as Dehotsarg Teerth, since He gave up His mortal body here (*Deha*).

Sri Krishna Neejadham Teerth

The white enclosure has white

marble footprints of Lord Krishna to commemorate His visit to this sacred place. Hence, this spot is also known as Bhagwan Sri Krishna Charan Paduka. When I saw the footprints of Krishna, I felt sure He was nearby.

Lord Krishna has arrived on the banks of the River Hiran. He is resting under a tree. He has just witnessed Lord Balarama assume His original serpent form of Lord Sheshanag and leave the Earth to return to Vaikunta. He realises His time has also come. He glances upwards and sees all the Gods and Goddesses welcoming the Serpent King, Lord Sheshanag. He also knows that they are eagerly awaiting His return.

Sage Narada comes and bows to Lord Krishna, "Narayana! Narayana! Lord Sheshanag has returned to the Holy Abode Vaikunta. We are all awaiting your return."

Saying this, he bows once again and departs. Lord Krishna enters River Hiran. He closes His eyes in deep meditation. He ascends towards Vaikunta. There is thunder and lightning everywhere. The entire universe reverberates. All the Gods and Goddesses stand near the entrance to Heaven and drop flowers at His lotus feet, worshipping Him. They sing and chant the thousand holy names of Lord Vishnu. There is celebration and joy everywhere. Lord Krishna has returned to His Holy Abode, Vaikunta.

It is the end of Dwapara Yuga and the onset of Kali Yuga.

HIRAN, KAPILA, SARASWATI TRIVENI SANGAM

As I went back from Sri Prabhas Golok Dham towards Balka Teerth, on my left I saw the sacred Triveni Sangam. This Sangam is also known as Hiran Kapila Saraswati Triveni Sangam since it is a confluence of the three sacred rivers Hiran, Kapila, and Saraswati with the Arabian Sea. There were hundreds of devotees bathing here.

Lord Krishna has left His mortal body and proceeded towards His Celestial Abode, Vaikunta. There is no one to witness this incident except the Gods and Goddesses from Heaven. After a few days, the locals who had found all the Yadavas dead near Balka Teerth, begin to hunt for Lord Krishna, since He is nowhere to be seen. People scan the entire Balka Teerth area, but in vain. They now begin to move outwards, away from Balka Teerth. They divide themselves into four groups. Each group heads in one direction. One group heads towards Sri Prabhas Golok Dham. They search everywhere. Finally they find the mortal body of Lord Krishna on the banks of the Hiran. They take the body to Triveni Sangam to perform the cremation. Thousands of people assemble at Triveni Sangam. Everyone wants to have one final glimpse of the Supreme Lord in His earthly form. The women are weeping at the loss of their mischievous Child. The men are grieving for the departure of their righteous King. The birds and animals are sensing the loss of their Cowherd. The trees have shed their leaves. The heavy rains that follow symbolically represent the tears of the entire universe.

After this sacred cremation, people have begun to believe that anyone who bathes in these holy waters will get a passage to heaven. It is believed that since this sacred spot was the last place Lord Krishna visited before He began His heavenly journey, anyone who bathes here will also attain heaven when he leaves his mortal body.

Thus ends the stay of Lord Krishna in His mortal form on earth and marks the beginning of His journey to His Holy Abode, Vaikunta. There were a few people in Brij Bhoomi and Dwarka who had the pleasure of seeing Him and watching His divine pastimes. However, there are millions of people who would like to see Him now, but may not know how to achieve this. There are also millions of people who would not like to be born again in this material world, but would like to stay in the spiritual world, the Holy Abode of the Supreme Lord.

So how can one achieve this?

It is stated in the *Srimad Bhagavatam* that when a person dies, he will take birth as per his desires and his 'karma'. How does one liberate oneself from this cycle? How does a person ensure that his soul is liberated from being born again? How does he reach the kingdom of God? *Srimad Bhagavatam* states that for a person to reach the kingdom of God, he should meditate on and chant God's name and worship God at the time of death. However, how will a person know when he is dying, in order to chant the holy name? The solution is simple! Throughout your life, always remain immersed in the divine thoughts of God and chant His holy name. Always think of Him and pray to Him to take you to His Holy Abode.

As Lord Krishna Himself tells Arjuna in *Bhagavad Gita*:

"*Manmana bhava madbhakto madyaji mam namaskuru,*
Mam evaishyasi satyam te pratijane priyo asi me."

("Always think of Me, just become My devotee, worship Me and offer your obeisance unto Me. You will certainly come to Me, I truly promise you because you are dear to Me.")

(*Bhagavad Gita* 18.65)

Epilogue

•••

Lord Krishna!

What images does your mind conjure when you hear this divine name?

The divine Incarnation who was born on the stroke of midnight to Devaki and Vasudev in a prison cell in Mathura?

The innocent Newborn, who was carried across a raging Yamuna from Mathura to Gokul on a stormy night by His father Vasudev?

The divine Infant who was strong enough to confront demons like Putana, Kakasura, Shakatasura, and Trinavarta and kill them with a single blow?

The mischievous Child who stole butter and curds from the gopis' homes?

The divine Child who ate mud, but showed the entire cosmos to His mother when He was asked to open His mouth?

The naughty Boy who stole and hid the gopis' clothes?

The courageous Cowherd who subdued the venomous serpent Kaliya and danced on its hood?

The handsome Boy who stole Radha's heart and charmed Her with His words?

The divine Musician who played His flute so melodiously that the fauna of Brij Bhoomi came to listen to Him?

The lissom Dancer who danced Ras Lila, through the night, with Radha and the gopis?

The brawny Cowherd who killed powerful demons like Bakasura, Aghasura, Dhenukasura, and many others?

The strapping young Prince who killed His maternal uncle and ended his tyrannical rule in Mathura?

The dutiful King who carried away and married Rukmini to save Her from getting married to Shishupal against Her wishes?

The devoted Friend who took a handful of puffed rice from Sudama and showered him with riches in return?

The master Diplomat who tried His best as the mediator between the Pandavas and the Kauravas to avert the Kurukshetra war?

The Supreme Lord who bestowed spiritual wisdom in the form of the *Bhagvad Gita* on Arjuna at the start of the Kurukshetra war?

The crafty Statesman who meticulously planned the deaths of Bhishma, Drona, Duryodhana, and many others during the Kurukshetra war?

The powerful Emperor of Dwarka who ruled Dwarka for 97 long years?

The champion of *Dharma* (righteousness and justice) who was ready to lead His own clan towards self-destruction to protect *dharma*?

Which of them is the real Krishna? All of them and more. It is not difficult for the Supreme Lord, the eighth incarnation of Lord Vishnu, to perform all these roles with equal panache. Lord Krishna is known as the Poorna Avatar of Lord Vishnu. The common interpretation of this word is 'complete incarnation', which means that Krishna has all the qualities of Vishnu and He is as powerful as the the Protector of the Universe and there is no difference between the two. The other interpretation of the word

Poorna is 'complete in all respects'. If you look at most of the other incarnations of Lord Vishnu, they have been one-dimensional or most, two-dimensional. Narasimha was the fiercest among all avataras, but can you imagine Him being the 'mediator of peace' between the Pandavas and the Kauravas?

Vamana was the shrewdest among all, but can you picture Him annihilating demons like Putana, Trinavarta, Aghasura, and Bakasura?

Parashurama was the mightiest among all incarnations but can you see Him exhibit the sensitivity that Krishna exhibited towards Radha and the gopis?

Rama, also rightly known as 'Maryada Purushottam', was the epitome of righteousness in the entire cosmos so we cannot envisage Him playfully stealing butter and curds from the homes of gopis!

Buddha was the embodiment of non-violence so it is difficult to think of Him persuading Arjuna to battle against his own kith and kin to protect righteousness.

In contrast, Krishna is a multi-faceted Personality — a dutiful son, charming lover, courageous prince, loyal friend, master diplomat, devoted king — all rolled into one!

Lord Krishna explains Himself beautifully in His recitation of the *Bhagavad Gita*:

"Pitaham asya jagato mata dhata pitamahah,
Vedyam pavitram omkara rig saama yajur eva cha"

"I am the Father of this Universe, the Mother, the Supporter, and the Grandfather. I am the Object of Knowledge, the Purifier, and the Syllable 'Om'. I am the 'Rig', 'Sama' and 'Yajur' Vedas."

(*Bhagavad Gita* 9.17)

Travelogue

...

If you are a devotee of Lord Krishna, who wishes to visit all the holy places mentioned in this book, this section provides you with some tips and guidance for planning an optimal route.

BEST SEASONS TO VISIT

The climate at all the places in Brij Bhoomi (Uttar Pradesh) and Kurukshetra are extreme and tropical. Summers are extremely hot and winters are exceptionally cold. It rains here between July and September. The best time to visit these places would be between October and March. Since the Brij Bhoomi Parikrama (during which devotees cover the entire Brij Bhoomi on foot) is performed during the Karthik season, which falls during Diwali, this would probably be the ideal time to visit.

The climate of Dwarka and Somnath is equally hot and humid. It also receives heavy rains between July and September. The best period to visit these places is between November and February since the winters are very cool and pleasant.

IMPORTANT FESTIVALS

Some of the important festivals celebrated in Brij Bhoomi are Krishna Janmashtami (in the month of Shravana), Jhulan Yatra (in the month of Shravana), Radhashtami (in the month of Bhadrapada), Laatmaar Holi (in the month of Phalgun) and Annakut (in the month of Karthik). Brij Parikrama is also popular during the month of Karthik.

The most important festival in Kurukshetra is the Kurukshetra Festival, which is celebrated in December every year, to commemorate the birth anniversary of the Srimad Bhagavat Gita. This festival is also known as 'Gita Jayanti' and 'Mahabharath Festival'. The most important festival in Dwarka is Krishna Janmashtami, the birth anniversary of Lord Krishna. This is celebrated in the month of Shravana. Holi, the festival of colours, is celebrated in the month of Phalgun.

LOCATION AND TRAVEL

Mathura, which is the 'heart' of Brij Bhoomi, is located 150 km to the southeast of New Delhi and 58 km to the northwest of Agra. Though Agra is the nearest airport to Mathura, the former is not well connected to other Indian cities. A better option would be to go to New Delhi and travel to Mathura by road.

Kurukshetra, in the present state of Haryana, is located 160 km to the north of New Delhi. A road journey of three hours would seem to be the ideal option for those planning to commute from New Delhi to Kurukshetra.

Dwarka is 380 km to the west of Ahmedabad. One could reach Ahmedabad and take a bus, taxi, or train from there. This would be a good option since Ahmedabad is well connected to other Indian cities by rail, road, and air. The nearest airport to Dwarka is Jamnagar, at a distance of 145 km. You can travel from Jamnagar to Dwarka within a couple of hours by road. However, Jamnagar is not very well connected to other Indian cities.

Somnath is located at a distance of 225 km to the southeast of Dwarka. The best way to travel from Dwarka to Somnath would be by road. Since a major portion of the drive is along the coast of the Arabian Sea, it is extremely scenic and beautiful.

ITINERARY

Since Lord Krishna's life was spent in the current states of Uttar Pradesh and Gujarat, which are separated by a few hundred kilometres, I have divided the tour into two parts. You can first go to New Delhi and from there, travel south-eastwards, to explore all the towns of Brij Bhoomi by road. On your return to New Delhi, you can travel north-westwards to visit Kurukshetra by road.

Next, you can go to Ahmedabad from New Delhi either by air, or by rail. From Ahmedabad, you can proceed to Dwarka, Porbandar, and Somnath by road. If you plan to go from New Delhi to Ahmedabad by air, you can visit all the places in 17 days. If you go to Ahmedabad from New Delhi by train, you can visit all places in 18 days.

BRIJ BHOOMI AND KURUKSHETRA

Get to New Delhi which is well connected to other major cities and towns of India by air, rail, and road. Start your journey with a trip to Brij Bhoomi from New Delhi by road.

Day One

Leave New Delhi in the morning and proceed to Mathura which is 150 km away. You will reach Mathura by noon. In the afternoon, visit all the places in Mathura. You can start with a visit to the famous Krishna Janmasthan. From there, you can visit Potara Kund which is nearby. Later you can visit Kansa Qila and Rang Bhoomi. Conclude your day with a visit to Vishram Ghat in the evening. Many devotees place *diyas* (lamps) in the Yamuna at Vishram Ghat in the evening and it is a beautiful sight to see.

Day Two

Visit the places that are to the east of Mathura, across the River Yamuna. You can start your day with a visit to Raval (10 km) which is the birthplace of Radha. From here, visit Mahavan, which is five kilometres from Raval. From Mahavan, proceed to Gokul, which is just two kilometres away. In the afternoon, proceed eastwards and visit Baldeo, five kilometres from Gokul. On your way back to Mathura, you can visit Madhuvan which is five kilometres from Mathura.

Day Three

Visit the places that are to the west of Mathura. Start the day with a visit to Goverdhan (25 km from Mathura). You can next visit Manasi Ganga and Mukharvind Mukut Temple. You can visit all the other temples and *kunds* in Goverdhan. Conclude your Goverdhan trip with a visit to Uddhav Temple and Kusum Sarovar which are located on the outskirts of Goverdhan town and on the way to Radha Kund. From here, proceed to Radha Kund which is five kilometres to the north of Goverdhan.

Day Four

Start the morning with a visit to Barsana, which is 50 km to the northwest of Mathura. In the afternoon, continue your journey northwards and visit Nandagaon which is 10 km from Barsana.

Day Five and Six

Visit Vrindavan, 15 km from Mathura. Since there are many important places to be seen in Vrindavan, you will need two days here. The places that I have described in the book are listed in the right sequence for planning a visit. There is abundant room to park your car at ISKCON and Rangaji temple. Since most of the roads in Vrindavan are very narrow, it is best to park your car at one of these two places and then cover all places on foot, or by cycle-rickshaw.

Day Seven

Leave Mathura in the morning and reach Kurukshetra in the evening.

Day Eight and Nine

You can visit the Sri Krishna Museum, Bhadrakali Temple, Sthaneshwar Mahadev, Ban Ganga (Dhyalpur), Bhor Saidan, Ban Ganga (Narkatari), and Jyotisar on your first day here. Remember to see the light and sound show at Jyotisar in the evening. On the second day, you can visit Sannihit Sarovar, Brahma Sarovar, and all the temples near Brahma Sarovar.

Day Ten

Leave Kurukshetra in the morning by road and reach New Delhi by noon.

GUJARAT

Reach Ahmedabad which is well connected to other major cities and towns of India by air, rail, and road. Visit all the holy places at Dwarka, Porbandar, and Somnath from Ahmedabad by road.

Day One

Leave Ahmedabad in the morning by road. You will reach Dwarka (380 km) in the evening.

Day Two

Visit all the temples that are located in Dwarka town. You can start your day with a visit to the famous Dwarkadheesh Temple. From here, you can walk across to Gomti Ghat and visit all the temples located near Gomti Ghat.

Day Three

Start your day with a visit to Bet Dwarka. On the way back, visit the places which are on the outskirts of Dwarka town and located between Bet Dwarka and Dwarka — Gopi Talav and Rukmini Temple.

Day Four

Leave Dwarka and reach Porbandar (Sudamapuri) by noon. Porbandar is 95 km from Dwarka and on the way to Somnath. Visit the famous Sudama Temple. Leave for Somnath which is 225 km from Dwarka. You will reach Somnath by evening.

Day Five

Visit all the places in Somnath.

Day Six

Leave Somnath in the morning and reach Ahmedabad by evening. From Ahmedabad, proceed to your home town.

Maps

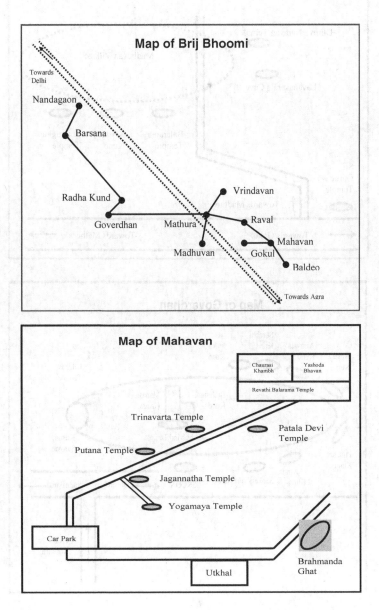

Map of Brij Bhoomi

Towards Delhi

Nandagaon
Barsana
Radha Kund
Goverdhan
Mathura
Vrindavan
Raval
Mahavan
Madhuvan
Gokul
Baldeo

Towards Agra

Map of Mahavan

Chaurasi Khambh	Yashoda Bhavan
Revathi Balarama Temple	

Trinavarta Temple

Patala Devi Temple

Putana Temple

Jagannatha Temple

Yogamaya Temple

Car Park

Utkhal

Brahmanda Ghat

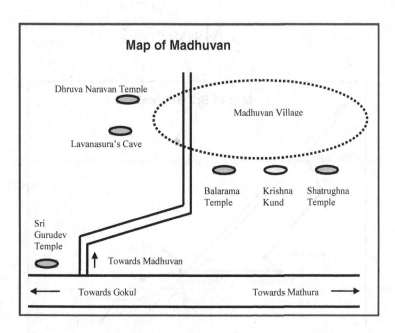

Map of Madhuvan

Dhruva Narayan Temple

Madhuvan Village

Lavanasura's Cave

Balarama
Temple

Krishna
Kund

Shatrughna
Temple

Sri
Gurudev
Temple

↑ Towards Madhuvan

← Towards Gokul

Towards Mathura →

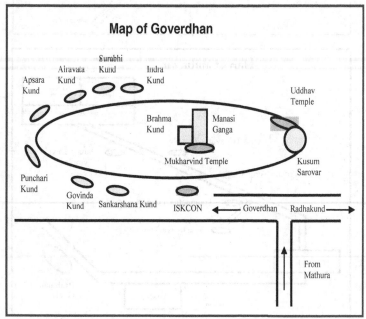

Map of Goverdhan

Surabhi
Kund

Airavata
Kund

Apsara
Kund

Indra
Kund

Uddhav
Temple

Brahma
Kund

Manasi
Ganga

Mukharvind Temple

Kusum
Sarovar

Punchari
Kund

Govinda
Kund

Sankarshana Kund

ISKCON

← Goverdhan

Radhakund →

↑ From
Mathura

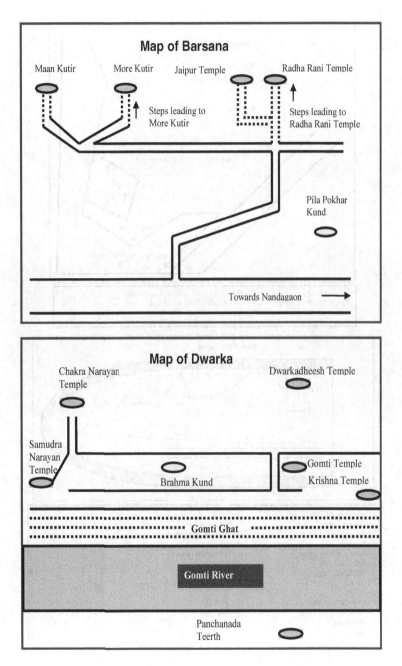

Map of Barsana

Maan Kutir More Kutir Jaipur Temple Radha Rani Temple

Steps leading to
More Kutir

Steps leading to
Radha Rani Temple

Pila Pokhar
Kund

Towards Nandagaon →

Map of Dwarka

Chakra Narayan
Temple

Dwarkadheesh Temple

Samudra
Narayan
Temple

Gomti Temple
Krishna Temple

Brahma Kund

Gomti Ghat

Gomti River

Panchanada
Teerth

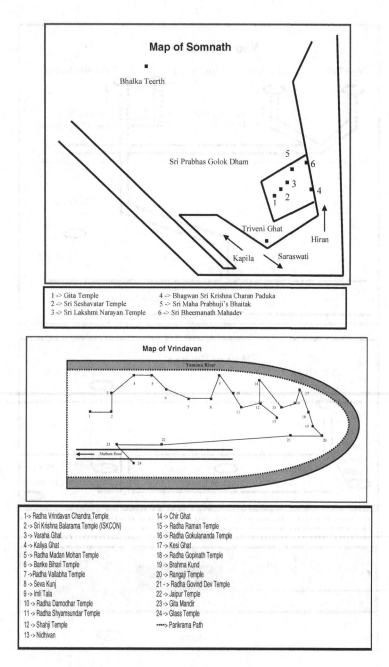

Map of Somnath

Bhalka Teerth

Sri Prabhas Golok Dham

5
6
3
2
1
4

Triveni Ghat

Hiran

Kapila   Saraswati

1 -> Gita Temple
2 -> Sri Seshavatar Temple
3 -> Sri Lakshmi Narayan Temple
4 -> Bhagwan Sri Krishna Charan Paduka
5 -> Sri Maha Prabhuji's Bhaitak
6 -> Sri Bheemanath Mahadev

Map of Vrindavan

Yamona River

Mathura Road

1-> Radha Vrindavan Chandra Temple
2 -> Sri Krishna Balarama Temple (ISKCON)
3 -> Varaha Ghat
4 -> Kaliya Ghat
5 -> Radha Madan Mohan Temple
6 -> Banke Bihari Temple
7 ->Radha Vallabha Temple
8 -> Seva Kunj
9 -> Imli Tala
10 -> Radha Damodhar Temple
11 -> Radha Shyamsundar Temple
12 -> Shahji Temple
13 -> Nidhivan
14 -> Chir Ghat
15 -> Radha Raman Temple
16 -> Radha Gokulananda Temple
17 -> Kesi Ghat
18 -> Radha Gopinath Temple
19 -> Brahma Kund
20 -> Rangaji Temple
21 - > Radha Govind Dev Temple
22 -> Jaipur Temple
23 -> Gita Mandir
24 -> Glass Temple
----> Parikrama Path

Acknowledgements and Thanks

...

"Sri Mahabharata" by Prof. L.S. Seshagiri Rao

"Magic Flute" by K.M. Munshi

"Krishna Kathayein" by Ramanand Sagar

Guides: Mathuresh Bharadwaj (Brij Bhoomi) and Vikram (Kurukshetra)

Drivers: (Late) Ashwani, Swaroop and Singh

Countless helpful local people at all the sacred places - with a special mention of the priests at Radha Rani Janmasthan Temple (Raval), Gaudiya Math (Goverdhan), ISKCON Temple (Goverdhan), Sri Radha Vrindavan Chandra ISKCON Temple (Vrindavan), More Kutir (Barsana), Bhor Saidan (Kurukshetra), Curator at Sri Krishna Museum (Kurukshetra)

My family members, for the continuous support that I received from them throughout my spiritual journey

OTHER PLACES:

There are many sacred places that are associated with these towns but do not form an integral part of the story of Lord Krishna. However, these places are equally holy and worth a visit. If you plan to visit the towns described in this book, then it is worthwhile to visit these places too:

Nageshwar Mahadev (Jyotirlinga), Sri Bhadkeshwar Mahadev, and Sri Siddeshwar Mahadev at Dwarka

Kirti Mandir at Porbandar (Sudamapuri)

Somnath Temple (Jyotirlinga), Sri Kamnath Mahadev, Sharada Peetha, Suraj Mandir and Sri Parashuram's Tapo Bhoomi at Somnath

Kamal Nabhi at Kurukshetra

ଔ Hare Krishna ୨

JAICO PUBLISHING HOUSE

Elevate Your Life. Transform Your World.

ESTABLISHED IN 1946, Jaico Publishing House is home to world-transforming authors such as Sri Sri Paramahansa Yogananda, Osho, The Dalai Lama, Sri Sri Ravi Shankar, Robin Sharma, Deepak Chopra, Jack Canfield, Eknath Easwaran, Devdutt Pattanaik, Khushwant Singh, John Maxwell, Brian Tracy and Stephen Hawking.

Our late founder Mr. Jaman Shah first established Jaico as a book distribution company. Sensing that independence was around the corner, he aptly named his company Jaico ('Jai' means victory in Hindi). In order to service the significant demand for affordable books in a developing nation, Mr. Shah initiated Jaico's own publications. Jaico was India's first publisher of paperback books in the English language.

While self-help, religion and philosophy, mind/body/spirit, and business titles form the cornerstone of our non-fiction list, we publish an exciting range of travel, current affairs, biography, and popular science books as well. Our renewed focus on popular fiction is evident in our new titles by a host of fresh young talent from India and abroad. Jaico's recently established Translations Division translates selected English content into nine regional languages.

Jaico's Higher Education Division (HED) is recognized for its student-friendly textbooks in Business Management and Engineering which are in use countrywide.

In addition to being a publisher and distributor of its own titles, Jaico is a major national distributor of books of leading international and Indian publishers. With its headquarters in Mumbai, Jaico has branches and sales offices in Ahmedabad, Bangalore, Bhopal, Bhubaneswar, Chennai, Delhi, Hyderabad, Kolkata and Lucknow.

SINCE 1946